BEYOND BORDERS

States have long denied basic rights to non-citizens within their borders, and international law imposes only limited duties on states with respect to those fleeing persecution. But even the limited rights previously enjoyed by non-citizens are eroding in the face of rising nationalism, populism, xenophobia, and racism. *Beyond Borders* explores what obligations we owe to those outside our political community. Drawing on contributions from a broad variety of disciplines – from literature to political science to philosophy – the volume considers the failures of law and politics to guarantee rights for the most vulnerable and attempts to imagine new forms of belonging grounded in ideas of solidarity, empathy, and responsibility in order to identify a more robust basis for the protection of non-citizens at home and abroad. This title is also available as Open Access on Cambridge Core.

Molly Land is the Catherine Roraback Professor of Law at the University of Connecticut School of Law. Her research focuses on the intersection of human rights, science, technology, and innovation.

Kathryn Libal is an Associate Professor of Social Work and Human Rights and Director of the Human Rights Institute at the University of Connecticut. Her publications have focused on human rights, social work, and refugees and asylum seekers.

Jillian Chambers is a Juris Doctor Candidate at the University of Connecticut School of Law, where she is the Symposium Editor of Volume 53 of the *Connecticut Law Review* and Executive Brief Writer for the Connecticut Moot Court Board.

T0384793

Beyond Borders

THE HUMAN RIGHTS OF NONCITIZENS AT HOME AND ABROAD

Edited by

MOLLY LAND
University of Connecticut School of Law

KATHRYN LIBAL
University of Connecticut School of Social Work

JILLIAN CHAMBERS
University of Connecticut School of Law

CAMBRIDGE
UNIVERSITY PRESS

Shaftesbury Road, Cambridge CB2 8EA, United Kingdom

One Liberty Plaza, 20th Floor, New York, NY 10006, USA

477 Williamstown Road, Port Melbourne, VIC 3207, Australia

314–321, 3rd Floor, Plot 3, Splendor Forum, Jasola District Centre, New Delhi – 110025, India

103 Penang Road, #05–06/07, Visioncrest Commercial, Singapore 238467

Cambridge University Press is part of Cambridge University Press & Assessment,
a department of the University of Cambridge.

We share the University's mission to contribute to society through the pursuit of
education, learning and research at the highest international levels of excellence.

www.cambridge.org
Information on this title: www.cambridge.org/9781108823975

DOI: 10.1017/9781108914994

First published 2021
First paperback edition 2024

A catalogue record for this publication is available from the British Library

Library of Congress Cataloging-in-Publication data
NAMES: Beyond Borders: the Human Rights of Noncitizens at Home and Abroad (Conference) (2017 :
University of Connecticut, Stamford) | Land, Molly, 1974– editor. | Libal, Kathryn, 1968– editor. | Chambers,
Jillian Robin, 1996– editor.
TITLE: Beyond borders : the human rights of noncitizens at home and abroad / edited by Molly Land, University
of Connecticut School of Law; Kathryn Libal, University of Connecticut School of Social Work; Jillian
Chambers, University of Connecticut School of Law.
DESCRIPTION: Cambridge, United Kingdom ; New York, NY : Cambridge University Press, 2021. |
Includes index.
IDENTIFIERS: LCCN 2021026053 (print) | LCCN 2021026054 (ebook) | ISBN 9781108843171 (hardback) |
ISBN 9781108823975 (paperback) | ISBN 9781108914994 (epub)
SUBJECTS: LCSH: Aliens–Congresses. | Human rights–Congresses. | LCGFT: Conference papers and
proceedings.
CLASSIFICATION: LCC K3274.A6 B49 2017 (print) | LCC K3274.A6 (ebook) | DDC 342.08/3–dc23
LC record available at https://lccn.loc.gov/2021026053
LC ebook record available at https://lccn.loc.gov/2021026054

ISBN   978-1-108-84317-1   Hardback
ISBN   978-1-108-82397-5   Paperback

In loving memory of Lyndsay Nalbandian

Contents

Notes on Contributors

Kristy A. Belton is a writer and storyteller whose work focuses on issues of belonging, human rights, and social justice, especially as pertains to the Caribbean. She holds a PhD in Political Science from the University of Connecticut and serves as Director of Professional Development for the International Studies Association. Belton is the recipient of numerous awards for her work on statelessness and migration, and she is the author of *Statelessness in the Caribbean: The Paradox of Belonging in a Postnational World* (Penn Press, 2017), among other publications.

Jacqueline Bhabha, JD, MSc, is Professor of the Practice of Health and Human Rights at the Harvard T. H. Chan School of Public Health and the Director of Research at the François-Xavier Bagnoud (FXB) Center for Health and Human Rights at Harvard University. She also serves as the Jeremiah Smith Jr. Lecturer in Law at Harvard Law School and adjunct lecturer in public policy at the Harvard Kennedy School. She is the author of *Child Migration and Human Rights in a Global Age* (Princeton University Press, 2014) and *Can We Solve the Migration Crisis?* (Polity Press, 2018), and is the editor or coeditor of books on statelessness, adolescence, child migration, Roma rights, access to higher education, and reparations.

Brad K. Blitz is Professor of International Politics and Policy and Head of the Department of Education, Practice and Society at University College London. He was previously Director of the British Academy/DFID Programme on Modern Slavery. His research focuses on displacement, citizenship, governance, and human rights. He is currently Co-Investigator on a £15 million "hub" on Gender, Justice and Security, funded by the Global Challenges Research Fund (GCRF); and Co-Investigator on Life after Deportation, a study of refused and current asylum-seekers returned to Mexico and Guatemala from the United States. His publications include *Migration and Freedom: Mobility, Citizenship, and Exclusion* (Edward Elgar, 2016).

Tendayi Bloom is a political and legal theorist with a particular interest in dimensions of noncitizenship. She engages on these topics in UN and civil society processes relating to migration governance. She is the author of *Noncitizen Power: Agency and the Politics of Migration* (Bloomsbury, forthcoming) and *Noncitizenism: Recognising Noncitizen Capabilities in a World of Citizens* (Routledge, 2018). Her coedited works include *Statelessness, Governance, and the Problem of Citizenship* (Manchester University Press, 2021; with L. Kingston) and *Understanding Statelessness* (Routledge, 2017; with K. Tonkiss and P. Cole). She lectures in Politics and International Studies at the University of Birmingham, UK.

Yajaira Ceciliano-Navarro is a PhD candidate in the Department of Sociology at the University of California, Merced. She has a bachelor's degree in Psychology and a master's degree in Labor Psychology from the University of Costa Rica (UCR). She worked at Academic Latin American Faculty of Social Science (FLACSO) in Costa Rica, where she was a coordinator of projects related to immigration, education, youth, and gender in countries such as Argentina, Colombia, Mexico, and the Central American region. As a doctoral candidate, she is researching the effects of deportations in Latin American countries and incarceration in the Central Valley.

Jillian Chambers is a Juris Doctor candidate at the University of Connecticut School of Law, where she is the Symposium Editor of Volume 53 of the *Connecticut Law Review* and Executive Brief Writer for the Connecticut Moot Court Board. Her student note, "*Carpenter*, the Fourth Amendment, and Third-Party Workarounds," is being published in the *Connecticut Law Review*. Following graduation, she will be clerking at the Connecticut Supreme Court for the 2021–2022 term.

Eleni Coundouriotis is Professor of English and Comparative Literary and Cultural Studies at the University of Connecticut. Her scholarship focuses on the engagement of literature with history in the postcolonial novel and human rights narratives. She is the author of *Narrating Human Rights in Africa* (Routledge, 2021), *The People's Right to the Novel: War Fiction in the Postcolony* (Fordham University Press, 2014), and *Claiming History: Colonialism, Ethnography and the Novel* (Columbia University Press, 1999).

Susan Bibler Coutin holds a PhD in anthropology from Stanford University and is Professor of Criminology, Law and Society and Anthropology at the University of California, Irvine, where she also is Associate Dean for Academic Programs in the School of Social Ecology. She is the author of *Exiled Home: Salvadoran*

Transnational Youth in the Aftermath of Violence (Duke University Press, 2016), *Nations of Emigrants: Shifting Boundaries of Citizenship in El Salvador and the United States* (Cornell University Press, 2007), *Legalizing Moves: Salvadoran Immigrants' Struggle for U.S. Residency* (University of Michigan Press, 2000), and *The Culture of Protest: Religious Activism within the U.S. Sanctuary Movement* (Westview Press, 1993).

Azadeh Dastyari is Associate Professor in the School of Law at Western Sydney University. She researches in the areas of human rights, refugee rights, the law of the sea and constitutional law, with a particular focus on the experiences of vulnerable groups such as older persons, Indigenous Australians, and children. Her articles have been published in the *International Journal of Refugee Law* and the *Human Rights Law Review* among other places, and her most recent book is *United States Migrant Interdiction and the Detention of Refugees in Guantanamo Bay* (Cambridge University Press, 2015).

Tanya Golash-Boza is Professor of Sociology at the University of California, Merced, and the author of several books and dozens of articles on immigration, race, and racism. Her latest book *Deported: Immigrant Policing, Disposable Labor and Global Capitalism* (New York University Press, 2016) was awarded the Distinguished Contribution to Research Book Award from the Latino/a Studies Section of the American Sociological Association. In 2010, she won the Distinguished Early Career Award from the Racial and Ethnic Minorities Studies Section of the American Sociological Association. In 2019, she received the UC Merced Senate Award for Excellence in Faculty Mentorship.

Asher Hirsch is Senior Policy Officer with the Refugee Council of Australia, the national umbrella body for refugees and the organizations and individuals who support them, and is completing a PhD at Monash University in refugee and human rights law focused on Australia's migration control activities in Southeast Asia. He holds a Bachelor of Arts, a Master of Human Rights Law, a Juris Doctor, and a Graduate Diploma in Legal Practice. His articles have been published in the *Human Rights Law Review, Refugee Survey Quarterly*, and *Human Rights Review*, among other places.

Daniel Kanstroom is Professor of Law and Thomas F. Carney Distinguished Scholar at Boston College, Faculty Director of the Rappaport Center for Law and Public Policy, and Co-Director of the Center for Human Rights and International Justice. His work has appeared in the *Harvard Law Review*, the *Yale Journal of International Law*, *The New York Times*, and *The Washington Post*. His recent books include *Aftermath: Deportation Law and the New American Diaspora* (Oxford University Press, 2012) and *Deportation Nation* (Harvard University Press, 2007), and he has edited volumes with M. Brinton Lykes (New York University Press, 2015) and Cecilia Menjívar (Cambridge University Press, 2013). His forthcoming book is *Deportation World* (Harvard University Press, 2022).

Molly Land is the Catherine Roraback Professor of Law and Human Rights at the University of Connecticut School of Law. Her research focuses on the intersection of human rights, science, and technology. She has authored more than twenty-five articles or book chapters and coedited or coauthored three books, including *New Technologies for Human Rights Law and Practice* (with Jay Aronson, 2018), available under an open access license from Cambridge University Press. A former Fulbright Scholar at the University of Bonn, Professor Land earned her JD at Yale Law School.

Kathryn Libal is Director of the Human Rights Institute and Associate Professor of Social Work and Human Rights at the University of Connecticut. Her publications have focused on human rights, social work, and the rights of refugees and asylum seekers, including contributory volumes on *Human Rights in the United States: Beyond Exceptionalism* (with Shareen Hertel, Cambridge University Press) and *Refugees and Asylum Seekers: Interdisciplinary and Comparative Perspectives* (with S. Megan Berthold, Praeger). She examines the localization of human rights norms and practices in the United States and the politics and practices of voluntarism and social activism to support the rights of refugees, asylum seekers, and migrants.

Jamie Chai Yun Liew is an immigration and refugee lawyer and Associate Professor at the University of Ottawa, Faculty of Law. She has appeared in front of the Immigration and Refugee Board, the Federal Court of Canada, and the Supreme Court of Canada. Her research focuses on how law and public policy marginalize immigrants, migrants, refugees, refugee claimants and stateless persons. Her current research examines how law constructs stateless persons in Canada and Malaysia. Her forthcoming book "Ghost Citizens" examines the post-colonial construction of in situ stateless persons as foreigners.

Luis Rubén González Márquez is a PhD student of Sociology at the University of California, Merced. Previously he studied History and Sociology in El Salvador and Ecuador. He has worked as a researcher in the National Teachers Training Institute (INFOD) of El Salvador and as Adjunct Professor in the University of El Salvador. For his doctoral studies in 2019–2021, he was awarded a Fulbright-LASPAU scholarship for the development of higher education in the Americas. His current research is about labor mobilization, political violence, and transnational production in Latin America.

Serena Parekh is Associate Professor of Philosophy at Northeastern University in Boston, where she is the director of the Politics, Philosophy, and Economics Program. Her primary philosophical interests are in social and political philosophy, feminist theory, and continental philosophy. She is the author of three books, including her most recent book *No Refuge: Ethics and the Global Refugee Crisis* (Oxford University Press, 2020). Her other books include *Refugees and the Ethics of Forced Displacement* (Routledge, 2017) and *Hannah Arendt and the Challenge of Modernity: A Phenomenology of Human Rights* (Routledge, 2008).

Jaya Ramji-Nogales is Associate Dean for Academic Affairs and the I. Herman Stern Research Professor at Temple University's Beasley School of Law. Her recent publications include *Migration Emergencies*, which uncovers the role of international law in constructing migration emergencies, and *Undocumented Migrants and the Failures of Universal Individualism*, which critiques human rights law as insufficiently attentive to the interests of undocumented migrants. She is the coauthor, with Andrew I. Schoenholtz and Philip G. Schrag, of *The End of Asylum*, a forthcoming book that analyzes changes to the US asylum system under the Trump administration.

Acknowledgments

We are grateful to the numerous people and institutions that made this book possible. We are indebted to our contributors, who first gathered in April 2017 at the University of Connecticut's (UConn) Stamford Campus to discuss the relationship between citizenship and human rights through an interdisciplinary lens. In particular, we thank Eleanor Acer, who was our keynote speaker at the conference. We are also grateful to Connecticut Students for a Dream, who organized a session with conference participants on the day before the conference to introduce us to their work and the challenges they face on a daily basis.

The conference and the publication of this book under an open access license were made possible by the Senator Joseph I. Lieberman Conference & Lecture Series on Human Rights Practice. Cambridge University Press's Gold Open Access license allows anyone anywhere around the world to read, download, and utilize the material in this volume directly from Cambridge University Press under a Creative Commons license. We are proud of this arrangement and hope that it becomes the norm for all scholarly work that relates to human rights and human flourishing.

We are deeply appreciative of the financial support provided by the University of Connecticut's Office of Global Affairs and the Human Rights Institute, as well as crucial logistical and administrative support provided for the 2017 conference by Rachel Jackson, Lyndsay Nalbandian, Nana Amos, Susan Rosman, Carolyn Golden, Cara Workman, Kathy Harrison, Terrence Cheng, Zahra Ali, and Heather McDonald. We are especially grateful to the conference steering committee for their thoughtful feedback and advice as we planned the conference: Nehama Aschkenasy, Jon Bauer, Mary Cygan, Samuel Martinez, Glenn Mitoma, Ingrid Semaan, and Rich Watnick. We are also thankful for the ongoing support of Dan Weiner, Vice President of Global Affairs, for his support of this volume and the associated conference, as well as his unfailing promotion of human rights at UConn. Our thanks also to Co-Lab for their design of the conference poster and for their permission to use that design for the cover of this volume.

In particular, we owe a profound debt to Cathy Buerger, who, as part of her responsibilities as a postdoctoral fellow with the Human Rights Institute, played an invaluable role in bringing the conference to fruition. Without her intellectual leadership in collecting and curating research materials associated with the conference as well as her enthusiasm and organizational skills in bringing the conference together, this volume would not have been published.

Molly Land would like to thank the School of Law for summer fellowship support for her research on these issues and Taylor Faranda Korthuis for her research assistance in planning the conference. Kathryn Libal would like to acknowledge the School of Social Work for its ongoing support for her activities in the Human Rights Institute and the Office for the Vice President of Research for financial assistance in the preparation of the index for this volume. Jillian Chambers would like to acknowledge her professors at both the School of Law and the Human Rights Institute for their mentorship, encouragement, and commitment to providing students with meaningful opportunities to grow as writers and practitioners.

It almost goes without saying that a project like this demands sacrifice from family members at critical points of the editorial process. Our deepest thanks to our families for their love, patience, and support throughout the production of this volume.

Finally, we dedicate this volume to Lyndsay Nalbandian, whose love, support, and unfailing good cheer touched countless lives at the Institute and the University. You are sorely missed.

Introduction

The Human Rights of Non-citizens

Molly Land, Kathryn Libal, and Jillian Chambers

Biden will turn Minnesota into a refugee camp – and he said that – overwhelming public resources, overcrowding schools and inundating your hospitals. You know that. It's already there. It's a disgrace what they've done to your state. It's just – it's absolutely – it's a disgrace, OK?

These were the words of the President of the United States at a September 2020 campaign rally in Duluth, Minnesota.[1] These words are not only emblematic of now-standard fearmongering about the economic impact of accepting refugees. They also shine a spotlight on what we believe is a fundamental shift in discourse around non-citizens that has been building for some time, driven by populist, nativist, and racist tropes of the "other" – a shift from a language of compassion to one of indifference or apathy. According to the President, it is "disgraceful" to give refuge to those who are suffering, or to provide medical and other aid to those without.

This book is an attempt to respond to that shift by exploring what, if any, obligations we as humans have to other humans. Featuring contributions drawn from a range of disciplinary perspectives, the chapters in the first part of this book seek to shed light on the original promise of human rights law and how that promise has failed – spectacularly so in many places – to provide a basis for ensuring rights. Human rights law, a supposedly universal body of law that applies to every individual, has long tolerated limits on human rights protections for non-citizens.[2] States

[1] J. Rose, "What Are the Presidential Candidates' Views on Immigration?," *Delaware Public Media*, October 14, 2020, www.delawarepublic.org/post/what-are-presidential-candidates-views-immigration.

[2] D. Weissbrodt, "Human Rights of Noncitizens," in R. E. Howard-Hassmann and M. Walton-Roberts (eds.), *The Human Right to Citizenship: A Slippery Concept* (Philadelphia: University of Pennsylvania Press, 2015), pp. 21–29; A. Abizadeh, "Closed Borders, Human Rights, and Democratic Legitimation," in D. Hollenbech (ed.), *Driven from Home: Protecting the Rights of Forced Migrants* (Washington, DC: Georgetown University Press, 2010), pp. 147–166;

deny many basic rights to non-citizens within their borders, and international law imposes only limited duties on states with respect to those fleeing persecution.[3] Furthermore, even those limited rights previously enjoyed by non-citizens are eroding in the face of rising nationalism, populism, xenophobia, and racism. Given such disparate treatment of non-citizens, the promise of *universal* human rights law appears relatively empty.[4]

Perhaps more importantly, however, this volume also seeks to go beyond a discussion of the promise and failure of human rights law, to help us imagine new forms of belonging across borders. If citizenship as a basis for rights is inadequate as a mechanism for universal protection,[5] what other values or commitments might ground action to realize rights for the most vulnerable? The chapters in the second half of this book explore these themes, again from a variety of disciplinary perspectives, considering, among other things, the ideas of solidarity and non-citizen rights as concepts that might ground belonging across borders.

The book is drawn from presentations at an April 2017 conference on the human rights of non-citizens, held at the University of Connecticut in Stamford, Connecticut, sponsored by the Senator Joseph I. Lieberman Conference & Lecture Series on Human Rights. Both the conference and the collection are interdisciplinary in order to allow broad access to the topic of the rights of non-citizens, with the contributors intervening from their own disciplinary perspectives about the question of who gets to have rights and why. As such, the chapters are also necessarily limited in scope. The literature on human rights and citizenship in each of the disciplines included in this volume – political science, philosophy, sociology, law, anthropology, literature – is extensive. We have sought to be selective and provocative, including pieces designed to start conversations, rather than complete them.

Although each chapter approaches the topic from a different starting point, they cohere around two central themes – first, the deficiencies of the current approach to rights across borders and, second, the importance of bottom-up approaches to reimagining belonging that center on the lived experience of rights and responsibilities. The book is organized around these two central themes.

The first half of the volume addresses the problems of our current response to the rights of non-citizens both within and outside of state borders and the inadequacy of citizenship as the only foundation for making meaningful claims to rights

E. T. Achiume, "Re-Imagining International Law for Global Migration: Migration as Decolonization?" (2017) 111 *AJIL Unbound* 142–146, at 142.

3   D. S. Fitzgerald, *Refuge beyond Reach: How Rich Democracies Repel Asylum Seekers* (New York: Oxford University Press, 2019); S. Parekh, *No Refuge* (New York: Oxford University Press, 2020), pp. 131–141.

4   Weissbrodt, "Human Rights of Noncitizens."

5   A. Brysk and G. Shafir, "Introduction: Globalization and the Citizenship Gap," in A. Brysk and G. Shafir (eds.), *People Out of Place: Globalization, Human Rights, and the Citizenship Gap* (New York: Routledge, 2004), pp. 3–9.

protection. The chapters in this part illustrate the deficiencies of a state-centric view of who has rights and the terrible harms this approach inflicts on the most vulnerable – creating in effect a system of global apartheid.

The contributions in the second half of the book explore alternative foundations for rights, including empathy, solidarity, empowerment, and responsibility. Empathy and solidarity are emotional responses that can provide the necessary impetus for political action to protect and empower the vulnerable. Empowerment does not necessarily have to be tied to political membership but can be manifested through participation in an economic community. Those who act must take responsibility for the harms of their own actions. And the law can embody these principles not only in substance but in process; the very process of law creation can contribute to the development of conditions needed for rights to be realized across borders.

A few caveats are in order, however. First, although all of the pieces in this collection address the rights of non-citizens, they focus on different aspects of non-citizenship. In general, the chapters use the term "refugee" to refer to individuals who meet the international definition of this term, whether or not they have been officially recognized as refugees by the UN Office of the High Commissioner for Refugees.[6] Individuals who meet the definition of a refugee are refugees even if their status has not yet been adjudicated.[7] In addition, basic human rights should be afforded to all, including those who do not qualify for recognition as refugees.[8] Some of the contributions also address the problem of statelessness and the political and logistical challenges of identifying who lacks effective protection of a state. The tenth chapter in this collection discusses the rights of "noncitizens" as a way of signaling all of the myriad ways in which individuals are affected by states of which they are not citizens.

Second, the contributions in this volume are not studies of citizenship in the traditional sense. A rich interdisciplinary literature theorizes the varied meanings and enactments of citizenship that have emerged in the modern nation-state system.[9] The chapters in this volume engage questions of the legal status of citizens

---

[6] United Nations High Commissioner for Refugees, *Handbook on Procedures and Criteria for Determining Refugee Status under the 1951 Convention and the 1967 Protocol Relating to the Status of Refugees* (Geneva, Switzerland: United Nations High Commissioner for Refugees, 2011), ¶ 28.

[7] United Nations High Commissioner for Refugees, *Note on Determination of Refugee Status under International Instruments EC/SCP/5* (August 24, 1977), ¶ 5, www.unhcr.org/excom/scip/3ae68cc04/note-determination-refugee-status-under-international-instruments.html (noting that "determination of refugee status can only be of a declaratory nature" and that "any person is a refugee within the framework of a given instrument if he meets the criteria of the refugee definition in that instrument, whether he is formally recognized as a refugee or not").

[8] Weissbrodt, "The Rights of Noncitizens."

[9] See, e.g., E. F. Isin and G. M. Nielsen (eds.), *Acts of Citizenship* (London: Zed Books, 2008); Brysk and Shafir (eds.), *People Out of Place*; Howard-Hassmann and Walton-Roberts, *The Human Right to Citizenship*; B. N. Lawrence and J. Stevens (eds.), *Citizenship in Question: Evidentiary Birthright and Statelessness* (Durham, NC: Duke University Press, 2017).

(formal citizenship) and the social, political, cultural, and symbolic practices of becoming and being a citizen (substantive citizenship), focusing on the non-citizen through a human rights lens.[10] Chapter 7 by Eleni Coundouriotis and Chapter 11 by Susan Bibler Coutin address how citizenship is enacted and new forms of belonging emerge through what some have called "lived citizenship," a concept that stresses the phenomenological and performative aspects of citizenship. As Kirsi Kallio, Bronwyn Wood, and Jouni Häkli note, such work contrasts citizenship "based on status and the respective rights granted by the state" and attends to "less formal modes of political participation and ways of enacting citizenship beyond the largely institutionalized practices within states."[11]

Furthermore, there are many aspects of the topic the volume does not address, including the experience of non-citizens with quasi-membership rights, such as work authorization but without political rights, or the experience of resettled refugees or permanent residents. It also largely does not address the experience of those who may have political citizenship, but for whom the rights of citizenship have been denied due to racism or other forms of oppression.[12]

Securing the human rights of non-citizens is one of the most pressing global social problems of the twenty-first century. Like climate change and the global economy, addressing the human rights implications of global migration – and forced migration in particular – transcends the limits of any one state and requires both domestic and international commitments and action. This volume attempts to provoke conversations across disciplines about how we can ground such commitments and action for those with whom we do not share a political community.

PART I: THE FAILURE OF RIGHTS

The first section of the book discusses the imperfections of citizenship as a basis for rights. A historic number of refugees, asylum seekers, asylees, undocumented migrants, and immigrants with varied statuses reside and work within states where they do not have citizenship.[13] And, in the post-Cold War era, they share new forms of insecurity and precarity due to a rise in xenophobia and racist backlash against

---

[10] E. F. Isin, "Theorizing Acts of Citizenship," in Isin and Nielsen (eds.), *Acts of Citizenship*, pp. 15–43.

[11] K. P. Kallio, B. E. Wood, and J. Häkli, "Lived Citizenship: Conceptualizing an Emerging Field" (2020) 24(6) *Citizenship Studies* 713–729 at 714.

[12] Brysk and Shafir, "Introduction," pp. 6–7.

[13] The International Organization of Migration estimates that there are 272 million international migrants (3.5% of the world's population), of which approximately two thirds are labor migrants, in 2020. This figure surpasses earlier estimates that by 2050 there would be 230 million international migrants. IOM UN Migration, *World Immigration Report 2020* (Geneva, Switzerland: International Organization for Migration, 2020), https://publications.iom.int/ system/files/pdf/wmr_2020.pdf at 2.

refugees and immigrants in many countries.[14] Zero-sum politics around the world frame the issue of non-citizens' rights as "us against them," and politicians manipulate fears of economic and physical insecurity to justify hardened borders.[15]

The result is that many countries are now instituting procedures that effectively deprive migrants and refugees of even the limited rights they might once have had.[16] These can be seen as part of a larger trend to "illegalize" migration in the past few decades, following an earlier century of creating legal mechanisms for global migration.[17] As Catherine Dauvergne notes, "It has proven extraordinarily difficult to meaningfully extend human rights norms to those with 'illegal' status."[18] States' efforts to limit "illegal migration" have occurred simultaneously with increasingly codified and restrictive asylum law norms at state levels, enabling states to "narrow the constraint on sovereignty to the smallest point possible."[19] Nancy Hiemstra and Alison Mountz highlight that in the United States, immigration legislation passed in 1996 is casting a long shadow on immigration enforcement practices today, where the full force of crafting conditions of "illegality" is brought to bear on racialized groups.[20]

In recent decades, as well, states have sought to deter asylum seekers through policies of mandatory detention and deportation. The United States and many European countries have aimed to prevent migrants from making claims of asylum at ports of entry and have enacted a queuing process that forces would-be claimants to wait for extended periods of time at sea or a land border in inhumane conditions.[21] David Scott Fitzgerald has signaled that rich democracies actively repel asylum seekers, making refuge "beyond reach" for most.[22] Yet policies to deter or repel are evident not only at EU, Australian, and U.S. borders, but also increasingly

---

[14] See, e.g., M. Czaika and A. Di Lillo, "The Geography of Anti-Immigrant Attitudes across Europe, 2004–2014" (2018) 44(15) *Journal of Ethnic and Racial Studies* 2453–2479; J. O. Baker, D. Cañarte, and L. E. Day, "Race, Xenophobia, and Punitiveness among the American Public" (2018) 59(2) *The Sociological Quarterly* 363–383.

[15] M. Hooghe and R. Dassonville, "Explaining the Trump Vote: The Effect of Racist Resentment and Anti-Immigrant Sentiments" (2018) 51(3) *PS: Political Science and Politics* 528–533; P. C. Gattinara, "Europeans, Shut the Borders! Anti-refugee Mobilisation in Italy and France," in D. della Porta (ed.), *Solidarity Mobilisations in the "Refugee Crisis": Contentious Moves* (Cham, Switzerland: Palgrave MacMillan, 2018), pp. 271–297.

[16] R. Vandevoordt, "Resisting Bare Life: Civil Solidarity and the Hunt for Illegalized Migrants" (2020) *International Migration* 1–16.

[17] C. Dauvergne, *Making People Illegal: What Globalization Means for Migration and Law* (Cambridge: Cambridge University Press, 2008), p. 4.

[18] Ibid., p. 5.

[19] Ibid.

[20] N. Hiemstra and A. Mountz, "Slippery Slopes into Illegality and the Erosion of Citizenship in the United States," in Howard-Hassmann and Walton-Roberts (eds.), *The Human Right to Citizenship*, p. 165.

[21] C. Dickerson, "Inside the Refugee Camp on America's Doorstep," *New York Times*, October 23, 2020, www.nytimes.com/2020/10/23/us/mexico-migrant-camp-asylum.html.

[22] Fitzgerald, *Refuge beyond Reach.*

in many Global South states as well, as Yajaira Ceciliano-Navarro, Tanya Golash-Boza, and Luis Rubén González Márquez elaborate in Chapter 6.

The prevalent assumption that rights are tied to citizenship leaves countless people without protection as they flee violence, persecution, and famine. This assumption also coexists uncomfortably with the reality of the current moment, in which many people live and reside outside their country of nationality. Furthermore, the countries that fight hardest to close their borders are often also responsible for the very conditions and polices that have caused or contributed to displacement and migration, such as the United States with respect to historic role in destabilization of Central American governments and economies.[23] Systematically denying human rights to those in situations of vulnerability – both within a state's borders and outside of them – is unjustified from both a moral and a practical perspective.

Finally, assuming that citizenship is the primary foundation for the enjoyment of rights also fails to recognize the countless ways in which citizenship itself is under assault today. From new state policies seeking to strip individuals of their citizenship status to immigration policies that deprive those in mixed-status families of the rights to which they are supposedly entitled – citizenship is no longer the foundation we believed it to be.[24] Likely it never was. The pressures of globalization and humanitarian crisis are simply making this more evident than ever before. By bringing contemporary scholarship on the rights of non-citizens to bear on current debates about rights and citizenship, the book is intended to help contribute to a dialogue about the very urgent problems states around the world are facing in grappling with migration, flight, and the failure of law and institutions.

One of the critical concerns of this collection is the inadequacy of domestic and international laws and institutions intended to protect those who have sought refuge beyond borders or who are stateless. As Weissbrodt points out, the rights of non-citizens are addressed in all the major human rights treaties and yet the chasm between legal principle and lived reality for non-citizens, and especially undocumented migrants, asylum seekers, and refugees, continues to grow.[25] Both international law and the international institutions that administer migration (the UN High Commissioner for Refugees, International Organization of Migration, and International Labor Organization) are ill equipped to address what is a profound global challenge.[26] This is a sober assessment shared by scholars and practitioners as we approach the United Nations' 75th anniversary.

---

[23] M. G. Garcia, *Seeking Refuge: Central American Migration to Mexico, the United States, and Canada* (Berkeley: University of California Press, 2006), pp. 13–43.
[24] R. E. Howard-Hassmann, "Introduction: The Human Right to Citizenship," in Howard-Hassmann and Walton-Roberts (eds.), *The Human Right to Citizenship*, pp. 1–18.
[25] Weissbrodt, "Human Rights of Noncitizens."
[26] P. Nyers, "Humanitarian Hubris and the Global Compacts on Refugees and Migration" (2019) 5(2) *Global Affairs* at 171–178.

The United Nations has recognized this crisis of global governance regarding international migration and systematic violations of non-citizens' rights taking place around the world. In September 2016, the United Nations initiated a summit to convene world leaders and representatives of UN and nongovernmental organizations to make international migration, and particularly the situation of refugees, an international priority. The New York Declaration created a framework for future deliberations and, by late 2018, many UN member states had developed and agreed to a Global Compact for Safe, Orderly and Regular Migration (GCM) and a Global Compact on Refugees (GCR).[27] Although these compacts have been heralded as important steps in international law, it remains to be seen how they will guide international migration policy and practice at the national and supranational levels. The GCM highlights that human rights norms and processes are fundamental to the compact:

> The Global Compact is based on international human rights law and upholds the principles of non-regression and non-discrimination. By implementing the Global Compact, we ensure effective respect for and protection and fulfilment of the human rights of all migrants, regardless of their migration status, across all stages of the migration cycle. We also reaffirm the commitment to eliminate all forms of discrimination, including racism, xenophobia, and intolerance, against migrants and their families.[28]

The UN General Assembly passed a resolution affirming the Global Compact on Refugees on December 17, 2018.[29] The preamble highlights that the agreement demonstrates states' and other stakeholders' "political will and the ambition to operationalize the principle of burden- and responsibility-sharing" and to "mobilize the international community as a whole."[30] Peter Nyers charges that these compacts reflect a form of "humanitarian hubris" by assuming the need to "manage migration and asylum in the first place" and that "governments and international agencies are capable of managing global movements in a 'safe, orderly, and regular' manner."[31] Nyers points to another source of hubris as "the precept that protecting the interests of host states – states of refuge – should be a leading objective of the global compacts."[32] This latter critique is a central concern running through the chapters

---

[27] United Nations, "Global Compact for Safe, Orderly and Regular Migration, A/RES/73/195," December 19, 2018, www.un.org/en/ga/search/view_doc.asp?symbol=A/RES/73/195; "ILO and IOM Sign Agreement to Strengthen Collaboration on Migration Governance," October 23, 2020, www.iom.int/news/ilo-and-iom-sign-agreement-strengthen-collaboration-migration-governance.

[28] United Nations, "Global Compact."

[29] Ibid.

[30] Ibid., p. iii.

[31] Nyers, "Humanitarian Hubris," p. 172.

[32] Ibid.

included in Part I, which examines the failure of rights to be recognized or secured by governments and international organizations.

Chapter 2 by Kristy A. Belton and Jamie Chai Yun Liew examines the limitations of the global–national governance nexus for non-citizens, focusing on how states increasingly are "unmaking citizens." The authors argue that a patchwork of national laws governing who can be a citizen – including variations of citizenship acquired at birth or through naturalization – renders citizenship "an inadequate foundation upon which to base human rights." Legal barriers to citizenship have been created and fortified that exclude individuals because they are indigenous, female, or members of an ethnic minority, while other laws deprive individuals of citizenship based on criminal behavior or national security interests. Thus, citizenship – already an arbitrary concept that is often rendered ineffective by political or bureaucratic forces – is today even more precarious as a foundation for rights, as governments are increasingly depriving citizens of their claims to formal belonging on the grounds of national security or the war on terror.

The chapter highlights that "citizenship is not necessarily a neutral and stable status upon which to base rights, freedoms, and protections" because the law that grounds citizenship is not itself neutral. Modern citizenship law is based on international political practice that favors state sovereignty. Thus, although treaties and conventions would come to recognize the significance of citizenship through the human right of nationality, "no international organization exists, whether as creator, arbiter, or enforcer, of citizenship laws for any state." Belton and Liew write persuasively that "[p]erhaps citizenship was never meant to be more than an international ordering principle of people(s) and we have tied notions of human rights, equality, and justice to a concept that was never built to hold them."

Chapter 3 by Jacqueline Bhabha, "Zero Humanity: The Reality of Current US Immigration Policy toward Central American Refugee Children and Their Families," illustrates the way in which even basic obligations owed to refugees within a state's territory are currently being eroded. Bhabha examines the Trump administration's policy of family separation to illustrate the impacts of anchoring rights on citizenship, and she calls for international action to remedy the deficiencies of national practice. Bhabha details the intensification of policies of deterrence since 2016 to block or prevent "humanitarian migrant children and families" entry into the United States, force them to leave the United States while awaiting asylum adjudication, or leave them to languish for long periods in harsh detention conditions. She argues that these policies are not only inhumane and in violation of binding domestic and international legal obligations, but also "futile." She underscores that the so-called zero tolerance policies, which have an explicit intent to "deter" asylum seekers, including children, from entering the United States, are in fact "zero humanity" policies.

One way the United States is able to perpetuate its "zero humanity" policies, Bhabha explains, is by its failure to ratify international treaties that would impose higher obligations in its treatment of children, such as the Convention on the Rights of the Child. Without ratification, the Trump administration's family separation policy "would doubtless have elicited more vigorous international protest had the UN Committee on the Rights of the Child been afforded oversight." And although a US court was able to halt family separation as unconstitutional, government officials were unable to comply with the order to reunify children with their families because it had no "clear or centralized tracking system." Bhabha also depicts the administration's efforts to overturn *Flores*,[33] the seminal Supreme Court case governing child migration detention. This chapter illustrates the nuances of "law" as a tool. Law has tremendous power to provide a platform for halting discriminatory government practices, but it can also be used to challenge long-standing precedent like *Flores* on which families have come to rely, camouflaging exclusionary politics under a veneer of neutrality.

Chapter 4 by Azadeh Dastyari and Asher Hirsch, "Australia's Extraterritorial Border Control Policies," further illustrates the inadequacy of law to ensure rights. Technically, states are obligated under international treaties to provide certain rights to individuals once they reach the state's territory. States are rendering this obligation increasingly meaningless by extending the reach of their immigration policies beyond their borders to ensure that no refugees reach their territory and exercise these rights. The authors highlight how "non-entrée policies" are more readily enforced in Australia because of its isolation and lack of land borders. They outline measures to stop irregular arrivals of refugees by air and sea, which have increased in intensity in the past decade despite human rights advocacy. Consistent with other chapters in this part, including those of Belton and Liew, Bhabha, and Ceciliano, Golash-Boza, and Rubén González (discussed later), Dastyari and Hirsch underscore that Australia's policy response toward refugees aligns with "the view that a refugee is a potential threat, rather than someone fleeing from harm." Here they amplify Nyers' point that states in the Global North have deployed a non-entrée regime "under the guise of an orderly and regular system" and are most concerned with protecting host states' interests.[34]

Dastyari and Hirsch showcase the ways in which Australia has been avoiding its treaty obligations by exploiting loopholes through their non-entrée measures such as extraterritorial processing and detention, interdiction at sea, and carrier sanctions. Dastyari and Hirsch argue, however, that Australia's refugee response is still illegal under the Refugee Convention, because while "states may not have a duty to grant asylum, they do have an obligation to provide access to their asylum procedures." This access is key to refugees having their rights recognized and fulfilled and for Australia to avoid running afoul of its binding legal obligations.

---

[33] *Reno v. Flores*, 507 U.S. 292 (1993).
[34] Nyers, "Humanitarian Hubris," p. 172.

Chapter 5 by Brad K. Blitz, "Protection through Revisionism? UNHCR, Statistical Reporting, and the Representation of Stateless People," begins by identifying yet another gap in international protections for non-citizens – the way that stateless individuals are counted by the UNHCR. Blitz argues that international efforts to respond to the problem of statelessness have replicated and reinforced disparities by focusing on de jure statelessness. Blitz charts the history of how the UNHCR defined and collected information about stateless individuals, demonstrating that its internal decisions and methodologies adopted a narrow definition of statelessness that exhibited deference to the (often limited) way in which states counted "statelessness." Blitz also critiques the results-based turn to standards and indicators as creating systemic incentives to underestimate statelessness.

Blitz goes beyond identifying gaps, however, to generate recommendations for how the UNHCR might reform its approach, advocating a bottom-up approach that foregrounds the experiences of stateless individuals themselves. He argues forcefully that numbers matter, not only because of what they reflect about the world, but also because of their political authority. As he explains, "[w]ho is counted also tells us about governmental and institutional priorities and exposes biases about *what* counts, and how resources *should* be allocated." According to Blitz, current approaches "reflect an increasingly top-down logic that ignores the lived experience of stateless people and undermines the provision of humanitarian protection to some who may need it." Instead of a top-down managerialist approach to "success," Blitz advocates focusing instead on how changes on the ground impact individuals and limit their ability to rely on citizenship to protect their rights. Definitions of statelessness and measures of success should foreground the lived experience of those who are stateless themselves.

Chapter 6 offers a critical vision of restrictive internal and external immigration policies as part of a much larger system of global apartheid. In "Reflections on Anti-immigration Narratives and the Establishment of Global Apartheid," Yajaira Ceciliano-Navarro, Tanya Golash-Boza, and Luis Rubén González Márquez examine the construction, organization, and maintenance of global apartheid ideology "around narratives that criminalize immigrants and immigration." The authors underscore that restrictionist immigration policies in the Global North reflect a segregationist ideology that "adopts subtle mechanisms of control, removal, and exploitation of migrants worldwide," which in turn preserves wealth for a small minority. Deterrent and punitive moves such as these result in the transformation of "freedom of movement" into a costly and dangerous process, where moving becomes a "privilege and not a right." Examining the ways in which mechanisms of control, removal, and exploitation of immigrants is steeped in racist, segregationist logics allows us to see how these policies operate to allow wealthier countries to control the movement of non-White populations.

The analogy offered by the authors to South African apartheid is helpful because it sheds light on how law (and the state) can codify and justify exclusionary principles and practices, as well as how resistance to law can constitute resistance to injustice. Refusal to observe border controls and even the very act of transit over boundaries reject global forms of apartheid and constitute a demonstration of agency – or "acts of citizenship."[35]

Taken together, the chapters in this part underscore the limits of both global and domestic governance in securing the human rights of asylum seekers and refugees. They highlight the magnitude of injustice that is perpetuated by prioritizing national interests over the welfare of asylum seekers, refugees, and other migrants. Maintaining draconian border controls and waging policies of deterrence, the Global North enforces a kind of global apartheid that has ramifications not only in the present, but also for future generations.

PART II: BELONGING ACROSS BORDERS

Why do we – or should we – act to protect people who are suffering, when those people are not part of our political community and when their suffering is distant, both geographically and metaphorically? What underpins the human rights commitment to universality, the idea that every individual everywhere should have rights regardless of their political membership? Scholars across a range of disciplines have provided a variety of answers to these questions, some of which are highly pragmatic. Michael Perry, for example, points to ideas such as religion, altruism, and self-interest as motivating the "spirit of brotherhood" that is called for in Article 1 of the Universal Declaration of Human Rights.[36] The altruistic perspective, Perry explains, rests in an individual's self-perception of themselves as an altruist – as one who believes all life matters and is simply "wired" to care about suffering.[37]

Others point to empathy and other-identification as providing a basis for acting to protect those outside one's own political community. Lynn Hunt, for example, argues that the emergence of the novel in the eighteenth century was instrumental in promoting the idea of equality and expanding the capacity of the reader to have empathy with those separated by lines of class and other status.[38] Novels, according to Hunt, provided the foundation for the idea of universal rights because they allowed the reader to see others "as like them, as having the same kinds of inner emotions."[39] As Alison Brysk has written, human rights is centrally about the mobilization of care, which itself "rests on empathy, and empathy requires humanization."[40] Serena

---

[35] Isin and Nielsen, *Acts of Citizenship*.

[36] M. J. Perry, "Why Act Towards One Another 'In a Spirit of Brotherhood?': The Grounds of Human Rights," in M. Goodale (ed.), *Human Rights at the Crossroads* (Oxford: Oxford University Press, 2013), p. 45.

[37] Ibid., pp. 55–56.

[38] L. Hunt, *Inventing Human Rights: A History* (New York: W. W. Norton, 2007), p. 40.

[39] Ibid.

[40] A. Brysk, "'Why We Care': Constructing Solidarity," in Goodale (ed.), *Human Rights at the Crossroads*, pp. 163, 167.

Parekh[41] and Kathryn Sikkink[42] – writing respectively as a philosopher and a political theorist – have invoked Iris Marion Young's work on injustice to promote ideas of responsibility to others as a basis for engaging in collective and individual action to protect the human rights of all.

The second half of this collection engages with these ideas of empathy and responsibility to explore arguments for protecting the rights of others from a variety of different vantage points. Eleni Coundouriotis' analysis of the work of Peter Balakian in Chapter 7 introduces this discussion by examining the role of narrative in creating conditions that enable a discussion about belonging and rights. Chapters 8, 9, and 10 by Daniel Kanstroom, Serena Parekh, and Tendayi Bloom, respectively, suggest possible grounds for new forms of belonging, including solidarity, economic rights, and non-citizen rights. The final two chapters in this part, Chapters 11 and 12 by Susan Bibler Coutin and Jaya Ramji-Nogales, respectively, discuss the way forward. They propose bottom-up methods for constructing international law and political action that may be better able to accommodate and channel responsibilities across borders.

Chapter 7, "Imagining New Forms of Belonging: The Futurity of the Stateless," reflects on the importance of narrative in constructing community and defining bonds of belonging. According to Coundouriotis, literary analysis can help us navigate difficult questions of law and policy by prodding the reader's imagination and ability to think outside the box. Coundouriotis examines Peter Balakian's memoir *Black Dog of Fate* to explore the role of testimony in relating past to future. As she explains, "Testimony makes legible the futurity of statelessness and invites creative engagement to elaborate on new aspirations." Accounting for the past is what allows us "to make a claim for future belonging."

This chapter is also a contemporary illustration of literature's ability to mobilize empathy as a foundation for such claims. According to Coundouriotis, narrative is essential in allowing the reader to identify with the experience of another. Empathy, as opposed to compassion and sympathy, is an active practice of becoming vulnerable. It requires one to identify with aspects of the experience of another person. Identifying with those in precarious and vulnerable circumstances can be terrifying: One worries it may negate one's own pain, or that the experience of empathy will be painful itself, or will create new pain due to an awareness of one's powerlessness. Balakian's work engages the reader in the practice of empathy by allowing the reader to identify with Balakian, which not only makes legible the experience of violation but also "refuses to other the victim of genocide."

Considering Balakian's oeuvre as a whole, Coundouriotis traces a path in his work from engagement with history to responsibility for the future. His poetry, for example, links crises such as genocide and environmental catastrophe "by analogy

---

[41] S. Parekh, *No Refuge* (Oxford: Oxford University Press, 2020).

[42] K. Sikkink, *The Hidden Face of Rights: Towards a Politics of Responsibilities* (New Haven, CT: Yale University Press, 2020).

and poetic image to the plight of the stateless, making it hard to refuse the urgent predicament of the stateless in our contemporary moment." Balakian's works thus "afford a type of recognition cast as discovery that urges us to witness and hence interrupt the ways the past continues into the present. Through this witness, the stateless find new interlocutors with whom to claim belonging." Coundouriotis argues that this "broadened sense of participation in history" in the reader "links explicitly to an ethos of human rights: everything is pegged on the idea that human rights give legibility to the type of responsible subjectivity that extends belonging to the stateless."

The next three chapters explore other foundations for such claims of future belonging. These contributions pick up the theme of empathy but move beyond, exploring the role of rights, law, and the market in promoting or undermining relationships of belonging. Chapter 8, "'Either I Close My Eyes or I Don't': The Evolution of Rights in Encounters between Sovereign Power and 'Rightless' Migrants," explores cases in which governments have prosecuted individuals who have provided migrants and refugees with basic humanitarian assistance – Cédric Herrou, a French olive farmer who provided assistance to unauthorized migrants in France; two German ship captains who rescued distressed migrants at sea; and Scott Warren, who provided food and water for people trying to cross the Sonoran Desert in the United States. In each of these cases, the individuals who were prosecuted invoked principles higher than the law in justification of their actions. And in some, the courts appeared to recognize such higher principles. In Herrou's case, Kanstroom explains, the *Conseil constitutionnel* in France invalidated Herrou's conviction, invoking the principle of fraternity as a value that must be balanced with state efforts to safeguard public order.

Kanstroom's work illuminates the possibility that principles such as fraternity and solidarity might ground efforts to create relationships across borders, including to compel action on behalf of those who are not a part of our political community. The cases he explores also illustrate the way in which rights can emerge not only via the nation-state but also through the actions of individuals. Rights emerge, according to Kanstroom, "from encounters between raw state sovereign power and ostensibly extra-legal, humanitarian actions for those at the lowest ebb of their power and with the least legal status." According to Kanstroom, the principle of fraternity "imbues charity with implications of universal obligation."

The cases he examines also provide a basis for giving those bonds legal and not just moral weight. The decision of the *Conseil constitutionnel* in Herrou's case recognizes the idea that acting to protect the safety of someone who otherwise would have no claim on us can override the sovereign's otherwise nearly invincible prerogative in the context of national security. Kanstroom argues that "noncitizens, especially the unauthorized and ostensibly 'rightless,' are uniquely positioned to challenge, to critique, and to improve the meaning of law in constitutional democracies and of international human rights."

These cases – and the judicial system's response to individual defiance of unjust laws – illustrate not only the possibility of other ways of expressing rights outside of citizenship but also the risks that insistence on policing these boundaries could pose for the legitimacy of the constitutional order. In this way, Kanstroom's chapter is in dialogue with the arguments of Tendayi Bloom, who later in the volume argues that the state's legitimacy derives not just from its accountability to its citizens, but also the extent to which it attends to its relationships with and thus its obligations to noncitizens. Kanstroom similarly argues, "Since legitimate lawmaking both responds to and generates communicative power from, as it were, below, noncitizens play a central role in translating communicative power into administrative power and law."

The third chapter in this part, Chapter 9 by Serena Parekh, "Do Non-citizens Have a Right to Have Economic Rights? Locke, Smith, Hayek, and Arendt on Economic Rights," explores the idea of economic rights and the ability to meaningfully participate in the economy as a prerequisite for the enjoyment of human rights. Parekh begins by re-reading Locke, Smith, and Hayek, arguing that these scholars – known best for their defenses of the free market – in fact anticipated involvement of the state in the market in order to ensure individual equality and minimum economic guarantees.

Focusing on the experiences of individuals who are present within a country but unable to participate in the market because they lack work authorization (as opposed to those outside of a country seeking admission), Parekh then argues that Arendt's ideas about the need for a "right to have rights"[43] can be extended to participation in the market. Parekh flips the usual neoliberal conception of economic citizenship in which individuals voice their opinions through participation in the market and the mechanism of consumer choice.[44] According to Parekh, economic rights are not a manifestation of citizenship, but its precursor. Parekh argues, echoing Arendt, that "being human is not enough to have one's economic rights protected." Instead, "non-citizens need a right to have economic rights, that is, a right to belong to an economic community." Whether or not one can actually enjoy human rights has less to do with one's citizenship than one's place in the global economy.

Chapter 10 makes an explicit claim for rights based on non-citizenship. In "Human Rights Are Not Enough: Understanding Noncitizenship and Noncitizens in Their Own Right," Tendayi Bloom argues in favor of the concept of "noncitizen" rights. Rather than seeing citizenship as the sole foundational relationship between an individual and a state and non-citizenship as its absence, she contends that there is another foundational relationship, that of non-citizenship. Moreover, this

---

[43] H. Arendt, *Origins of Totalitarianism* (2nd ed., New York: Harcourt, 1978); *see also* S. DeGoyer et al., *The Right to Have Rights* (London: Verso, 2018).

[44] K. A. Faulk, "Solidarity and Accountability: Rethinking Citizenship and Human Rights," in Goodale (ed.), *Human Rights at the Crossroads*, pp. 98, 102.

"institutional, necessarily non-contractual, relationship of noncitizenship" gives rise to substantive rights and obligations of its own. As states seek to ensure that their citizens have access to goods, they "may also *actively impair* access to these goods for others." As she explains, "a state has specific and institutional obligations towards those people who bear the burden of its existence and of its actions." Writing from the vantage point of political theory, Bloom's argument is that relationships of both citizenship and non-citizenship are essential to state construction and state legitimacy.

By emphasizing responsibility, Bloom's contribution is in conversation the work of several human rights scholars seeking to reinvigorate the concept of responsibility. In her recently published book *No Refuge*, Parekh argues that we must move beyond a frame of "rescue" toward a frame of political responsibility for conditions of structural injustice that deny refugees the minimum conditions of human dignity.[45] The states that established the current refugee system "have created a situation in which the vast majority of refugees are effectively unable to get refuge in any meaningful sense; that is, they are not able to access the minimum conditions of human dignity."[46] This is a structural injustice that *we* – the citizens of those states and Parekh's audience for her book – "share political responsibility for."[47] This is not the responsibility that one might have for a "direct injustice"[48] like the US family separation policy, but rather a responsibility for an injustice that has resulted from the aggregate acts of people living their lives, which is then "*assigned* depending on how we are related to the injustice."[49] Kathryn Sikkink, in her recent work focusing on responsibility, has argued that some harms cannot be remedied without individual and collective action.[50] As a result, "for the enjoyment and implementation of rights, other agents, including individuals, must take some responsibilities for the fulfillment of rights."[51] Recent work by Tendayi Achiume ties this responsibility to the entrenched global inequality caused by colonization.[52] She argues that "Third World peoples" are not in fact political strangers to "First World political communities" – they "were brutally initiated into First World political communities under European colonialism and remain within these communities today."[53] Based on this, she argues that "First World states have no right to exclude Third World persons" and that "Third World persons are entitled to First World inclusion."[54]

[45] Parekh, *No Refuge*, p. 12
[46] Ibid., p. 159.
[47] Ibid.
[48] Ibid., p. 167
[49] Ibid., p. 172.
[50] Sikkink, *The Hidden Face of Rights*, p. 45.
[51] Ibid., p. 52.
[52] Achiume, "Re-Imagining International Law," p. 143; *see also* E. T. Achiume, "Migration as Decolonization" (2019) 71(6) *Stanford Law Review* 1509–1574.
[53] Achiume, "Migration as Decolonization" at 1533.
[54] Ibid. at 1551.

The work of Bloom and these other scholars also helps us understand how to direct this responsibility. To varying degrees, they argue that responsibility arises from our deep interdependence with others, regardless of (or even as a result of) borders. Empathy or fraternity may provide impetuous for action, but it does not necessarily help decide where action is needed.[55] Bloom's argument, however, is that responsibility is tied to impact: "A stronger noncitizen relationship gives rise to stronger claims." This is resonant in the cases examined by Kanstroom as well. It is not undifferentiated suffering that Herrou rails against with his acts of civil disobedience – rather, it is suffering that is caused by the injustice of French law. When asked by a judge, "Why do you do all this," Herrou described French migration enforcement as "ignoble," explaining: "My inaction and my silence would make me an accomplice, I do not want to be an accomplice."[56]

The final two contributions begin a discussion about how to move forward in constructing new bonds of belonging that can sustain political action on behalf of non-citizens. Chapter 11 by Susan Bibler Coutin, "Uncertainty and Educational Mismatch: Schooling and Life Pursuits in Contexts of Illegalization," illustrates the precarity associated with a life without citizenship or equivalent status, and it contrasts this precarity with immigrants' own understandings of what kinds of affiliations give rise to an entitlement to enjoy rights in a society. Coutin analyzes the complicated mismatches between the lives of immigrant youth and their families and the forms of subjectivity created through US immigration enforcement initiatives. These initiatives have subjected unauthorized immigrants from Mexico and Central America to illegalization, which gives rise to experiences of stigmatization and discrimination, as well as material precarity. Coutin focuses on the process by which individuals, families, and communities are "constituted" by the state and other actors as "illegal" and "undeserving" as an "ongoing part of daily life." Immigrant youths' lives in her qualitative study were rendered precarious by the state limiting access to key social institutions, including higher education, employment, health care, family, and safety. Public condemnation of undocumented immigrants for allegedly undermining the rule of law, however, differed sharply from interviewees' senses of their own merit, who saw themselves as deserving even though they remained vulnerable to detention and deportation.

Coutin's interviews profoundly illustrate the negative effects of this process of illegalization for youth in California during two different periods (2006–2010 and 2014–2017). But the interviews also reveal that youth have created new forms of

[55] P. Bloom, *Against Empathy: The Case for Rational Compassion* (New York: Harper Collins, 2016), p. 34.

[56] K. G. Brown, "France Prosecuting Citizens for 'Crimes of Solidarity,'" *Aljazeera*, January 25, 2017, www.aljazeera.com/indepth/features/2017/01/france-prosecuting-citizens-crimes-solidarity-170122064151841.html.

durable, meaningful belonging, even among those who did not qualify for Deferred Action for Child Arrivals (DACA) status. Through the youths' stories, Coutin was able to point to the mechanisms through which "educational institutions were potentially empowering," but also that schools, colleges, and universities could be sites where "illegalization, precarizaton, and uncertainty occurred." Coutin suggests that similarities in experiences of those who came before or after DACA was enacted point to the inadequacy of temporary measures, which are "insufficient to counter both the intensity of illegalization, and the financial pressures of paying for college." Coutin calls for us to imagine a reality when college campuses can be "truly sanctuaries" that make achieving a higher education accessible for all youth regardless of immigration status or income.

Finally, Chapter 12 by Jaya Ramji-Nogales, "Constructing Human Rights: State Power and Migrant Silence," also begins by charting the gaps in current law. Ramji-Nogales traces the evolution of the concept of rights in international law, both the promise of its ideals and the disappointment of reality. Despite claims to be universal, the state-centric nature of international human rights law "prioritizes the power of the state while erasing the interests of migrants." The purported universality of human rights "mask[s] political choices that prioritize certain interests over others."

Ramji-Nogales calls for a "radical rethinking" of human rights law through the vehicle of "a new human rights treaty focused on migrants rather than states." Although states are unlikely to be supportive of a new treaty, efforts to create a new treaty would have an expressive function and could also "help to frame the debate, persuade the public, and focus activist energies in lobbying states for change." More fundamentally, the project of a new treaty would help advance a rethinking of human rights law by foregrounding the voices and experiences of migrants themselves. She explains: "An emancipatory approach to international human rights law might instead take the human seriously, beginning from the perspective of the law's subject: the migrant. A reimagined canon would identify and foreground the voices of those in precarious situations, asking what protections are needed to minimize their vulnerability."

The pieces by Blitz and Ramji-Nogales, together with those by Coutin and Kanstroom, decenter the state and emphasize the voices of those most affected by the law's gaps. In chapters by both Kanstroom and Ramji-Nogales', the state is the cause of the harm, not its solution. Coutin draws from interviews with Salvadoran immigrants and DACA recipients, illustrating the impact of illegalization on migrants' lived experiences and how they have resisted these pressures and harms. Blitz and Ramji-Nogales emphasize the importance of centering on these experiences to create bottom-up solutions that can better respond to the harms of the law.

To the extent that human rights is seen as a solution in each of these chapters, it is a different (and potentially more powerful) vision of human rights than one typically sees. In each of these, human rights is not operating as law, but as a vehicle for care. This vision of human rights emphasizes the responsibilities that individuals have to

18

one another[57] – what Alison Brysk calls "care" – "giving attention and worth to someone else's experience, in a way that makes us available for solidarity with that person."[58] Care, in this view, is ultimately a political act and (as Kanstroom would attest) in some instances an act of civil disobedience. Brysk writes: "Care is how we speak love to power."[59] As Ramji-Nogales notes, "only by hearing and uplifting the voices of undocumented migrants can we push human rights law closer to its emancipatory potential, redeeming the humanity of migrants and citizens of destination states alike."

This vision of human rights as acts of care/empathy/solidarity is a vision of human rights not as law, but as action. Human rights are not ensured, but claimed. And it is the process of claiming those rights that helps create the sense of social responsibility needed to ensure rights.[60] In Ramji-Nogales' vision, for example, the value of a treaty is not in the law it might create, but in the networks and relationships that mobilization around a treaty might foster. Transnational advocacy to create international instruments promotes relationships between those in different political communities, thus providing a foundation for the development of greater shared understandings of the meaning of rights. This approach resonates with human rights scholars such as Alicia Ely Yamin, who emphasize the importance of rights-based practices, in addition to rights-based results. Thus, for Yamin, human rights are "social practices that create spaces for vital deliberation on how to arrange social institutions to meet population needs, especially of the most disadvantaged."[61]

Of course, this does not mean that law is irrelevant. As Chapters 2–4 illustrate, legal reforms are clearly needed. It does mean, however, that human rights cannot be achieved by law alone. Blitz's argument about the wrong turn that the UNHCR has taken in focusing solely on top-down technocratic arguments is law at its worst – what Yamin critiques as "top-down formalistic legal tools anchored by fixed understandings of norms."[62] Instead, Yamin argues for understanding human rights as "an incremental *process* by which they [human beings] can express their diverse views."[63] Richard Wilson has called this "the potential for human rights law to be a form of 'politics by other means,' rather than as wholly 'depoliticizing.'"[64] The chapters in this book make a compelling case that we must begin the work of prioritizing the voices of migrants and refugees caught in law's gaps. Even if the

---

[57] Faulk, "Solidarity and Accountability," p. 106.
[58] Brysk, "'Why We Care'," p. 163.
[59] Ibid., p. 164.
[60] Faulk, "Solidarity and Accountability," p. 105.
[61] A. E. Yamin, *Power, Suffering, and the Struggle for Dignity: Human Rights Frameworks for Health and Why the Matter* (Philadelphia: University of Pennsylvania Press, 2016), p. 65.
[62] Ibid., p. 247.
[63] Ibid.
[64] R. A. Wilson, "Tyrannosaurus Lex: The Anthropology of Human Rights and Transnational Law," in M. Goodale and S. E. Merry (eds.), *The Practice of Human Rights: Tracking Law between the Global and the Local* (Cambridge: Cambridge University Press, 2007), pp. 342, 355.

result of that work is uncertain, the process of re-centering holds significant promise on its own.

CONCLUSION

The chapters in this book together make a compelling case for the rights of non-citizens, examining the failures of our current moment, imagining new forms of belonging, and thinking critically about approaches that might bring us closer to the promise of universal enjoyment of rights. Thus, most directly, this book is about the laws and policies that affect those who are not members of a political community that can effectively protect their rights, and why – and how – those rights might be better protected.

More broadly, however, it is a book about why this matters. From the rise in populist governments around the world to the spread of disinformation and the COVID-19 pandemic, it is more evident than ever that the rights of all depend on the protection of the rights of the most vulnerable. As Brysk argues, "we are only as free as our weakest neighbor."[65] Exploring new rhetorics of relationship may provide at least a starting point for that conversation. Whether empathy, care, or solidarity, finding new ways to relate across metaphysical and geographic borders may help us to challenge the zero-sum strategies of political leaders seeking to consolidate power using populist techniques.[66] These new ways of relating can contribute to a foundation on which we can build political arguments for more effective ways to address the injustice of borders.

[65] Brysk, "'Why We Care'," p. 168.
[66] S. Scholz, *Political Solidarity* (Philadelphia: University of Pennsylvania Press, 2008).

PART I

The Failure of Rights

2

The Unmaking of Citizens

Shifting Borders of Belonging

Kristy A. Belton and Jamie Chai Yun Liew

INTRODUCTION

The world's population currently stands at 7.8 billion, and every day millions are born who automatically acquire the citizenship of a particular state. Few question the routineness of the citizenship acquisition process (whether through a citizen parent or through birth on a specific state's territory). Even fewer question the necessity of possessing citizenship or the state's sovereign right to determine who should belong and how. We generally take the particular rights, freedoms, and protections associated with citizenship for granted and cannot fathom what a world without citizenship, at least as currently conceived, would look like. Yet citizenship is not necessarily a neutral and stable status upon which to base rights, freedoms, and protections. It is also not a status available to all. As this chapter illustrates, citizenship is precarious and has never been a secure foundation upon which to base human rights. In the securitized world of the twenty-first century, this instability has heightened, especially for minorities.

To make this argument, the chapter is divided into three sections. The first section explains how citizenship arose in international practice and law and how states translated international practice into defined nationality laws in the domestic sphere. This section highlights how, before it became a status to which human rights attached, citizenship was, first and foremost, an international ordering principle. The second section demonstrates how states have historically excluded various groups, typically minorities, from enjoyment of full citizenship status, thereby endangering the access of these groups to human rights enjoyment. The third section provides contemporary examples of citizenship deprivation and denial, highlighting the myriad justifications that states use to deny and deprive people of citizenship.

CITIZENSHIP IN INTERNATIONAL AND DOMESTIC LAW

Citizenship may be understood in many ways. For the purpose of this chapter, it is defined as the legal bond of attachment between a person and a state. It serves as a mobile border, demarcating who is from where and how said person should be treated when outside the borders of her state. In the modern era, it has become an international ordering principle, which rests on the notion of states as self-contained political units that govern defined territories. The emergence of sovereign, independent states that governed their own internal affairs is typically traced to Europe and the Peace of Westphalia, which ended the Thirty Years' War.[1] The peace treaties cemented the demise of the overarching power of the Catholic Church and the Holy Roman Empire and heralded the advent of an international legal system where autonomous states became masters of their own domain and recognized each other's authority over territory.[2]

Although many trace the beginning of the present international world order to the Peace of Westphalia, scholars acknowledge that the concepts of statehood and state sovereignty were not simply constructed, endorsed, and applied at this point in time. Instead, the treaties sanctioned or confirmed an interstate system that was already developing, or in existence, out of necessity as a consequence of negotiating peace.[3] State sovereignty thus emerged as the dominant organizing principle of the Peace of Westphalia because of the growing recognition that polities were organizing themselves in this way.

Furthermore, these peace treaties not only addressed authority over territory but also endorsed authority over individuals, referring to "vassals," "subjects," "soldiers," "inhabitants," "servants," "people," and others.[4] Passages referring to such people in the peace treaties were written with the intention to provide protection. That is, state sovereignty included not only the unencumbered right to rule over people but the reciprocal responsibility of protecting them as well.

What began as political practice in early Europe solidified in international legal doctrine in the 1930s. The 1930 Convention on Certain Questions Relating to the Conflict of Nationality Law established that it was "in the general interest of the international community to secure that all its members should recognize that every

---

[1] Although this system of international law started in Europe, other polities were folded into this new world order through the expansion of European colonial empires. Polities that were not colonized reluctantly adopted this European model. As a result, by the early twentieth century, the European model of international legal order was universalized.

[2] J. H. Currie, *Public International Law* (2nd ed., Toronto: Irwin Law, 2008).

[3] D. Croxton, "The Peace of Westphalia of 1648 and the Origins of Sovereignty" (1999) 21(3) *The International History Review* 569–591.

[4] The Peace of Westphalia comprises a series of treaties signed between May and October 1648 in the cities of Osnabrück and Münster. See, for example, Treaty of Münster (Peace Treaty between the Holy Roman Emperor and the King of France and their respective Allies), October 24, 1648, http://avalon.law.yale.edu/17th_century/westphal.asp.

person should have a nationality,"[5] and it did not permit the loss of citizenship unless (or until such time that) a person acquired another one. Only a few years later, the 1933 Montevideo Declaration articulated that one of the criteria for statehood was the existence of a permanent population. This permanent population became the citizenry. Later United Nations human rights treaties[6] would institute the significance of citizenship through the establishment of a human right to a nationality.[7]

Citizenship is so important from an international legal framework that no right to be voluntarily stateless (without citizenship) exists; states are not allowed to deprive an individual of citizenship arbitrarily; and states are prohibited from allowing their citizens to become charges on other states. Citizenship is thus much more than a conduit for rights access. It is the basis upon which states formally set the borders of belonging and through which they are able to conduct what Ceciliano-Navarro, Golash-Boza, and Rubén González call a "global apartheid" in Chapter 6. Despite the importance of citizenship as an international ordering principle, no international organization exists, whether as creator, arbiter, or enforcer, of citizenship laws for any state. Instead, the state has the "reserve domain," or final say, on whether to grant, deny, or revoke citizenship, and on crafting the laws, processes, and legal institutions under which a person is deemed to be a citizen. It is within this "sovereign" space that the gap between the international human right to citizenship and its enjoyment in practice is most evident.

In general, there are two main ways to acquire citizenship globally: by birth and, to a lesser extent, through naturalization. Birthright citizenship can be obtained (a) by being born within a state or its territories (*jus soli*) or (b) by being born to a parent who has a particular citizenship (*jus sanguinis*). All countries around the world offer a form of *jus soli* or *jus sanguinis* citizenship, but not all provide it absolutely. Exceptions vary. In the *jus soli* arena, for example, states exclude birthright citizenship to children born of foreign diplomats. And in places such as the Dominican Republic, children born in the country to parents who are classified as "in transit,"

---

[5] Convention on Certain Questions Relating to the Conflict of Nationality Law, July 1, 1937, 179 L.N.T.S. 89. Articles 5–7 of the Convention on the Reduction of Statelessness, August 30, 1961, 989 U.N.T.S. 175, https://legal.un.org/ilc/texts/instruments/english/conventions/6_1_1961.pdf, also reiterate these principles.

[6] Citizenship and nationality are used interchangeably in this text, as is the practice in much of the literature on citizenship and statelessness.

[7] United Nations treaties that address the right to a nationality include the International Convention on the Elimination of All Forms of Racial Discrimination, December 21, 1965, 660 U.N.T.S. 195, art. 5; the International Covenant on Civil and Political Rights, December 16, 1966, 999 U.N.T.S. 171, art. 24; the Convention on the Rights of the Child, November 20, 1989, 1577 U.N.T.S. 3, art. 7; the Convention on the Elimination of All Forms of Discrimination against Women, December 18, 1979, 124 U.N.T.S. 13, art. 9; the International Convention on the Protection of the Rights of All Migrant Workers and Members of Their Families, December 18, 1990, A/RES/45/158, art. 29; and the Convention on the Rights of Persons with Disabilities, January 24, 2007, A/RES/61/106, art. 18.

which includes people with expired residency visas and undocumented workers, are excluded from acquiring citizenship via *jus soli*.

Still other states provide that both *jus soli* and *jus sanguinis* criteria must be met. For instance, France limits birthright citizenship to children born in France to a French parent or to a parent also born in France. Finally, some states offer a graduated process by which children born in the state to noncitizen parents may be eligible for citizenship by a certain age once residency requirements are fulfilled. For example, Israel allows persons between the ages of eighteen and twenty-one to acquire citizenship if they were born in Israel and resided there for more than five years. States such as Cambodia and Germany, on the other hand, only confer *jus soli* citizenship if a child is born to noncitizens who are residing there legally.

When it comes to *jus sanguinis* or acquisition of citizenship by "right of blood," restrictions may include limiting citizenship to the first generation or to those born of a citizen father. Canada, for example, limits *jus sanguinis* to the "first generation." Thus, if a Canadian citizen, who herself was born outside Canada, gives birth to a child outside Canada, her child will not be Canadian. In the Bahamas, only male citizens can pass on their citizenship to children born outside the country if they are married to a noncitizen. Bahamian women married to noncitizens who give birth to children outside the Bahamas have no similar right to pass on their citizenship. Numerous other exceptions exist that illustrate how citizenship is not an automatically acquired status for all at birth and is, therefore, an inadequate foundation upon which to base human rights. Furthermore, as the next section illustrates, states also exclude certain groups from citizenship when it serves their interests.

CITIZENSHIP AND ITS EXCLUSIONS

States have long erected barriers, indirectly and directly, to citizenship. Throughout history, and in modern times, legal categories of exclusions or exceptions have been created to prevent certain people from acquiring citizenship and to provide normative strength to the idea that only some are purportedly deserving of citizenship. In many cases, some may experience exclusion by virtue of intersecting statuses – because they are an Indigenous person who is also a woman, or a person who is of an ethnic minority group that has also been deemed a security risk to the state (consider the Kurds, for example). What follows are a few examples of groups who have not always found themselves fully captured within the state's borders of formal belonging. Many are, as Tendayi Bloom discusses in Chapter 10, individuals who are in both a citizen and a noncitizen relationship to the state.

Indigenous Peoples

Despite already living on the land when Europeans arrived, Indigenous peoples have not always been considered legal citizens of colonizing states. In Canada, for example, although the 1947 Citizenship Act provided that British subjects born in Canada prior to 1947 were Canadian citizens, First Nations and Inuit were not considered British subjects and therefore were not considered citizens. Furthermore, colonial governments created differential statuses for Indigenous peoples. In Canada, the Indian Act[8] created a system of reserves and registered Indigenous persons and defined how the Canadian government would treat certain Indigenous persons. A similar story played out in the United States and Australia where Native Americans and Aborigines were excluded from citizenship for much of these states' early history.[9] Indigenous peoples' experience thus shows how the law has constructed persons as not citizens or produced their citizenship in ways that differ from their legal traditions or entitlements.

Ethnic and Racial Minorities

States have also enacted measures to restrict access to citizenship to racialized persons or persons with a particular ethnicity. In the United States and Canada, for example, Asian people were subject to open hostility and discrimination that led to the enactment of legislation to prevent them from coming to North America. In the United States, the 1882 Chinese Exclusion Act prevented Chinese immigration to the United States.[10] Canada followed the Americans by first issuing a report by the Canadian Royal Commission on Chinese and Japanese Immigration that stated Asians were "unfit for full citizenship ... obnoxious to a free community and dangerous to the state."[11] Following this report, the Canadian Parliament voted to increase the Chinese head tax to $500, an entrance fee meant to deter the migration of Chinese people to Canada. Furthermore, during the Second World War, Japanese Canadians and Japanese Americans were interned in concentration camps all over North America. The experience of ethnic and racial minorities, also explored in Chapter 6 in the context of migration, highlights how the law can be used to actively discriminate against certain groups and prevent them from becoming citizens.

Women

Women, who typically make up more than half of any state's population, have historically been treated differently when it comes to the ability to acquire or lose

---

[8] Indian Act, Revised Statutes of Canada, 1985, c I-5.

[9] Note that with the passage of the US Indian Citizenship Act, June 2, 1924, Indigenous peoples, whether or not they wanted to become US citizens, were forced to become so.

[10] An Act to Execute Certain Treaty Stipulations Relating to the Chinese, May 6, 1882.

[11] Privy Council Office of Canada and the Canadian Royal Commission on Chinese and Japanese Immigration into British Columbia, Report of the Royal Commission on Chinese and Japanese Immigration (Ottawa: S. E. Dawson, 1902), http://publications.gc.ca/site/eng/9 .824969/publication.html.

citizenship, as well as to confer citizenship on their children. Historically, women were seen as the property of male citizens. As a consequence, they often lost their birthright citizenship upon marriage to a noncitizen because they were assumed to have taken on the foreign husband's citizenship. Although the 1957 Convention on the Nationality of Married Women prohibited this practice,[12] gender discrimination in nationality laws remains a problem today. Twenty-seven countries deny mothers the equal right to confer nationality on their children and around fifty have other gender-discriminatory nationality provisions that place their female citizens on an unequal footing with their male counterparts. Women's citizenship history and experience illustrate the property-like features of citizenship and underscore the patriarchal current that undergirds it.

The Stateless

Stateless people, or those who are not recognized under the operation of any state's nationality law, typically are born and reside within a state that excludes them from citizenship. More than fifteen million people are estimated to be stateless globally. They suffer a host of human rights violations and impingements upon their ability to be self-determining agents because they are citizens of nowhere.[13] Although multiple pathways to statelessness exist,[14] no international norm exists recognizing a person's right to be voluntarily stateless. In fact, international law is clear that each person should have a citizenship and that before a person is stripped of citizenship, she or he must have access to another state's citizenship first.

Even before the Universal Declaration of Human Rights asserted each person's right to a nationality, the 1930 Convention on Certain Questions Relating to the Conflict of Nationality Law established that it was "in the general interest of the international community to secure that all its members should recognize that every person should have a nationality."[15] Akin to the later 1961 Convention on the Reduction of Statelessness, the 1930 Convention does not permit the loss of citizenship unless or until such time that a person acquires another one.[16] Despite this, many states have resisted conferring citizenship on stateless persons, claiming they

---

[12] Convention on the Nationality of Married Women, February 20, 1957, 309 U.N.T.S. 65, https://treaties.un.org/doc/Treaties/1958/08/19580811%2001-34%20AM/Ch_XVI_2p.pdf.

[13] See K. A. Belton, *Statelessness in the Caribbean: The Paradox of Belonging in a Postnational World* (Philadelphia: University of Pennsylvania Press, 2017); K. A. Belton, "Statelessness: A Matter of Human Rights," in R. Howard-Hassmann and M. Walton-Roberts (eds.), *The Human Right to Citizenship: A Slippery Concept* (Philadelphia: University of Pennsylvania Press, 2015), pp. 31–42.

[14] See Belton, *Statelessness in the Caribbean*, pp. 30–38.

[15] Convention on Certain Questions Relating to the Conflict of Nationality Law, July 1, 1937, 179 L.N.T.S. 89.

[16] Ibid., art. 7; Convention on the Reduction of Statelessness, August 30, 1961, arts. 5–7.

are the citizens of other states even though they have no citizenship by operation of law to any state. The next section describes how even those with citizenship status may fall on the wrong side of state interests and lose this purportedly fundamental status.

CITIZENSHIP DEPRIVATION

It is one practice to deny individuals citizenship,[17] as in many of the aforementioned examples, and it is another practice to deprive individuals of the citizenship they hold. Citizenship deprivation (or withdrawal)[18] has its roots in former practices of exile and banishment. Although states are no longer permitted to allow their citizens to become charges on other states, they are allowed to withdraw citizenship on a number of grounds, including committing a crime or engaging in acts deemed "threatening" or "disloyal" to the state, seeking refuge elsewhere, converting to another religion, or failing to renew a passport, among other reasons.[19]

Moreover, the 1961 Convention on the Reduction of Statelessness,[20] which aims to reduce statelessness globally, is clear that citizenship deprivation is permissible when an individual has acted "inconsistently with his duty of loyalty to the Contracting state" by rendering services to another state, acting in a way that is "seriously prejudicial to the vital interests of the state," or declaring allegiance to another state, among other reasons.[21] As long as these grounds are not "arbitrary" (and it is not always clear what a state will deem arbitrary in practice), the state has the sovereign right to deprive a person of his/her citizenship and render the individual stateless.[22] Moreover, states that engage in citizenship withdrawal typically deny that they are rendering individuals stateless. They argue that the individuals deprived of citizenship are dual nationals or have the ability to apply for citizenship in another state through operation of that other state's law. As the following examples show, however, this is not always the case.

---

[17] Citizenship denial largely consists of preventing access to citizenship, whether through the refusal to grant identity documents (such as birth certificates) or the refusal to apply a given law to an individual to recognize him/her as a citizen.

[18] It is also known as citizenship stripping, citizenship revocation, denationalization, and denaturalization. Denationalization occurs when citizenship is taken away from someone who acquired citizenship through *jus soli* or *jus sanguinis* measures. Denaturalization occurs when citizenship is taken away from a naturalized citizen.

[19] *See* Belton, *Statelessness in the Caribbean*, pp. 30–38.

[20] Convention on the Reduction of Statelessness, August 30, 1961,.

[21] Ibid., art. 8.3(a).

[22] *See* S. Jaghai, "Citizenship Deprivation, (Non) Discrimination and Statelessness: A Case Study of the Netherlands (Institute on Stateless and Inclusion, 2017)," p. 9, https://files.institutesi.org/WP2017_07.pdf. As Jaghai observes, "There seems to be tension in the application of international law at the domestic level regarding the principle of non-discrimination and the prohibition that deprivation of nationality cannot lead to statelessness" (ibid., p. 14).

National Security

Despite the permissibility of citizenship deprivation in the international arena, and the fact that states have occasionally engaged in this practice historically,[23] it is only recently that citizenship deprivation laws have been more vigorously implemented and strengthened, and that countries that previously had no such laws have begun to introduce them. States are now looking to "nationality policy as a tool to tackle emerging national security threats."[24] For example, Austria, Azerbaijan, Bangladesh, Belgium, Israel, Russia, the Netherlands, the United Kingdom, the United States and others have either introduced citizenship deprivation measures in response to perceived national security threats or begun to more systematically apply and strengthen existing citizenship deprivation laws.[25]

The heightened security environment that ensued post 9/11 has allowed states to situate citizenship deprivation within a national security and crimmigration[26] policy rationale that challenges the permanency of citizenship and turns citizens into deportable foreigners or "dangerous aliens."[27] In this sense, citizenship deprivation has conceptually pushed citizenship into the realm of privilege rather than a right, and citizenship revocation has become a punitive tool.[28] Although the threat of a foreign enemy has always operated within a state's modus operandi, the figure of the foreign enemy is now extended to those that hold citizenship in Western states as part of the emergence of "homegrown" terrorism.[29] The identification of such "enemies" within has given Western states in particular the impetus to create and use legal mechanisms to engage in citizenship deprivation.[30]

Revocation grounds and proceedings vary by country. Some countries have legal provisions to denaturalize a citizen who obtained citizenship through fraud or misrepresentation. This is known as "civil denaturalization" in the United States

---

[23] *See* Belton, *Statelessness in the Caribbean*, chapter 2.

[24] L. van Waas and S. Jaghai, "All Citizens Are Created Equal, but Some Are More Equal Than Others" (2018) 65 *Netherlands International Law Review* 413–430 at 419.

[25] *See* ibid.; S. Pillai and G. Williams, "Twenty-First Century Banishment: Citizenship Stripping in Common Law Nations" (2017) 66 *International and Comparative Law Quarterly* 521–555. Both articles provide extensive details on the ways in which states are using citizenship withdrawal as a national security measure.

[26] J. Stumpf, "The Crimmigration Crisis: Immigrants, Crime, and Sovereign Power" (2006) 56(2) *American University Law Review* 367. Stumpf first coined this term to discuss the merging of criminal and immigration law where migrants are being criminalized through the immigration system.

[27] A. Macklin, "Citizenship Revocation, the Privilege to Have Rights and the Production of the Alien" (2014) 40(1) *Queens Law Journal* 1–54. *See also* Chapter 6.

[28] S. Lavi, "Citizenship Revocation as Punishment: On the Modern Duties of Citizens and Their Criminal Breach" (2011) 61(4) *Constitutionalism and the Criminal Law* 783–810.

[29] C. Forcese, "A Tale of Two Citizenships: Citizenship Revocation for 'Traitors and Terrorists'" (2014) 39(2) *Queens Law Journal* 551–570.

[30] P. Lenard, "Democracies and the Power to Revoke Citizenship" (2016) 30(1) *Ethics and International Affairs* 73–91.

and was practiced under the administrations of both George W. Bush and Barack Obama, but it has increased, and become further institutionalized, under Donald J. Trump's administration. For instance, in February 2020, the US Department of Justice established a "Denaturalization Section," which purportedly targets "terrorists, war criminals, sex offenders, and 'other fraudsters.'"[31]

Increasingly, legislation is being amended to include reasons of national security, broadly worded, to encompass a wide array of threats or activities. One prominent and recent example is Jack Letts, more popularly known as "Jihadi Jack." Letts was a dual citizen of the United Kingdom and Canada. Letts was reportedly raised in the United Kingdom, converted to Islam at the age of sixteen, and joined ISIS, or the Islamic state abroad, a jihadist terror group known for its brutal mass killings.[32] Letts' overseas activities are not substantiated, but in an interview with BBC, he stated that he was an enemy of the United Kingdom, that he thought he was doing something good, and that he had made a big mistake.[33] While he was imprisoned in a Kurdish jail in northern Syria in August 2019, the United Kingdom revoked Letts' citizenship.

The move to strip Letts of UK citizenship blindsided Canada. The Minister of Public Safety in Canada commented, "Canada is disappointed that the United Kingdom has taken this unilateral action to off-load their responsibilities," but also added that they had "no legal obligation to facilitate" the return of Canadian citizens detained in Syria.[34] Former defense minister of the United Kingdom, Tobias Ellwood, agreed, stating that citizenship revocation "shunts the responsibility elsewhere" when many persons were "radicalised here in the UK."[35] The UK Home Office held, however, that "[t]his power is one way we can counter the terrorist threat posed by some of the most dangerous individuals and keep our country safe."[36]

While Letts is fortunate because he held dual citizenship, there are two normative implications to the United Kingdom's move to revoke citizenship of someone it deems as a terrorist threat. The first is that it legitimizes the very act of revocation even where it does not leave a person stateless. It thus makes citizenship probationary and precarious. Second, it legitimizes the use of citizenship deprivation as a form of banishment or punishment and allows the state to avoid responsibility for the acts of its citizens.

---

[31] R. Prasad, "What Does Trump's New Denaturalisation Section Do?" *BBC News*, February 28, 2020, www.bbc.com/news/world-us-canada-51681840.

[32] D. Sabbagh, "Jack Letts Stripped of British Citizenship," *The Guardian*, August 18, 2019, www.theguardian.com/world/2019/aug/18/jack-letts-stripped-british-citizenship-isis-canada; "Jihadi Jack: IS Recruit Jack Letts Loses UK Citizenship," *BBC News*, August 18, 2019, www.bbc.com/news/uk-49385376.

[33] "Jack Letts, Islamic State Recruit: 'I Was Enemy of UK,'" *BBC*, June 21, 2019, www.bbc.com/news/uk-48624104.

[34] "Jihadi Jack: IS Recruit Jack Letts Loses UK Citizenship."

[35] Ibid.

[36] Ibid.

Another prominent but more problematic example is that of Shamima Begum, a twenty-year-old woman who at age fifteen left the United Kingdom to join the Islamic state,[37] In February 2019, the United Kingdom revoked her citizenship. The Special Immigration Appeals Commission, a tribunal that hears national security cases, reasoned that Begum could be stripped of her citizenship because she would not be left stateless despite the fact that Bangladesh had stated that it did not recognize her as a citizen.[38] The Commission held that Begum was "a citizen of Bangladesh by descent."[39] Begum's lawyer has appealed the decision.

This practice reinforces the normative move to legitimize citizenship deprivation where national security concerns exist, but, troublingly, it also shows how the legal definition of statelessness may be eroding. In particular, the legal finding that Begum was a national of another state was not based on any evidence, but on speculation that she could be granted citizenship by another state (in this case, Bangladesh) by an examination of its laws.

Criminal Behavior

Aside from national security or terrorism concerns, citizenship withdrawal may be premised upon individuals' criminal behavior. Take for example the case of *Canada v. Budlakoti*.[40] Budlakoti was born and raised in Canada. Due to his criminal convictions, Budlakoti was found inadmissible under Canada's *Immigration and Refugee Protection Act*. Budlakoti challenged this finding by asserting he was a Canadian citizen. The Immigration Division of the Immigration and Refugee Board (IRB), however, held that he was not a citizen as per the *Citizenship Act* since he fell into the exception that children born of parents under the employment of a foreign government do not enjoy birthright citizenship.

The Immigration Division determined that Budlakoti's parents were working for officials of the Indian Consulate in Canada at the time he was born, therefore making him ineligible for citizenship by birth. Budlakoti unsuccessfully challenged this decision. In asserting he would be stateless as a result of the Immigration Division's findings, the Federal Court of Appeal held that "[h]e is not yet stateless" since Budlakoti "can take steps to apply for citizenship in India and in Canada."[41] This finding is particularly troubling given that the Court acknowledged that the Indian Consulate had refused to recognize Budlakoti as a citizen and that the Canadian government was involved in litigation to make him removable from Canada.

---

[37] "Shamima Begum Loses First Stage of Appeal over Citizenship," *BBC*, February 7, 2019.
[38] Ibid.
[39] Ibid.
[40] *Budlakoti v. Canada (Citizenship and Immigration)*, 2015 FCA 139.
[41] Ibid. 23.

Minority Status

States have also used the tool of citizenship deprivation against political opponents, human rights defenders, protestors, and minority groups (as defined by their religion, ethnicity, race, or culture). For example, Rohingya have been stripped of their citizenship and denied any entitlement to citizenship in Myanmar since 1982. Many Rohingya are stateless as a result of a deliberate change in citizenship law that turned them into illegal immigrants within their own country. The loss and denial of citizenship is not a benign act. At a minimum it means Rohingya cannot open a bank or a cell phone account, register births, marriages or deaths, and, more seriously, it has also meant difficulties in accessing health care, education, employment, and freedom of movement.

More concerning is that citizenship deprivation has cast the Rohingya as outsiders and justified their oppression and institutionalized exclusion, leading to genocide. The state has thus harnessed the legal fact of statelessness to engage in violence, displacement, and killing of its Rohingya population. Indeed, on January 23, 2020, in response to legal action taken by Gambia, which had accused Myanmar of genocide, the International Court of Justice took a significant step by issuing a preliminary order that instructed Myanmar to take immediate measures to prevent the genocide of its stateless Rohingya Muslim minority.[42]

Citizenship withdrawal also takes on an ethnic dimension in the Dominican Republic, which has a long history of discriminating against individuals of Haitian descent among its citizenry. In 2013, the Dominican state systematically institutionalized this discrimination by revoking the citizenship of approximately 200,000 Dominicans of Haitian descent through Constitutional Court decision TC/0168/13.[43] This decision permitted civil registries to audit birth registry books as far back as 1929 to find out whether a person's ancestor had used a non-authorized document[44] to secure a legal status within the Dominican state. If said ancestor was deemed to have used an unauthorized document, then that person's Dominican descendants were stripped of citizenship.

Due to international concern about the judicial decision and its retroactive effect, the Dominican government implemented a path to regularization for those citizens

---

[42] *Application of the Convention on the Prevention and Punishment of the Crime of Genocide (The Gambia v. Myanmar)* (January 23, 2020), www.icj-cij.org/en/case/178/orders.

[43] *Sentencia TC/0168/13*, Dominican Republic: Constitutional Court (September 23, 2013), www .refworld.org/cases,DR_CC,526900c14.html.

[44] There has been much debate on whether the permits that granted individuals the right to work on the sugarcane plantation served as "authorized" documents or not. For more on citizenship deprivation in the Dominican Republic, see Belton, *Statelessness in the Caribbean*, chapter 4. For information on how similar discriminatory civil registries practices play out in the Malaysian context, see J. Liew, "Homegrown Statelessness in Malaysia: The Administratively Stateless and the Promise of the Principle of Genuine and Effective Links" (2019) 1(1) *Statelessness and Citizenship Review* 95–135.

who had been rendered stateless. This regularization plan created different classes of denationalized persons, led to the deportation of many, and has yet to fully restore citizenship to those who have legitimate claims to it.

Whereas in the Dominican case a regularization plan was established for those stripped of citizenship, Bahrain has chosen deportation for many of those it has stripped of citizenship. Since 2012, at least 990 Bahrainis have lost their citizenship through court decisions or executive orders, leaving most persons stateless and leading to their deportation. Among those stripped of citizenship are human rights defenders, political activists, journalists, and religious scholars. Recently, a mass trial convicting 139 people of terrorism charges led to the wholesale revocation of citizenship of those persons. This trial demonstrates that Bahrain's authorities are increasingly relying on citizenship withdrawal as a tool of repression and as a means to eliminate opposition.

CONCLUSION

Although citizenship as a status is an accepted international ordering principle, it is not, and never has been, a status that is equally accessible to all. For those who were denied citizenship from birth, citizenship has always been unattainable. For others, their belonging to a particular minority group – both historically and today – has prevented their access to full citizenship in practice, even if they were (or are) nominally recognized as citizens under domestic law. Citizenship is not only unevenly applied as a principle in practice, but it is not a stable, enduring, or permanent status either. Those who have been stripped of citizenship under the rationale of national security and other such prerogatives can attest to this.

Perhaps citizenship was never meant to be more than an international ordering principle of people(s) and we have tied notions of human rights, equality and justice to a concept that was never built to hold them. As several authors in this volume attest, concepts of citizenship and noncitizenship perpetuate distorted perceptions of who belongs and how they should be treated. In essence, by bestowing states with the sovereign prerogative to define who belongs where, we have allowed an exclusionary and precarious status to hold far too much influence over people's life chances and furthered global conditions of injustice.

3

Zero Humanity

The Reality of Current US Immigration Policy toward Central American Refugee Children and Their Families

Jacqueline Bhabha

INTRODUCTION

Many months have passed since the Trump administration's initial ruthless separation of more than 4,300 babies and children from their parents at the United States' southern border.[1] Since that time, partly under the guise of public health concerns prompted by the COVID-19 pandemic, the administration has continued to impose draconian rights-violative policies on migrant children – not just family separation but summary deportation.[2] Irrespective of changing circumstances, the underlying administrative philosophy – that deterrence is the solution to humanitarian emergencies that drive forced migration – remains in place. This philosophy subordinates American constitutional values and international obligations to non-citizens to the instrumental goal of reducing access to US soil for people fleeing life-threatening violence, however strong their claim to protection.

By doggedly implementing policies that block, detain, deport, and humiliate humanitarian migrants, the United States is participating in what the authors of Chapter 6 in this volume have usefully termed "a system of global apartheid." Moreover, just as South African apartheid encouraged the development of a movement to overthrow racist state oppression, local and underground at first but global over time, so is global apartheid encouraging the development of alternatives to racist migration exclusion. Smuggling networks, caravans, global migration compacts, trafficking rings, Facebook-mediated migration itineraries, and heroic

---

[1] "Attorney General Announces Zero-Tolerance Policy for Criminal Illegal Entry," *United States Department of Justice, Office of Public Affairs,* April 6, 2018, www.justice.gov/opa/pr/attorney-general-announces-zero-tolerance-policy-criminal-illegal-entry.

[2] "Family Separation Policy Continues Two Years after Trump Administration Claims It Ended," *Southern Poverty Law Center,* www.splcenter.org/news/2020/06/18/family-separation-policy-continues-two-years-after-trump-administration-claims-it-ended; C. Dickerson, "10 Years Old, Tearful and Confused after a Sudden Deportation," *NY Times,* May 21, 2020, www.nytimes.com/2020/05/20/us/coronavirus-migrant-children-unaccompanied-minors.html.

individual voyages are just some of the current modalities. Others will develop over time, as vigorous and ambitious populations, intent on saving their lives and sharing the all-too-visible bounty generated by a global capitalist commons, refuse enduring and oppressive sequestration. But, as it was in South Africa, the process is protracted and arduous, and hugely costly in terms of human lives and suffering. As they tried to access safety, nearly 19,000 people drowned in the Mediterranean from 2014–2019,[3] 2,243 perished in the deserts between the United States and Mexico, and tens of thousands faced excruciating detention conditions in rogue jails in Libya.[4]

The US-bound exodus of Central American children and their families, from some of the poorest and most violent countries in the world, and the US government's responses provide a case study of global apartheid in action. In what follows, after outlining the United States' key legal obligations toward non-citizens, I will track some of the policies deployed by the Trump administration to block or otherwise deter the entry of humanitarian migrant children and families. I will suggest that these policies are not only inhumane and in violation of binding legal obligations, but also futile. I will conclude by outlining what I consider more rights-respecting and effective alternatives.

The United States' International and Constitutional Obligations to Non-citizens

The United States is an outlier when it comes to ratification of international treaties. No better illustration exists than the situation regarding its stance on children's rights. Alone among member states of the United Nations, the United States has not ratified the 1989 UN Convention on the Rights of the Child (CRC), the cardinal international human rights treaty consolidating the principles that apply to children.[5] Central among these principles is the prohibition on discrimination and the obligation to make the child's best interests a primary consideration in actions and policies affecting them. Because these principles have been consistently applied by an overwhelming majority of countries for well over half a century, they may be considered customary international law, and therefore cannot be disregarded by the US government.

In practice, failure to ratify the CRC has reduced the leverage of international institutions such as the Committee on the Rights of the Child and UNICEF, and US-based child rights advocates, to press for enforcement of fundamental rights for

---

[3] "Migrant Deaths and Disappearances," *Missing Migrants Project: International Organization on Migration.* November 8, 2019, https://migrationdataportal.org/themes/migrant-deaths-and-disappearances.

[4] "Libya Immigration Detention," *Global Detention Project,* August 18, 2018, www.global detentionproject.org/countries/africa/libya#_ftn4.

[5] Convention on the Rights of the Child, November 20, 1989, 1577 U.N.T.S. 3, www.refworld .org/docid/3ae6b38fo.html.

migrant children. The egregious 2018 family separation border policy would doubt-less have elicited more vigorous international protest had the UN Committee on the Rights of the Child been afforded oversight.

The United States has, however, ratified other international treaties that generate powerful obligations towards persons within its jurisdiction irrespective of their citizenship status. They include the 1966 International Covenant on Civil and Political Rights (ICCPR),[6] the 1951 Convention Relating to the Status of Refugees,[7] and the 1984 Convention against Torture and other Cruel, Inhuman or Degrading Treatment or Punishment.[8] Treaties are considered the supreme law of the land under the US Constitution, so government actions have to be consistent with provisions in ratified treaties.[9] The implications of these obligations in relation to Central American children seeking protection in the United States from violence at home are multiple. One is the obligation not to subject children to arbitrary detention, whether in an immigration or any other context. Prolonged incarceration of children not charged with any criminal wrongdoing, with or without parents, violates this prohibition. Indeed, the UN High Commissioner for Refugees (UNHCR), the international agency charged with overseeing implementation of the Refugee Convention and the protection of refugees and asylum seekers, has explicitly held that "children should not be detained for immigration related purposes, irrespective of their legal/migratory status or that of their parents, and detention is never in their best interests."[10] The Human Rights Committee, the treaty body that oversees implementation of the ICCPR, addressed the issue of detention of a child and parent seeking asylum specifically in a case it adjudicated. It explained that, as a general rule, detention "should not continue beyond the period for which the State party can provide appropriate justification." Because Australia, the country in question, failed to show that detention was the least restrictive strategy available for achieving its intended objective, it had violated its obligations.[11]

Another treaty obligation binding on the United States is the prohibition on subjecting asylum seekers, including children, to punitive treatment.[12] Separating children from their parents clearly falls afoul of this prohibition, as does forcing

---

[6] International Covenant on Civil and Political Rights, December 16, 1966, 999 U.N.T.S. 171, www.refworld.org/docid/3ae6b3aao.html.

[7] UN Convention Relating to the Status of Refugees, July 28, 1951, 189 U.N.T.S. 137, www.refworld.org/docid/3be01b964.html.

[8] Convention Against Torture and Other Cruel, Inhuman or Degrading Treatment or Punishment, December 10, 1984, 1465 U.N.T.S. 85, www.refworld.org/docid/3ae6b3a94.html.

[9] U.S. Constitution, art., VI, cl. 2.

[10] United Nations High Commissioner for Refugees, *UNHCR Position Regarding the Detention of Refugee and Migrant Children in the Migration Context*, January 2, 2017, www.refworld.org/docid/5885c2434.html.

[11] *Baban v. Australia*, United Nations Human Rights Committee, ¶ 7.2 U.N. Doc. CCPR/C/78/D/1014/2001 (2003).

[12] Convention Relating to the Status of Refugees, July 28, 1951, 189 U.N.T.S. 137, www.refworld.org/docid/3be01b964.html, art. 31.

child asylum seekers to await their asylum hearings in places, such as the Mexico borderland, known to be crime and violence infested. More generally, under Article 24 of the ICCPR, the United States is obliged to provide children with special "measures of protection." From this one can infer that official policies targeting children in the United States, whatever their citizenship or immigration status, need, at a minimum, to protect their health, well-being, and development.[13] Policies that subject children to unsanitary conditions, traumatic experiences, or situations where essential health care is unavailable violate this fundamental obligation.

Family Separation

The welcome U-turn on the blanket Trump administration family separation policy, which ripped all children away from parents entering the country without prior authorization, came fairly promptly. On June 20, 2018, two months after the presidential order that legitimized the policy, the government was forced to neutralize it. Family separation on that scale only worked as long as it was a closely guarded secret.[14] Once photos of toddlers ripped from distraught parents, internment camps with children in cages, images of young children bottle feeding unrelated infants, and tapes of babies wailing while their jailers sardonically commented on the "orchestra" they were holding became public, the administration faced a watershed moment, even against the backdrop of its increasingly inhumane border control policies.[15]

The bipartisan storm of protest that erupted branded the government's version of migrant deterrence as un-American. And indeed, the widely circulated images evoked the darkest days of American history – family separation under slavery, abduction of Native American children from their families, internment without trial of Japanese Americans wrongly considered enemy aliens. The images also triggered alarming expert pronouncements about the devastating, and likely long-term, impact of the traumatic separation on the mental and emotional health of the affected children. Scholars of early childhood development characterized the experiences willfully imposed on the separated children as "toxic stress,"[16] known to affect neural pathways in the brain in young children and to lead to grave risks

---

[13] ICCPR, art. 24.

[14] A modified version of family separation, exacerbated by the COVID-19 pandemic, continues to this day.

[15] "Kirstjen Nielsen Addresses Families Separation at the Border: Full Transcript," *New York Times*, June 18, 2018, www.nytimes.com/2018/06/18/us/politics/dhs-kirstjen-nielsen-families-separated-border-transcript.html; G. Thompson, "Listen to Children Who've Just Been Separated from Their Parents at the Border," *ProPublica*, June 18, 2018, www.propublica.org/article/children-separated-from-parents-border-patrol-cbp-trump-immigration-policy.

[16] J. P. Shonkoff et al., "The Lifelong Effects of Early Childhood Adversity and Toxic Stress" (2012) 129(1) *Pediatrics* e232–e246.

such as emotional instability, high anxiety, suicidal ideation, and prolonged depression. Experts pointed out that the terror of separation from a parent and removal to an unfamiliar, punitive location for an indefinite time, without explanation or family contact, could cause life-long damage.[17] Predictably, accounts of serious mental distress ensued.[18]

Though the president has been forced to change course on family separation itself, it is not clear that his administrators will be able to rectify the immense harm done anytime soon. The instructions they are supposed to abide by are clear. On June 27, 2018, in a case brought by the American Civil Liberties Union, a district court judge in San Diego decided that family separation was unconstitutional, that separated children should be promptly reunified with their parents (within fourteen days for those under five, within thirty days for older children), that parents not yet in contact with their separated children should be provided with telephonic contact within ten days, and that no parents should be deported without their consent prior to reunification with their separated children.[19]

However, government officials were unable to comply with the court order. Astoundingly, no clear or centralized tracking system had been put in place to document and register each child taken from their parent into federal custody, no alien registration or other identifying number was given to parents to enable them to trace their children's whereabouts, no cross-referencing system linked separated parent and child, and no liaison with consular authorities was established to ensure diplomatic contact between vulnerable foreign nationals and their national representatives. As the San Diego judge hearing the ACLU case, Judge Dana M. Sabraw, bitingly commented: "The unfortunate reality is that under the present system, migrant children are not accounted for with the same efficiency and accuracy as property."[20] As a result the agonizing separation of parents and children continued for weeks, in some cases months. Even worse, some families seem to have been permanently separated as already deported parents, without access to lawyers or other advisers, encounter unsurmountable difficulties reuniting with children for whom they have been given no tracking details.[21]

The indiscriminate separation of parents and legal guardians from children accompanying them was stopped by public outcry. But, out of the glare of public

---

[17] *Hearing on Migrant Family Separation Policy before the House Committee on Energy and Commerce & Subcommittee on Oversight and Investigations*, 116th Congress 3 (2019) (statement of Jack P. Shonkoff, M. D.).

[18] *Ms. L v. Immigration and Customs Enforcement*, 310 F. Supp. 3d 1133, 1149–1150 (S.D. Cal. 2018).

[19] For excellent accounts of US policy in respect of migrant children, see L. Briggs, *Taking Children: A History of American Terror* (Berkeley: University of California Press, 2020); P. G. Schrag, *Baby Jails: The Fight to End the Incarceration of Refugee Children in America* (Berkeley: University of California Press, 2020).

[20] *Ms. L v. Immigration and Customs Enforcement*.

[21] Personal communication to author from ACLU lead counsel.

attention, family separation continues.[22] The new version of the policy, so-called For Cause separation, has affected thousands of children, including very young ones. This policy involves separation of children from nonparent relatives – grandparents, older siblings, and other relatives. A few reported cases describe separations from supposedly "unsuitable" parents – in one case a father whose only disqualifying feature was a shoplifting conviction, in another, a parent who was HIV-positive.[23] Once these children are separated from their relatives – allegedly to guard against abuse or the risk of trafficking – they are placed in facilities that have attracted strong criticism. A particularly searing indictment was offered by an experienced and widely respected Columbia Law School expert. In her testimony before the US House of Representatives Committee on Oversight and Reform, Elora Mukherjee included the following account:

> In June 2019, a small team of lawyers, a doctor, and I met with nearly 70 immigrant children detained . . . in Texas . . . . The children . . . were dirty and distressed, held for days and weeks without access to soap, showers, toothbrushes, clean clothing, adequate nutrition, or adequate sleep. Over the past year, at least seven children are known to have died in federal immigration custody or shortly after being released. These tragedies occurred after nearly a decade of no reported child deaths. Every day, children are ripped apart from their family members at our borders and detained without access to their loved ones. These separations leave young children isolated for days, weeks and months without their parents, grandparents, aunts, siblings and other familial adult caregivers.[24]

The lawyer's testimony to Congress included searing quotations from some of the children interviewed. A typical excerpt: "I started taking care of [a five-year-old girl] . . . after they separated her from her father. I did not know either of them before that. She was very upset. The workers did nothing to try to comfort her. I tried to comfort her and she has been with me ever since. [This five-year-old girl] sleeps on a mat with me on the concrete floor. We spend all day every day in that room. There are no activities, only crying" (age 15, female).[25]

The rollout of "zero humanity" immigration policies by the Trump administration continues. Indeed it is accelerating, building on the grim foundations laid very early on by this administration – the incoherent executive orders banning Muslims,[26] the elimination of the Central American minors' program designed to

---

[22] S. Pierce, *Immigration-Related Policy Changes in the First Two Years of the Trump Administration* (Washington, DC: Migration Policy Institute, 2019), p. 2.

[23] Personal communication from ACLU counsel to author at Harvard University conference on November 13, 2019.

[24] *Hearing on the Trump Administration's Child Separation Policy: Substantiated Allegations of Mistreatment before the House Committee on Oversight and Reform*, 116th Congress (2019) (statement of Elora Mukherjee, Professor, Columbia Law School), p. 2.

[25] Ibid., p. 9.

[26] "Protecting the Nation from Foreign Terrorist Entry into The United States," Executive Order 13769, March 6, 2017, www.whitehouse.gov/presidential-actions/executive-order-protecting-

provide alternative routes to safety for children fleeing gang warfare and drug murders in the countries of the Northern Triangle,[27] the withdrawal of temporary protected status in the United States for law-abiding and self-supporting survivors of calamities in Honduras, El Salvador, and Haiti.[28]

A central plank of the Trump administration's immigration control agenda moving forward is large-scale and prolonged child migrant imprisonment. The government's justification for this is twofold: a need to address unmanageable border arrivals and an intention to stop what it considers the perverse incentive, generated by the current child release policy, to transport children on dangerous journeys. Paradoxically, then, the government claims that by preventing children at serious risk of gang violence from accessing safety, it is protecting them from harm. But at the same time, post-pandemic border control policies have done exactly the opposite. They have forced children seeking asylum back across the border with no attention to their needs or vulnerabilities, they have subjected families awaiting processing of their asylum claims to indefinite delays as they await their turn in dangerous Mexican borderlands, and, despite court orders mandating release of child migrants from detention, they continue to hold significant numbers of children in crowded and unsanitary facilities.

So far, the Trump administration has been unable to implement child migrant detention on a comprehensive and "deterrent" scale because of *Flores*, the much-cited Supreme Court settlement that addresses child migration detention.[29] *Flores* became a household name during the family-separation debacle. When Supreme Court cases become household names, it is reasonable to suggest that a watershed US political event has taken place. So it was with *Dred Scott*, *Brown v. Board of Education*, and *Roe v. Wade*. And so it is with *Flores*. The administration is currently attempting to reverse *Flores* to clear the way for indefinite detention of migrant children with their families.

The *Flores* case has been on the books for thirty-five years. It started off as a challenge to the indefinite detention of unaccompanied child migrants in harsh facilities where children were commingled with unrelated adults. It has continued as a platform for challenging the circumstances in which migrant children, both

---

nation-foreign-terrorist-entry-united-states-2/; "Raising the Global Travel Security Bar: DHS Announces New Travel Restrictions on Six Countries and Updated Process for Evaluating Foreign Country Compliance," *Department of Homeland Security*, January 31, 2020, www.dhs .gov/news/2020/01/31/raising-global-travel-security-bar-dhs-announces-new-travel-restrictions-six.

[27] "Status of the Central American Minors Program," *United States State Department, Office of the Spokesperson*, November 8, 2017, www.state.gov/status-of-the-central-american-minors-pro gram/.

[28] Continuation of Documentation for Beneficiaries of Temporary Protected Status Designations for El Salvador, Haiti, Honduras, Nepal, Nicaragua, and Sudan, 84 Fed. Reg. 59403 (November 4, 2019), www.federalregister.gov/documents/2019/11/04/2019-24047/continuation-of-documentation-for-beneficiaries-of-temporary-protected-status-designations-for-el.

[29] *Reno v. Flores*, 507 U.S. 292 (1993).

unaccompanied and accompanied by their families, are denied their liberty in the absence of any criminal charges, but merely because of their immigration status.

Flores's complex and tortuous history spans the past three decades of violence in Central America, from the murderous civil wars of the 1980s to the pervasive gang criminality of the twenty-first century, violence in which the United States has continually been deeply implicated. In the 1980s, the United States was a key supporter of paramilitary activity shoring up the Central American dictatorships by providing them with military training, arms, and other forms of support. Many young adults targeted by military were forced to flee; Jenny Flores was one of thousands of children left behind in El Salvador, who traveled unaccompanied to reunify with a US-based parent.[30]

In the 1990s and through the twenty-first century, the United States has been the entity responsible for the export of gang violence from its metropolitan cities, a clear example of the spill-over effect of misguided and poorly considered punitive measures against young migrants. As discussed in more detail later, the violence has turned the so-called Northern Triangle countries of Central America, Guatemala, Honduras, and El Salvador into murder capitals of the world. The gang export process originated with the deportation from US cities, primarily Los Angeles, of sizeable numbers of convicted young Central American migrants, who had been brought to the United States as infants. These young immigrants, many living in impoverished neighborhoods and in families with parents working very long hours to make ends meet, had become ensnared in the drug and gang warfare in inner city Los Angeles. After serving their criminal sentences, they were ordered deported. By forcibly sending these long resident offenders to "homes" to which they had no ties, the United States was operating a discriminatory form of double jeopardy – piling on the draconian sanction of deportation after the young migrants had already served their criminal sentences. The United States was also creating what Dan Kanstroom memorably terms a new "American diaspora," a community of deracinated youth who found status and a means of survival through the launch of gang warfare in the impoverished environments to which they were forced back.[31]

A new chapter in the story of punitive and misguided policies targeting child migrants from Central America is now starting with the attack on *Flores*. The fascinating history of the *Flores* case, a decades-long battleground for the protracted fight over the length and conditions of child migrant confinement, is brilliantly recounted by Phil Schrag in his new book, *Baby Jails*.[32] He highlights the contestation between constitutional principle (children's liberty interests), represented by activist immigrant rights advocates, and administrative discretion in the service of

---

[30] Schrag, *Baby Jails*.
[31] D. Kanstroom, *Aftermath: Deportation Law and the New American Diaspora* (Oxford: Oxford University Press, 2012).
[32] Schrag, *Baby Jails*.

migrant exclusion, represented by government lawyers and their agents. As Schrag shows, government actors have attempted to keep publicity and legal representatives at arm's length from asylum seekers in desperate need of lawyers by siting migration detention facilities in remote locations. But immigrant rights advocates have vigorously countered, organizing round-the-clock schedules to ensure pro bono client representation and track detention conditions. The book describes government officials purposely moving child migrants to undisclosed new locations just before their hearings without informing appointed lawyers to undercut the possibility of legal representation. But it also recounts determined counter-moves, such as congressional interns surreptitiously videoing conditions in detention facilities to publicize them. The message is that defending non-citizens' basic rights to humane treatment requires much more than recitation of constitutional principle – extraordinary dedication and ingenuity have been the bedrock of moves to counter the administration's rollback of basic legal obligations.

As of this writing, the administration has applied for a court order to reverse the *Flores* settlement that governs the terms of child migrant detention. *Flores* prohibits the incarceration of migrant children for more than twenty days, irrespective of whether or not they are with their parents. It also requires that migrant children in state custody be held in certified facilities, specifically licensed to provide appropriate care.[33] If the government is successful in reversing *Flores*, it will be able to indefinitely detain migrant children with their families. The fact that family detention space is being expanded to accommodate 20,000 children is ominous. It remains to be seen whether the courts and American public will tolerate this cruel policy shift any more than they did its predecessor, family separation.

Externalizing Humanitarian Responsibility

Apart from the contested litigation centered on the *Flores* settlement, the Trump administration is pursuing additional exclusion and deterrent strategies, all of which violate migrant children's rights to protection and safety, and all of them under legal challenge. The common denominator for these policies is externalization – a process by which the United States exploits its economic and political heft to dislodge its humanitarian obligations onto its much poorer and more unstable neighbors.

Ferocious violence in Central America shows no signs of abating. Homicide rates in the Central Triangle remain the highest in the world – 62 homicides per 100,000 people in El Salvador (#1), 42 per 100,000 in Honduras (#5), and 26 per 100,000 in

---

[33] For a detailed account of the *Flores* settlement and its changing provisions, see Schrag, *Baby Jails.*

Guatemala (#16).[34] The region is particularly dangerous for women and children. According to the UNHCR, 82 percent of Central American women asylum seekers reported that they would face torture or persecution if returned to the region.[35]

In the face of life-threatening circumstances, migration deterrence simply does not work. Children and their families are continuing to flee and to seek protection in the United States. More than 76,020 unaccompanied children and more than 473,000 adults and children traveling in family units were apprehended at the Unites States' southern border in 2019, the highest numbers ever recorded.[36]

Having failed with family separation, the administration has turned to other strategies. In 2018, then-Attorney General Jeff Sessions announced a proposal to radically curtail the scope of asylum by excluding from protection survivors of persecution by private actors, including murderous spouses and brutal gangs.[37] The bar for gaining asylum in those cases was already high – applicants had to demonstrate that they could not get protection from their governments, that they could not secure safety by traveling to distant sites within their own countries, and that the harm they feared rose to the very high threshold of "persecution." So only a small proportion of the most extreme cases of domestic and gang-related violence were successful – no open door or "flood" of asylum grants had ever existed. But this new policy bars access completely. In so doing it signals a reversal of decades of American refugee practice.

The attack on asylum access has been further accelerated by three other momentous developments. The first is the June 26, 2018, majority Supreme Court judgment in *Hawaii* v. *Trump* that upheld the administration's ban on all access to the United States for nationals from several majority-Muslim countries. As Stephen Legomsky, a widely revered legal scholar, has noted, the Supreme Court has, time and again, "declared itself powerless to review even those immigration provisions that explicitly classify on such disfavored bases as race, gender, and legitimacy."[38]

American citizen children will no longer be able to be joined in their country by parents, grandparents, or siblings who are, for example, Iranian or Syrian. People fleeing the devastating (US-supported) conflict in Yemen that has left 12,000 civilians dead and spread famine and disease to millions will no longer be able to join their relatives long settled in the United States. Young people from the marked

---

[34] "Intentional Homicides (per 100,000 people)," *United Nations Office on Drugs and Crime, International Homicide Statistics*, https://data.worldbank.org/indicator/VC.IHR.PSRC.P5?most_recent_value_desc=true.

[35] "UNHCR Warns of 'Looming Refugee Crisis' in the Americas," *UN High Commissioner for Refugees*. October 28, 2015, www.unhcr.org/5630fc6a9.html.

[36] "Southwest Border Migration FY 2019," U.S. *Customs and Border Protection*, November 14, 2019, www.cbp.gov/newsroom/stats/sw-border-migration/fy-2019.

[37] *Matter of AB-*, 27 I&N Dec. 316 (A.G. 2018), Interim Decision #3929, www.justice.gov/eoir/page/file/1070866/download.

[38] S. H. Legomsky, "Immigration Law and the Principle of Plenary Congressional Power" (1984) 1984 *Supreme Court Review* 255–307 at 255.

countries, however able, will be denied access to US universities, and patients seeking advanced medical care will have to turn elsewhere. Another, less-remarked-upon, consequence of the Supreme Court's judgment is its devastating impact on the LGBTI community. A significant minority of asylum applicants from the excluded countries have turned to the United States for safety in the face of barbarous anti-gay policies in their home countries – homosexuality is punishable by death in Iran, Syria, and Yemen.[39] This door is now closed.

To further its externalization strategy, the administration has developed several other policies designed to block, deter, or return humanitarian migrants, policies that have a disproportionate impact on Central American children and their families. In January 2019, months after the family separation policy was halted, but with the same deterrent intent, the US government introduced the mis-named "Migration Protection Protocols" (MPP), more accurately known as the "Remain in Mexico Policy."[40] For the first time, border officials are forcing child refugees and their families, who present themselves at the United States' southern border to apply for asylum, to return to Mexico. There, in a no-man's-land known to be riddled with drug traffickers and criminal cartels, certified as a "Do Not Travel" area by the US State Department, the asylum seekers have to spend months waiting for their hearings to be listed. US asylum officials, protesting the new policy, described it in a court petition they lodged: "Prior to the MPP, our country's processing of asylum applications ensured that people fleeing persecution would not be … returned to a territory where they may face persecution or threat of torture."[41] This externalization practice recalls the infamous Haitian maritime interdiction policies of the 1980s and 1990s. According to October 2019 estimates, more than 66,000 Central American humanitarian migrants have been affected, of whom approximately 5,000 are under five years old.[42] According to firsthand reports, 50 percent of those returned report being kidnapped in Mexico; systematic sexual violence has also been reliably documented.[43] These reports and other confirmed cases of shootings and ransoms have not, to date, forced a revision of US border practice.

---

[39] "#Outlawed: The Love That Dare Not Speak Its Name," *Human Rights Watch*, http://internap .hrw.org/features/features/lgbt_laws/.

[40] "Migration Protection Protocols," *Department of Homeland Security*, January 24, 2019, www .dhs.gov/news/2019/01/24/migrant-protection-protocols.

[41] Local 1924, Amici Brief 2, *Innovation Law Lab* v. *McAleenan*, No. 19-15716 (9th Cir. June 26, 2019).

[42] "US Move Puts More Asylum Seekers at Risk: Expanded 'Remain in Mexico' Program Undermines Due Process," *Human Rights Watch*, September 25, 2019, www.hrw.org/news/ 2019/09/25/us-move-puts-more-asylum-seekers-risk#; R. Mishor and K. Hampton, "The Worst Immigration Policy You've Never Heard of," *The Hill*, January 8, 2020, https://thehill.com/ opinion/immigration/477329-migrant-protection-protocols-the-worst-immigration-policy-youve-never.

[43] "Delivered to Danger: Illegal Remain in Mexico Policy Imperils Asylum Seekers' Lives and Denies Due Process," *Human Rights First*, August 2019, www.humanrightsfirst.org/sites/ default/files/Delivered-to-Danger-August-2019%20.pdf.

At the same time as it is forcing vulnerable humanitarian migrants seeking protection back into Mexico, the US government is also severely rationing the rate at which US border officials accept asylum applications, a process referred to as "metering." This intentional rationing of an urgent humanitarian service exacerbates delay and fuels the sense of "crisis." Predictably, demand for asylum processing increasingly outstrips the ever more limited supply of officials charged with asylum processing responsibility.

Meanwhile, those asylum seekers who understandably try to circumvent this dramatic bottleneck by attempting to enter between official entry points and apply for asylum thereafter are subject to prosecution for illegal entry, the hard edge of the "zero tolerance" policy. In short, damned if you do, and damned if you don't. The well-established international norm protecting access to asylum irrespective of the manner of entry on the territory, clearly codified in the 1951 Refugee Convention, has been eliminated. It remains to be seen whether this frontal attack on established humanitarian law and principle will be upheld by the courts, but while it is in operation, it further undermines the access to protection for non-citizen children fleeing Central American violence.

It is not just Mexico's northern border that is affected. Under threat of crippling economic sanctions, the Trump administration has pressured Mexico to block refugee entry at its southern border by deploying, for the first time ever, its national guard forces. As of June 2019, Mexico had sent 15,000 untrained soldiers to police the border. In June 2019 alone, more than 30,000 Central Americans, including unaccompanied children, were detained in this way, which has led to overcrowding at 300 percent overcapacity in some Mexican detention centers.[44] The Mexican government is now planning to close down these facilities, presumably by emulating US conduct and sending asylum seekers back across the border into Guatemala.[45] Children fleeing gangs and other forms of violence now face much more costly and dangerous smuggling strategies to secure safety.

A third externalization measure is probably the most devastating to Central American children's chances of securing safety abroad.[46] Adopting Europe's "safe third country" approach that forces asylum seekers to apply for protection in the first safe country they enter, even if they have family or other ties elsewhere, the Trump

---

[44] M. Meyer and A. Isacson, *The "Wall" Before the Wall: Mexico's Crackdown on Migration at Its Southern Border* (Washington, DC: WOLA, 2019), www.wola.org/analysis/mexico-southern-border-report/.

[45] J. Valencia, "Mexico Closes 5 Immigrant Detention Centers," *Arizona Public Media*, March 7, 2019, https://news.azpm.org/p/news-topical-border/2019/3/7/147445-mexico-closes-5-immigrant-detention-centers/.

[46] Z. Kanno-Youngs, "Federal Judge Strikes Down Trump Administration's Asylum Rule," *New York Times*, July 1, 2020, www.nytimes.com/2020/07/01/us/politics/trump-asylum-ruling-immigration.html.

administration is proposing to completely block land entry via the southern border to all asylum seekers. If implemented, this would mean that only refugees rich enough to fly or organize visas for themselves would have the possibility of getting to the United States to seek asylum. In a macabre, Monty Pythonesque twist, the job of providing sanctuary to humanitarian migrants fleeing violence would then be left to the murder capitals of the world – Guatemala, El Salvador, and Honduras – all of whom have signed cooperative agreements to this effect with the United States. In addition, new proposals advanced by the Trump administration would gut the asylum process even further, compounding the impact of safe third country exclusion procedures with draconian restrictions to the substantive grounds required as proof of eligibility for refugee status.[47]

No European country, many of them addressing immigration pressures proportionately greater than the United States, has intentionally incarcerated migrant children or denied access to the asylum procedure to irregular entrants. Why? Not because they have unlimited reception capacity, not because they lack a deeply xenophobic element in their electorates, not because arguments about deterrence and moral blackmail as pragmatic migration control tools do not circulate. Countries do not incarcerate migrant children or eliminate the possibility of asylum for irregular entrants as a matter of fundamental moral and legal principle.

These policies and proposals highlight the growing outlier, even rogue status of the United States in the international sphere. American exceptionalism has long been acknowledged in relation to gun ownership, capital punishment, mass incarceration, and – in recent history – unapologetic use of torture. But this country's long history of celebrating its immigrant identity was a welcome aspect of US exceptionalism. Trump's infliction of harm on current populations of distress migrants eviscerates the best aspects of the American polity itself.

Rights-Respecting and Feasible Alternatives

It is worth considering the alternatives to these inhumane policies. International law, US constitutional obligations, and common humanity demand a radically different approach to children fleeing life-threatening violence. The fact that these children are non-citizens has no relevance to their claim for enforcement of rights – legal rights, human rights, fundamental rights. Outrage at the family separation policy demonstrated that, across the political spectrum, the claim that the well-being of vulnerable children can legitimately be used as a deterrent to border crossing is untenable. Widespread global political consensus and international norms establish the opposition to child migrant detention and to punitive action against children

---

[47] Z. Kanno-Youngs, "Asylum Officers Condemn What They Call 'Draconian' Plans by Trump," *New York Times*, July 15, 2020, www.nytimes.com/2020/07/15/us/politics/asylum-officers-trump.html.

charged with no criminal infractions. What is required, then, instead of punitive and deterrent policies?

There are much better alternatives. The first, and most crucial, involves a constructive and collaborative regional approach – not one that coerces neighbors to accept refugees destined for the United States (as the asylum cooperation agreements described earlier do), but one that deploys the United States' substantial resources – financial, political, and technical – to the urgent task of making the Northern Triangle countries safe again for children.

This is no easy task. The rule of law has been shattered by conflict, drug cartels, and the export of gang violence through deportations from the United States. Courageous local judges attempting to punish kleptocracy at the highest government levels have been forced to flee for their lives. These challenges are exacerbated by rural to urban migration caused by environmental damage. Children in overcrowded and under-resourced cities need safe and well-resourced schools, parents with jobs, effective health care, and playgrounds not threatened by gangs. Both self-interest and the reparative obligations that result from decades of engagement with military regimes should drive substantial US investment in building these resources. Roberto Suro, a respected Central American expert, has pointed out that the Trump administration's total 2019 budget for the wall, immigration enforcement, and detention ($44 billion) is close to the combined GDP of El Salvador and Honduras ($48 billion).[48] A portion of those huge sums deployed to encourage Northern Triangle economic development would greatly contribute to improved local conditions and attendant decreases in migration pressure. A civic intervention program introduced by the Obama administration in one of Honduras's most notorious neighborhoods produced excellent results. At an annual cost of $100 million, an integrated set of schemes in Rivera Hernández, the most violent neighborhood in San Pedro Sula, the murder capital of the world for four years in a row, reduced the risk of crime and alcohol or drug abuse among targeted youth by 77 percent compared to their untargeted peers. The violence prevention program also increased conviction rates for those charged with homicide from a previous low of 4 percent to a record 50 percent. Most significantly, over the two-year period of intervention, the violence prevention program reduced by more than half the number of Honduran youth arriving at the US–Mexico border.[49] This was one initiative in one neighborhood. Similar past initiatives in El Salvador have also been successful. Instead of canceling them, the administration should scale them up. This would improve youth safety and reduce migration pressures.

---

[48] R. Suro, "We Need to Offer More Than Asylum," *New York Times*, July 14, 2018, www.nytimes .com/2018/07/14/opinion/sunday/migration-asylum-trump.html.

[49] S. Navarro, "Op-Ed: How to Secure the Border. Spoiler Alert: A Wall Won't Do It," *Los Angeles Times*, April 23, 2017, www.latimes.com/opinion/op-ed/la-oe-nazario-what-works-to-end-illegal-immigration-20170423-story.html.

Closer to home, at a fraction of the cost of prolonged incarceration, the administration could replace family detention pending a final immigration decision with supervised family release and a much speedier and better administered asylum process. As noted, previous efforts to do this have yielded excellent results. Recent data from the Department of Justice shows that 89 percent of all asylum applicants attended their final court hearing to receive a decision on their application,[50] and among families and unaccompanied children who have access to legal representation, "compliance" with immigration court obligations is 98 percent.[51] The United States could learn from its peers – other wealthy migration destination states addressing large-scale child migration – by providing legal representation and guardianship to unaccompanied children to ensure simpler and speedier court proceedings and more rational and just living arrangements. Guardians could ensure that children are accommodated in safety, with families or in childcare facilities, while they await decisions in their cases, and that they have access to appropriate educational and health facilities. Legal representatives could sift meritorious from unmeritorious cases, obviating the need for lengthy and costly court adjournments, negotiating safe returns home where this is in the best interests of the child, and ensuring prompt resolution by other means as appropriate, to the benefit of all parties. No one benefits from the uncertainty, cost, and misery generated by prolonged limbos.

Most critically, the United States should accept that, until it is abated by vigorous and effective development investments, the current humanitarian disaster facing children from the Central Triangle countries warrants special immigration policies. Instead of trumpeting the myth that physical or institutional barriers will prevent at-risk children from fleeing, the United States should institute deliberate and regulated policies to facilitate orderly child entry.

Many of the unaccompanied children who seek humanitarian entry in the United States have well-founded fears of persecution – they should qualify for refugee status. But the recent executive changes to US policy described earlier have restricted their chances, excluding those threatened by gang violence, for example, from qualifying for asylum.

For Central American children fleeing violence who have documented relatives in the United States, there should be refugee processing by US consulates in Central America. This would ensure safe travel, removing children from harm at home and en route. A program to do this that worked successfully was cancelled by the Trump administration.[52] It should be reinstated.

---

[50] "Workload and Adjudication Statistics," *United States Department of Justice*, February 3, 2020, www.justice.gov/eoir/workload-and-adjudication-statistics.

[51] "Priority Immigration Court Cases: Women with Children," *TRAC Immigration, Syracuse University*, https://trac.syr.edu/phptools/immigration/mwc/.

[52] Pierce, *Immigration-Related Policy Changes*, p. 17.

In addition, the United States could follow historical precedents – the Kindertransport for Jewish children fleeing the Nazis, the Pedro Pan movement for Cuban children fleeing Castro – and institute refugee resettlement programs, establishing reasonable annual quotas and a transparent, fair, and efficient system of admission for the most vulnerable Central American children. The Office of Refugee Resettlement could work with local US communities, tapping into the extensive bedrock of civic capacity and willingness to accommodate, support, mentor, and nurture refugee children. Canada's civic sponsorship program and Germany's remarkable network of engaged communities and municipalities provide excellent precedents.

Finally, the United States could deploy its unrivalled educational resources to encourage subsidized scholarship programs for at-risk children and adolescents. Many immigrant and children's rights advocates in schools and colleges would enthusiastically support such an initiative – the much celebrated Erasmus program in Europe, which has facilitated mobility for adolescents from Romania, Bulgaria, and Hungary to educational institutions in Germany, the United Kingdom, and Sweden, provides a powerful precedent.[53] Nothing but benefit for US educational institutions and their students, the broader community, and of course the at-risk Central American children and youth could flow from such initiatives.

As in other complex social fields, what is needed to address the challenges generated by contemporary distress migration (a constant in human history) is clarity and equity. Clarity about who is eligible for protection, for work authorization, for family reunification, for receipt of a visa; equity in relation to the right to mobility, access to timely and fair procedures and legal representation, and protection of basic human rights.

Our societies have extensive unmet needs for manual and low-skilled labor, needs that are not matched by proportionate work visas – as a result, millions are employed in an irregular immigration status, a clear inequity.[54] Our societies have extensive availability of educational opportunity given declining domestic fertility rates – yet only very wealthy non-citizen adolescents and young people (unless they are highly talented "scholarship" material) can access this opportunity, a clear inequity. Our societies are built on the founding notion that families are a fundamental social unit, the best context for child rearing – yet millions of children are separated from loving families for immigration reasons, a clear inequity. Our societies uphold the right not

[53] "The 30th Anniversary and You," *European Commission*, https://ec.europa.eu/programmes/erasmus-plus/anniversary/30th-anniversary-and-you-_en.

[54] M. Sumption and D. G. Papademetriou, *Legal Immigration Policies for Low Skilled Foreign Workers* (Washington, DC: Migration Policy Institute, 2013), www.migrationpolicy.org/research/legal-immigration-policies-low-skilled-foreign-workers; "Highly Skilled Migrants Are No Longer Welcome in America. Maybe," *The Economist*, June 23, 2020, www.economist.com/united-states/2020/06/23/highly-skilled-migrants-are-no-longer-welcome-in-america-maybe.

to be forced back home if there is a threat to life or freedom – yet millions are denied the opportunity to exercise that right, a clear inequity.

The proliferation of conflicts, the increase in environmental harms associated with climate change, the growing and increasingly evident social inequity across regions, and demographic transformations are complex factors that all impinge on migration and which must be addressed as part of the answer to unregulated and life-threatening movements of people. Migration cannot be fixed by migration strategies alone. There are no quick fix solutions, as the Trump administration has learnt to its cost.

In response to the large-scale flows of desperate distress migrants from Syria and other parts of the Middle East, Asia, and Africa into Europe in 2014 and 2015, the member states of the United Nations embarked on a systematic process to review global migration and refugee flows. In the fall of 2018, they signed two "global compacts," one on refugees and one on migrants.[55] The compacts address many of the complexities bedeviling current migration policy – the lack of responsibility sharing for refugees, the dearth of legal and safe access to migration for many deserving and able populations, the imperative of linking migration and refugee policies with development strategies, and the urgency of attending to the human rights and needs of child migrants, whether accompanied by their families or unaccompanied. A central goal was to create integrated, global strategies for managing migration, sharing responsibility, and more adequately responding to the needs of the many constituencies implicated in contemporary migration.

Two years down the line from the initial, vigorous engagement with the global compacts' project, it is not clear that demonstrable progress has been achieved. The notion that migration management should be linked to development goals – and in particular to Sustainable Development Goal 10.7 that calls on state parties to "[f]acilitate orderly, safe, regular and responsible migration and mobility of people, including through the implementation of planned and well-managed migration policies" – is a powerful one.[56] It sets a useful framework for action and for policy development. Several of the alternative policy approaches outlined here are consistent with this development approach. However, opinions differ when it comes to evaluating progress. Although some analysts are disappointed, critical of the fact that little political will has been galvanized and few if any significant improvements in

---

[55] United Nations, *Global Compact for Safe, Orderly, and Regular Migration*, July 13, 2018, https://refugeesmigrants.un.org/sites/default/files/180713_agreed_outcome_global_compact_for_migration.pdf; United Nations General Assembly, *Report of the United Nations High Commissioner for Refugees: Part II. Global Compact on Refugees*, U.N. Doc. A/73/12 (Part II) (September 13, 2018), www.unhcr.org/gcr/GCR_English.pdf.

[56] United Nations General Assembly, *Transforming Our World: The 2030 Agenda for Sustainable Development*, U.N. Doc. A/RES/70/1 (October 21, 2015), available at: www.refworld.org/docid/57b6e3e44.html; "SDG 10: Reduce Inequality Within and Among Countries," *United Nations Office on Drugs and Crime*, www.unodc.org/unodc/en/about-unodc/sustainable-development-goals/sdg10_-reduce-inequalities.html.

migration safety or humanitarian protection and resettlement have been secured, others suggest the opposite – that given the unrealistic nature of the global compact recommendations to start with, there are grounds for cautious optimism about incremental steps toward progress in both refugee integration and life-saving migration management.

The US government has signed on to the Global Compact on Refugees, though its annual rate of acceptance of resettled refugees is at an all-time low. The US government has withdrawn from the Global Compact on Migration, however, reflecting the isolationism of its current foreign policy and the failing commitment to sustainably improving the migration management system. Both these developments – the low resettlement rates and the failure to engage with constructive approaches to improved migration management – bode ill for the thousands of vulnerable Central American children and young people seeking safety from violence and the opportunity to lead productive and rewarding lives. They will create more business for people smugglers, higher casualties of fleeing children en route, and a greater burden of distress and trauma for thousands as they move from childhood to adulthood. But they will also strengthen the determination of child migrants and their supporters to press for alternatives, and to use all the means at their disposal to secure the rights and interests to which they are entitled.

4

Australia's Extraterritorial Border Control Policies

Azadeh Dastyari and Asher Hirsch

By international standards, the numbers of refugees arriving in Australia irregularly are small. Nevertheless, Australia has instigated extreme policies to deter and deny people seeking its protection. The impacts of these policies are felt by some of the world's most vulnerable individuals: refugees. For such individuals, the overall numbers are irrelevant because the harm caused to them is personal and real. Australia's policies are also undermining the international protection regime by setting a harmful example for other states who wish to deny refugees protection. In this way, Australia's impact on global protection is disproportionate to the size of the cohort of irregular arrivals.

The majority of spontaneous arrivals in Australia (i.e., the arrival of individuals without visas or other legal authority to enter the country) are refugees. A refugee is defined in Article 1(A)(2) of the Convention Relating to the Status of Refugees (Refugee Convention) as a person who, "owing to well-founded fear of being persecuted for reasons of race, religion, nationality, membership of a particular social group or political opinion, is outside the country of his nationality and is unable or, owing to such fear, is unwilling to avail himself of the protection of that country."

A person who meets this definition is considered a refugee with rights under international law from the moment they meet the definition, not from the moment their claim for protection is assessed. As the United Nations High Commissioner for Refugees (UNHCR) handbook makes clear:

> [a] person is a refugee within the meaning of the 1951 Convention as soon as he fulfils the criteria contained in the definition. This would necessarily occur prior to the time at which his refugee status is formally determined. Recognition of his refugee status does not therefore make him a refugee but declares him to be one. He does not become a refugee because of recognition, but is recognized because he is a refugee.[1]

---

[1] United Nations High Commissioner for Refugees, *Handbook on Procedures and Criteria for Determining Refugee Status under the 1951 Convention and the 1967 Protocol Relating to the Status of Refugees* (Geneva, Switzerland: United Nations High Commissioner for Refugees,

This distinction is significant because it means that a person who meets the definition of a refugee is a refugee even if they are prevented from accessing protection. That is, extraterritorial measures adopted by Australia, or any other country, which prevent the entry of a refugee, do not negate the status of the individual as a rights holder under international law.

In the last two decades, refugee arrivals in Australia have included Hazara and other Afghani refugees escaping the violence of the Taliban; Iraqi refugees fleeing sectarian violence in their war-torn state; and members of the LGBTQI community, political activists, evangelical Christians, and other persecuted minority groups fleeing the Iranian regime. Such individuals make the difficult and dangerous journey to Australia in search of safety because they have little choice.

Almost all such refugees pass through transit states in Southeast Asia, such as Indonesia and Malaysia, to reach Australia. They are unable to seek protection in these transit countries because these states have not ratified the Refugee Convention and therefore do not have any legal obligation to offer refugees protection. The refugees in transit states are often left without legal status in a precarious and at times dangerous situation. The ability of the refugees to come to Australia and find protection, therefore, is paramount for their safety.

Refugees arriving irregularly to Australia, however, have not been viewed favorably by successive Australian governments. Policies that deter and deny refugees access to Australian territory, regardless of their desperation or need, have enjoyed bipartisan support from both Australia's center-left Labor party and the center-right Liberal and National Coalition parties. Governments wishing to exercise a high degree of control over Australian borders have also been assisted by the country's geography. Australia's isolation and lack of land borders has helped it to implement a number of extraterritorial migration control measures, that is, actions outside of Australian territory that allow it to prevent the irregular arrival of refugees by both sea and air. These "*non-entrée* policies"[2] effectively stop would-be refugees from leaving their own countries, or keep refugees in countries that have not ratified the Refugee Convention and that have less capacity to protect refugees and uphold their rights.

Many of the extraterritorial border control measures adopted by Australia have focused on stopping irregular boat arrivals. Refugees arriving by boat, in particular, have been viewed as a grave risk to Australian society.[3] Stopping the refugee boats

---

2011), ¶ 28, www.refworld.org/docid/4f33c8d92.html; J. C. Hathaway and M. Foster, *The Law of Refugee Status* (2nd ed., Cambridge: Cambridge University Press, 2014), 25.

[2] J. C. Hathaway, *The Rights of Refugees under International Law* (New York: Cambridge University Press, 2005), 291.

[3] F. H. McKay, S. L. Thomas, and R. W. Blood, "'Any One of These Boat People Could Be a Terrorist for All We Know!' Media Representations and Public Perceptions of 'Boat People' Arrivals in Australia" (2011) 12(5) *Journalism* 607–626.

was a key election promise of the Coalition government in its re-election campaign in 2013. Australia has also introduced less publicized measures to prevent the entry of unauthorized non-citizens by air.

This chapter addresses some of the extraterritorial measures adopted by Australia to prevent the entry of certain people into Australian territory. In the first part, the chapter examines measures aimed at stopping irregular arrivals by air, including carrier sanctions, Airline Liaison Officers, and the use of technology. The second part assesses the measures taken by Australia to stop irregular boat arrivals, including third country detention and processing regimes in Nauru and Papua New Guinea and boat interdictions. The final part questions the legality or otherwise of Australia's actions.

Extraterritorial border control measures have proven highly effective in preventing the irregular arrival of refugees in Australia. They have, however, placed Australia in violation of its international obligations, prevented refugees from seeking protection thereby placing them in harm's way, and have resulted in great suffering for at-risk groups.

STOPPING THE PLANES

People seeking to claim protection in Australia have two options to enter Australia's territory and seek its protection: arrival by plane or by boat. The waters surrounding Australia are often treacherous and the boat journey to Australia can be deadly. Furthermore, people travelling irregularly by boat seldom have choice in the vessel used to carry them and can end up on unseaworthy boats that cannot cope with rough waters or precarious weather conditions. Although allowing asylum seekers and refugees to board a plane to Australia would be the safer option, Australia has gone to great lengths to ensure that those without a visa are unable to board an Australia-bound flight.

Carrier Sanctions

One of the most significant means by which Australia prevents the entry of refugees into its territory by air is through fines for airline operators in the form of carrier sanctions. Carrier sanctions are financial penalties imposed upon airlines and ships that transport passengers who do not hold the relevant permission to enter the country. By requiring carriers to check that passengers have authorization to enter a country prior to embarking, carriers effectively become border officials, controlling migration at the point of departure. Although carrier sanctions do not apply only to those who carry refugees, they disproportionally affect refugees seeking protection.

Carrier sanctions rely on an economic argument: The "fear of having their profit margin eroded by such penalties is supposed to encourage carriers to deny passage to

Australia to those who are inadequately or irregularly documented."[4] The Australian Migration Act of 1958 (Cth) makes it an offence to transport a non-citizen to Australia without a visa or documentation.[5] In addition, airlines and ship companies are responsible for removing passengers from Australia if they are refused entry after arrival.

To make it explicitly clear that carrier sanctions apply even to those with genuine protection claims, Section 228B(2) of Australia's Migration Act provides: "a non-citizen includes a reference to a non-citizen seeking protection or asylum (however described), whether or not Australia has, or may have, protection obligations in respect of the non-citizen because the non-citizen is or may be a refugee, or for any other reason." This makes it clear that airlines and other carriers will be fined even if the non-citizen they have brought to Australia is found to be a refugee and owed legal protection in Australia. This is in contrast to the policies of other countries.[6] For example, in the European Union, sanctions "may in some cases be waived if the passenger is found to be a refugee."[7] However, since carriers do not conduct refugee status determinations prior to boarding, the changes of an airline allowing refugee-claimant to board a plane – and thereby risk a fine – are slim.

Taylor argues that carrier sanctions have succeeded in reducing the number of refugees arriving by air: "The fact that the number of infringement notices actually served on carriers has been dropping markedly from year to year indicates that sanctions have had their intended effect."[8] Airlines are unlikely to be sympathetic to the claims of refugees seeking to board, and even if they are, they do not have adequate expertise to assess refugee claims before departure. Even for those who are sympathetic, the financial impact of carrier sanctions would eventually outweigh any humanitarian concern.[9]

Carrier sanctions mean that refugees are stopped outside of Australian territory – before they board the plane – and that the process of border control is carried out by a private company.[10] This privatization of border control adds an additional complication for those seeking protection. There are legal implications when private

[4]   S. Taylor, "Offshore Barriers to Asylum Seeker Movement: The Exercise of Power without Responsibility?," in J. McAdam (ed.), *Forced Migration, Human Rights and Security* (Oxford: Hart Publishing, 2008), p. 100.
[5]   Migration Act 1958, No. 62, 1958, §§ 229, 232.
[6]   A. Brouwer and J. Kumain, "Interception and Asylum: When Migration Control and Human Rights Collide" (2003) 21(4) *Refuge: Canada's Journal on Refugees* 6–24 at 10; Taylor, "Offshore Barriers to Asylum Seeker Movement," p. 101.
[7]   T. Baird, "Carrier Sanctions in Europe: A Comparison of Trends in 10 Countries" (2017) 19(3) *European Journal of Migration and Law* 307–334 at 326.
[8]   Taylor, "Offshore Barriers to Asylum Seeker Movement," p. 100.
[9]   Ibid., p. 101.
[10] S. Scholten, "The Privatisation of Immigration Control through Carrier Sanctions: The Role of Private Transport Companies in Dutch and British Immigration Control," in J. Niessen and E. Guild (eds.), *Immigration and Asylum Law and Policy in Europe* (vol. 38, Leiden, Boston: Brill Nijhoff, 2015).

commercial companies rather than a government official decide if a person has the right to cross the border. This is because states rather than private companies have the legal responsibility to refugees under international law, and it can be more difficult to hold states accountable when they exercise their power through private companies. As Gammeltoft-Hansen notes, "the argument that states incur any obligations under refugee law as a result of carrier controls has been rejected on the premise that these controls are a private matter, distinct from the state's own authorities and thus responsibility."[11] This makes asserting legal rights such as *non-refoulement*, increasingly difficult, successfully deterring many potential legal challenges.

Airline Liaison Officers

Although it has privatized border controls through carrier sanctions, Australia has not entirely relinquished its border control at airports to airlines. In order to assist airlines in meeting their carrier obligations, Australia has posted Airline Liaison Officers (ALOs) in more than sixteen airports throughout Asia and the Middle East, as these countries are often seen as transit countries for asylum seekers en route to Australia. By its own account, "Australia has one of the most experienced, respected and effective ALO networks in the world."[12]

The main function of ALOs is to "assist local immigration and airport authorities and airlines personnel to identify document fraud by checking documents and provide advice on authenticity."[13] As the Department of Immigration describes, "ALOs work with airlines, airport security groups and host governments, as well as colleagues from other countries, and have a dual role of preventing improperly documented passengers from travelling and facilitating the travel of genuine passengers at key overseas airports."[14] In 2014, ALOs prevented "173 improperly documented passengers from travelling to Australia."[15] It is not clear how many of these passengers had attempted to make asylum claims. "The Department of Immigration's arrangements with host country governments do not specify processes for dealing with asylum claims made by intercepted persons."[16]

---

[11] T. Gammeltoft-Hansen, *Access to Asylum: International Refugee Law and the Globalisation of Migration Control*, Cambridge Studies in International and Comparative Law (Cambridge: Cambridge University Press, 2011), p. 17.

[12] S. Morrison, "New Measures at Our Borders to Protect against Terrorist Threat," September 10, 2014, https://parlinfo.aph.gov.au/parlInfo/search/display/display.w3p;query=Id:%22media/press rel/3387218%22.

[13] Taylor, "Offshore Barriers to Asylum Seeker Movement," p. 95.

[14] Department of Immigration and Border Protection, *2014–2015 Annual Report* (2015), 92, www.border.gov.au/ReportsandPublications/Documents/annual-reports/DIBP-Annual-Report-2014-15-optimised.pdf.

[15] Ibid.

[16] Taylor, "Offshore Barriers to Asylum Seeker Movement," p. 97.

The aim of the ALO network is to "extend [the Australian] border all the way to embarkation points."[17] However, the direct impact of ALOs is difficult to quantify, as there is no record keeping of any refugee claims made at the departure point.[18] This has been noted at a roundtable with the UNHCR and the Council of Europe: "It is impossible to be precise about the number of refugees who are denied escape due to stringent checks by transport companies. The number is considered to be on the rise, however, not least since transport companies have been assisted by Governmental liaison officers in verifying travel documents."[19]

Use of Technology

Finally, to ensure compliance with its carrier sanctions and to further monitor and control its external borders, Australia maintains a range of surveillance technologies. The Department of Immigration's Annual Report 2014–2015 highlights a number of "Border Systems" it employs to monitor and control the movement of passengers en route to Australia. These include systems to identify "people who are of concern for a number of reasons, including health, character and national security"; to record "lost, stolen or cancelled and bogus foreign travel documents"; and to share "real-time travel document validation service between participating RMAS [regional movement alert system] economies – currently Australia, New Zealand, the USA and the Philippines."[20] As the Department notes, these systems ensure that "people tendering invalid travel documents [are] prevented from boarding a flight from any boarding point."[21]

Since 2005, Australia has required all airlines to process passengers through the Advance Passenger Processing ("APP") system.[22] The Department of Immigration outlines how this process works:

> Airlines bringing travellers to Australia are required to confirm that each traveller they uplift has an authority to travel to Australia, usually in the form of a visa. Airlines confirm this authority using the advance passenger processing (APP) system, which also reports details of all passengers and crew to the Department before arrival. This gives the Department and other agencies advance notice in real time of a person arriving by air and helps to facilitate immigration clearance of genuine travellers on arrival.[23]

[17] Morrison, "New Measures at Our Borders to Protect against Terrorist Threat."
[18] Taylor, "Offshore Barriers to Asylum Seeker Movement," p. 98; Brouwer and Kumain, "Interception and Asylum," p. 10.
[19] Brouwer and Kumain, "Interception and Asylum" at 11.
[20] Department of Immigration and Border Protection, *2014–2015 Annual Report*, p. 91.
[21] Ibid.
[22] Taylor, "Offshore Barriers to Asylum Seeker Movement," p. 99.
[23] Department of Immigration and Border Protection, *2014–2015 Annual Report*, p. 92.

Since 2006, Australia has also developed an extensive database of biometric data for all non-citizens.[24] In 2004, the Australian Parliament passed the Migration Legislation Amendment (Identification and Authentication) Act 2004 (Cth). This Act allows for the collection of personal identifiers from non-citizens, including fingerprints and handprints, photographs or other images of the face and shoulders, weight and height measurements, audio or video recordings, signatures and iris scans, and other items.[25] This data is shared with other partner nations and cross-referenced to identify any undesirable people. As the Department explains:

> Under the Five Country Conference (FCC) biometric data matching programme, the Department is developing capability to automate the exchange of non-FCC citizens' biometric data with other FCC partners. Automation of biometric data exchange has begun between Australia and the USA, and between Australia and the UK. Full automation of biometric data exchange, and the subsequent legal requirements to carry out this sharing, will be progressively rolled out to all FCC partners over the coming years.[26]

This data matching has led to the denial of visas to potential refugees. For example, the Australian government has published the following case study:

> An individual applied for a visitor visa at an overseas post on 24 February 2015. The individual's biometrics were captured and referred for FCC checking. One partner country returned an FCC match in March 2015 and advised that on 19 December 2008 the individual had been apprehended by immigration and customs officials and charged with being an undocumented arrival. The individual left the partner country on 27 March 2009 . . .. A second FCC country also returned a fingerprint match and revealed that the individual had applied for refugee protection there. In March 2005 the individual was reported inadmissible for being a member of an organised crime group that specialised in the theft of money and jewellery. It was also reported that the individual had been convicted on 10 August 2005 of an offence punishable by a maximum term of imprisonment of at least 10 years, or for which a term of imprisonment of more than six months was imposed . . .. The individual's application for an Australian visitor visa was refused at post on 8 April 2015.[27]

In this example, the potential refugee was not given a chance to present his case, had no rights to appeal, and no access to justice. It should be remembered that under

[24] Ibid., p. 51.
[25] Parliament of the Commonwealth of Australia, House of Representatives, *Explanatory Memorandum, Migration Legislation Amendment (Identification and Authentication) Bill 2004* (2003), ¶ 7, http://parlinfo.aph.gov.au/parlInfo/download/legislation/ems/r1750_ems_ad508d33-2128-4588-9020-c8660227eceo/upload_pdf/57737.pdf;fileType=application%2Fpdf.
[26] Department of Immigration and Border Protection, *2014–2015 Annual Report*, p. 50.
[27] Ibid., p. 51.

international law, being convicted of theft does not automatically make a person ineligible for refugee protection.[28] The example shows how these technologies of surveillance can work to keep out potential refugee claimants.

Those who are unable to board a plane to Australia are forced to seek refugee protection by boat. Indeed, it could be argued that the creation of visa controls and airline liaison officers has forced those seeking protection to use more dangerous pathways to protection. Those who are unable to obtain a visa have very few options at their disposal to protect themselves and their families. However, in response to the irregular arrival of refugees by boat, Australia has further hardened its border, implementing a range of discriminatory policies directed at boat arrivals.

STOPPING THE BOATS

Extraterritorial Processing and Detention of Asylum Seekers and Refugees Arriving by Boat

Much of Australia's current extraterritorial practices with regard to irregular boat arrivals were a response to the August 2001 arrival of the Norwegian-registered MV *Tampa* near Australian territory. MV *Tampa*, which was carrying 433 asylum seekers rescued at sea, attempted to enter Australian territorial waters and to disembark the rescued people on Australian territory of Christmas Island. The Australian government, then led by Prime Minister John Howard from the center-right Liberal party, in coalition with the National Party (which largely represents the more conservative rural communities in Australia), responded by deploying military (Special Air Services) personnel to take control of the vessel and forcibly transfer the passengers to Nauru for processing.

These events marked the commencement of a policy broadly known as the "Pacific Solution," under which any non-citizens, including refugees, interdicted at sea or arriving in certain parts of Australia without a valid visa to enter Australian territory, became vulnerable to transfer to Australia's economically struggling former protectorates of Nauru and Papua New Guinea for processing and detention.

Due to a drop in the number of boat arrivals, the number of asylum seekers transferred to Manus Island in Papua New Guinea decreased over time. By May 2005, there were no detainees in the Papua New Guinea facility. However, detention in Nauru continued until December 2007, when it was ended by Australia's newly elected center-left Labor government. The closure of the facilities in Nauru and Papua New Guinea was, however, short lived.

The Labor government announced the resumption of the transfer of asylum seekers to Nauru and Papua New Guinea in August 2012, and in July 2013 it was announced that no refugees processed in Nauru or Manus Island would ever be

---

[28] Hathaway and Foster, *The Law of Refugee Status*, p. 546.

resettled in Australia. Instead, asylum seekers would be sent to Nauru or Manus Island, and then, following the confirmation of refugee status, would either be expected to resettle in Nauru, Papua New Guinea, or a third country.

Australia has, however, found it difficult to resettle refugees from Nauru and Papua New Guinea. Cambodia agreed to resettle refugees from Nauru in exchange for $55 million from the Australian Government. Only seven refugees agreed to participate in the arrangement.[29] A highly publicized deal with the United States has also resulted in the resettlement of refugees from Nauru and Papua New Guinea.[30] As of August 22, 2019, a total of 619 refugees had been resettled in the United States.[31] An offer by New Zealand to resettle refugees from Australia's extraterritorial detention centers has been rejected by the Australian government.[32] The Australian government fears that the refugees resettled in New Zealand may be able to enter Australia later as a result of a special category visa for New Zealand citizens, which allows them to live and work in Australia indefinitely.[33] Between August 13, 2012, and September 1, 2019, 4,177 people were transferred to Nauru and Papua New Guinea, including children. In September 2019, 562 of the people transferred by Australia to Nauru and Papua New Guinea remained on the islands. No children remain on Nauru and Manus Island as of January 2020.

The cost of operating detention facilities in Nauru and Manus Island are borne entirely by Australia. Australia has contracted service providers and maintains a visible and active presence at the centers at all times. As the UNHCR notes, "it is clear that Australia has retained a high degree of control and direction in almost all aspects of the bilateral transfer arrangements."[34] The High Court of Australia has found that Australia secures, funds, and participates in the detention on Nauru, with Justice Bell further arguing that "[t]he Commonwealth funded the RPC and exercised effective control over the detention of the transferees through the contractual obligations it imposed on Transfield .... [D]etention in Nauru was, as a

---

[29] M. Walden, "Cambodia: Syrian Refugee Secretly Arrives from Australian Detention on Nauru," *Asian Correspondent*, May 26, 2017, https://asiancorrespondent.com/2017/05/cambo dia-syrian-refugee-secretly-arrives-australian-detention-nauru/.

[30] C. Packham, "Exclusive: Australia to Accept First Central American Refugees under U.S. Deal – Sources," *Reuters*, July 25, 2017, www.reuters.com/article/us-usa-trump-australia-refu gees-idUSKBN1AA0NO.

[31] H. Davidson, "Manus and Nauru Refugees in Australia on Medical Grounds Can Apply for US Move," *The Guardian*, September 6, 2019, www.theguardian.com/australia-news/2019/sep/06/ manus-and-nauru-refugees-in-australia-on-medical-grounds-can-apply-for-us-move.

[32] K. Murphy, "Jacinda Ardern Tells Scott Morrison New Zealand Remains Open to Resettling Nauru Refugees," *The Guardian*, December 5, 2019, www.theguardian.com/australia-news/ 2019/dec/05/jacinda-ardern-tells-scott-morrison-new-zealand-remains-open-to-resettling-nauru- refugees.

[33] Ibid.

[34] United Nations High Commissioner for Refugees, *UNHCR Monitoring Visit to the Republic of Nauru 7–9 October 2013* (November 26, 2013), p. 23 ¶ 128, www.unhcr.org/publications/legal/ 58117b931/unhcr-monitoring-visit-to-the-republic-of-nauru-7-to-9-october-2013.html.

matter of substance, caused and effectively controlled by the Commonwealth parties."[35]

The detention of asylum seekers in Papua New Guinea and Nauru has received a high degree of criticism from international organizations, including Human Rights Watch, the United Nations High Commissioner for Refugees, and Amnesty International. There have been several deaths of asylum seekers in the detention facility in Papua New Guinea, including the murder of a young Iranian man by guards and the deaths of two men, which a number of leading health professionals believe could have been prevented with better medical care.[36] The detention facility in Nauru has not been free from tragedy, either. Omid Masoumali, a young Iranian national seeking Australia's protection died after a 22-hour delay to fly him to Australia for burn treatment. Masoumali self-immolated following a UN visit to Nauru in protest against the conditions and continuing detention on the island.[37] Centers in both Papua New Guinea and Nauru have also been plagued by allegations of rape and other sexual assaults, including of children. Independent bodies have also observed overcrowding and poor conditions of detention,[38] a lack of fairness and transparency in refugee status determinations,[39] and repeated concerns regarding detainees' lack of safety.[40]

The UNHCR released a very strong condemnation of conditions for detainees on Australia's extraterritorial detention facilities, stating:

---

[35] *Plaintiff M68/2015 v. Minister for Immigration and Border Protection*, 257 CLR 42 (HCA 2016).

[36] B. Doherty, "Border Force Doctor Knew of Manus Asylum Seeker's Deteriorating Health before Death," *The Guardian*, August 9, 2017, www.theguardian.com/australia-news/2017/aug/09/border-force-doctor-knew-of-manus-asylum-seekers-deteriorating-health-before-death; G. Thompson et al., "Asylum Seeker's Death Blamed on 'Pathetic' Manus Island Blunder," *ABC News*, April 25, 2016, www.abc.net.au/news/2016-04-25/manus-island-blunder-blamed-for-asylum-seeker-death/7355858.

[37] Amnesty International, *Australia: Island of Despair: Australia's "Processing" of Refugees on Nauru* (October 2016), p. 19.

[38] Amnesty International, *This Is Breaking People: Human Rights Violations at Australia's Asylum Seeker Processing Centre on Manus Island, Papua New Guinea* (December 2013), www.refworld.org/pdfid/52aac41cb.pdf; Amnesty International, *This Is Still Breaking People: Update on Human Rights Violations at Australia's Asylum Seeker Processing Centre on Manus Island, Papua New Guinea* (May 2014), https://static.amnesty.org.au/wp-content/uploads/2016/09/This_is_still_breaking_people_update_from_Manus_Island.pdf; Senate Legal and Constitutional Affairs Legislation Committee et al., *Incident at the Manus Island Detention Centre from 16 February to 18 February 2014* (Parliament of Australia, 2014), www.aph.gov.au/Parliamentary_Business/Committees/Senate/Legal_and_Constitutional_Affairs/Manus_Island/Report.

[39] Human Rights Watch, *World Report 2015: Papua New Guinea* (New York: Human Rights Watch, 2015), www.hrw.org/world-report/2015/country-chapters/papua-new-guinea.

[40] Amnesty International, *This Is Breaking People*; Amnesty International, *This Is Still Breaking People*; Human Rights Watch, *World Report 2015*; Senate Legal and Constitutional Affairs Legislation Committee et al., *Incident at the Manus Island Detention Centre from 16 February to 18 February 2014*.

There is no doubt that the current policy of offshore processing and prolonged detention is immensely harmful . . .. Despite efforts by the Governments of Papua New Guinea and Nauru, arrangements in both countries have proved completely untenable.[41]

In 2016, the Papua New Guinea Supreme Court held in *Namah* v. *Pato* that detention of refugees and asylum seekers was unconstitutional under the right to liberty set out in the Papua New Guinean Constitution. The Court ordered both the Australian and Papua New Guinea governments to "take all steps necessary to cease and prevent the continued unconstitutional and illegal detention of the asylum seekers or transferees . . . on Manus Island."[42]

The detention center on Manus Island has now closed but there is little certainty regarding the fate of the refugees there as their resettlement appears untenable. A number of refugees have required medical attention following assaults from members of the local population after being released into the community, and there are deep concerns regarding the safety of the men transferred to Manus Island by Australia.[43] The men are vulnerable because of the animosity felt by some members of the local community toward them. As Grewcock explains, "the tensions between sections of the local Manus Island community and the detainees are rooted in the socio-economic impacts of locating the centre in one of the poorer regions of PNG."[44] Human rights groups also report that refugees have been attacked on a daily basis in Nauru after being released into the Nauruan community.[45]

Australia has paid a high cost for its extraterritorial status determination and detention regime for asylum seekers and refugees. In financial terms, the operation of detention facilities in Nauru and Manus Island cost Australia nearly $5 billion between 2012 and 2017.[46] The extraterritorial regime has also been highly damaging to Australia's international reputation with a negative impact on its diplomacy and

[41] United Nations High Commissioner for Refugees, "UNHCR Calls for Immediate Movement of Refugees and Asylum-Seekers to Humane Conditions," May 2, 2016, www.unhcr.org/en-au/572862016.pdf#zoom=95.

[42] *Namah* v. *Pato*, Papua New Guinea Supreme Court (2016), 8 ¶ 17.

[43] A. Dastyari and M. O'Sullivan, "Not for Export: The Failure of Australia's Extraterritorial Processing Regime in Papua New Guinea and the Decision of the PNG Supreme Court in Namah (2016)" (2016) 42 *Monash University Law Review* 308–338 at 308.

[44] M. Grewcock, "'Our Lives Is in Danger': Manus Island and the End of Asylum" (2017) 59(2) *Race & Class* at 78, https://doi.org/10.1177/0306396817717860.

[45] *See* "Claims Probed of Brutal Conditions for Refugees on Island of Nauru," *NPR*, August 11, 2016, www.npr.org/2016/08/11/489584342/claims-probed-of-brutal-conditions-for-refugees-on-island-of-nauru. *See also* M. G. Bochenek, "Australia: Appalling Abuse, Neglect of Refugees on Nauru," *Human Rights Watch*, August 2, 2016, www.hrw.org/news/2016/08/02/australia-appalling-abuse-neglect-refugees-nauru.

[46] R. Strating, "Enabling Authoritarianism in the Indo-Pacific: Australian Exemptionalism" (2020) 74(3) *Australian Journal of International Affairs* 301–321, https://doi.org/10.1080/103577 18.2020.1744516.

soft power.[47] The greatest cost of Australia's determination to process and detain asylum seekers and refugees offshore has, however, been borne by the asylum seekers and refugees themselves.

Interdiction at Sea

In addition to an extraterritorial processing and detention regime for people who arrive irregularly by boat, Australia has also attempted to prevent refugees from arriving by boat through an interdiction regime. "Interdiction" in this context means actions taken at sea to prevent vessels from reaching their intended destination, in this case Australia.[48]

Australia initially introduced an interdiction program named "Operation Relex" in 2001. While this regime was in effect, twelve vessels were detected attempting to reach Australia. Of these, four were successfully intercepted and returned to Indonesia, three ultimately sank, and the rest were intercepted and passengers were taken to Christmas Island, Nauru, or Papua New Guinea.[49]

Under the Labor Government, from 2007 to 2013, no boats were turned back. However on September 18, 2013, 11 days after the Liberal-National Coalition won back power in the federal election, then-Prime Minister Tony Abbott implemented "Operation Sovereign Borders," a "military-led response to combat people smuggling and to protect [Australia's] borders."[50] Operation Sovereign Borders involved a staunch commitment that all asylum seekers arriving by boat would be turned back to their country of departure. From September 2013 until July 2015, 20 boats carrying at least 633 passengers were intercepted and returned to their countries of departure, including to Sri Lanka, Vietnam, and Indonesia.[51] A number of these turnbacks involved "enhanced screening" at sea, which is a cursory assessment to determine if anyone being returned is a refugee. This policy of enhanced screening prevents asylum seekers from making a detailed refugee claim and denies them any procedural fairness.

---

[47] W. Maley, "Australia's Refugee Policy: Domestic Politics and Diplomatic Consequences" (2016) 70(6) *Australian Journal of International Affairs* 670–680.

[48] D. Guilfoyle, *Shipping Interdiction and the Law of the Sea* (Cambridge: Cambridge University Press, 2009), p. 4; A. Dastyari, *United States Migrant Interdiction and the Detention of Refugees in Guantánamo Bay* (New York: Cambridge University Press, 2015), p. 3.

[49] A. Schloenhardt and C. Craig, "'Turning Back the Boats': Australia's Interdiction of Irregular Migrants at Sea" (2015) 27(4) *International Journal of Refugee Law* 536–572 at 538, https://doi.org/10.1093/ijrl/eev045.

[50] Ibid., at 548.

[51] J. Phillips, "Boat Arrivals and Boat 'Turnbacks' in Australia since 1976: A Quick Guide to the Statistics," *Parliamentary Library, Parliament of Australia*, September 11, 2015, www.aph.gov.au/About_Parliament/Parliamentary_Departments/Parliamentary_Library/pubs/rp/rp1516/Quick_Guides/BoatTurnbacks.

The policy of enhanced screening was first introduced in 2012 by the Labor Government to apply to Sri Lankan boat arrivals, and was mostly undertaken in Australian territory on Christmas Island.[52] As part of Operation Sovereign Borders, the policy of enhanced screening was implemented while asylum seekers were detained on Navy and Custom vessels at sea. This policy involves:

> asking each of the asylum seekers a set of four questions and determining their refugee status on the basis of their answers to these questions (the asylum seeker's name, country of origin, where they had come from, and why they had left) without a right to appeal a negative decision.[53]

The risk that a person would be returned to face harm following such a cursory assessment of their claim is high, as seen when asylum seekers from Vietnam who were turned back by Australia were subsequently granted refugee protection by the UNHCR in Indonesia.[54]

Australia's policy of enhanced screening and turnbacks was highlighted in the case of *CPCF* v. *Minister for Immigration and Border Protection*,[55] in which a boat of 157 Tamil asylum seekers was intercepted en route to Australia from India. After initial attempts to return the asylum seekers to India, and a subsequent High Court challenge, the asylum seekers were taken to the extraterritorial processing center on Nauru. This is the only boat of asylum seekers not to be returned since the beginning of Operation Sovereign Borders.[56]

Both the physical act of interdicting boats at sea and the return of individuals to transit or refugee-producing countries place refugees and others seeking Australia's protection at risk of serious harm including further persecution and even death. There are grave concerns that the cursory status determination procedures undertaken at sea to identify individuals in need of protection are inadequate to safeguard refugees who must be protected from persecution.

EVALUATING THE LEGALITY OF AUSTRALIA'S POLICIES

Australia's response to refugees is consistent with the view that a refugee is a potential threat, rather than someone fleeing harm. Under international law, states do have a sovereign right to control their borders. Inherent in the principle of sovereignty are the principles of territorial supremacy and self-preservation. This

---

[52] M. Grewcock, "Back to the Future: Australian Border Policing under Labor, 2007–2013" (2014) 3(1) *State Crime Journal* 102–125 at 111.

[53] Schloenhardt and Craig, "'Turning Back the Boats,'" at 554.

[54] S. Sebban, "Turned Back by Australia, Vietnamese Recognised as Refugees in Indonesia," *The Sydney Morning Herald*, June 11, 2017, www.smh.com.au/world/turned-back-by-australia-vietnamese-recognised-as-refugees-in-indonesia-20170608-gwn475.html.

[55] *CPCF* v. *Minister for Immigration and Border Protection*, 255 CLR 514 (HCA 2015).

[56] Phillips, "Boat Arrivals in Australia: A Quick Guide to the Statistics."

principle of sovereignty allows states the "freedom to act unconstrained and the right to exclude foreigners from their territory."[57] Yet this absolute sovereignty has been partially relinquished through the voluntary ratification of international treaties. By agreeing to be bound by international treaties, including international human rights law, states have taken on additional obligations to uphold certain rights for both citizens and non-citizens within their jurisdiction. As Goodwin-Gill and McAdam note:

> The refugee in international law occupies a legal space characterised, on the one hand, by the principle of State sovereignty and the related principles of territorial supremacy and self-preservation; and, on the other hand, by competing humanitarian principles deriving from general international law (including the purposes and principles of the United Nations) and from treaty.[58]

International law, and in particular the right to seek asylum and obligations of the Refugee Convention, poses a challenge to the traditional concept of sovereignty. Although the right to seek asylum is provided in Article 14 of the Universal Declaration of Human Rights (UDHR),[59] it is often referred to as an empty right because it does not create a subsequent duty upon states to grant asylum.[60] Indeed, the Declaration on Territorial Asylum reiterates that the granting of asylum is an "exercise of [State] sovereignty."[61] Nevertheless, although states may not have a duty to grant asylum, they do have an obligation to provide access to their asylum procedures. Goodwin-Gill and McAdam argue that "while individuals may not be able to claim a 'right to asylum,' states have a duty under international law not to obstruct the right to *seek* asylum."[62]

In addition to the UDHR, the Refugee Convention and its 1967 Protocol provide further obligations on states with regard to their borders. By ratifying the Refugee Convention, states forfeit their claim to absolute control over their borders. One hundred and forty-six states, including Australia, have ratified the 1967 Protocol, which affirms the obligations of the Refugee Convention and removes its temporal and geographic limitations to post-Second World War Europe, transforming it into a set of global commitments. As Gammeltoft-Hansen argues, "refugee law places a constraint on the otherwise well-established right of any state to decide who may

---

[57] Gammeltoft-Hansen, *Access to Asylum*, p. 13.
[58] G. S. Goodwin-Gill and J. McAdam, *The Refugee in International Law* (3rd ed., Oxford: Oxford University Press, 2007), p. 1.
[59] Universal Declaration of Human Rights, December 10, 1948, United Nations General Assembly Res. 217A(III), art. 14.
[60] S. Kneebone, *Refugees, Asylum Seekers and the Rule of Law: Comparative Perspectives* (Cambridge: Cambridge University Press, 2009), p. 10.
[61] United Nations General Assembly Res. 2312 (XXIX), Declaration on Territorial Asylum (December 14, 1967), art. 1(1).
[62] Goodwin-Gill and McAdam, *The Refugee in International Law*, p. 358.

enter and remain on its territory."[63] In other words, while states are entitled to build walls, these walls must have doors for refugees.[64]

Refoulement of Refugees

One significant danger of Australia's extraterritorial actions is the *refoulement*, or return, of refugees to a place where they may face persecution. This is a significant risk when Australia returns boats to refugee-producing countries directly, such as when it interdicts and returns vessels to countries of origin such as Sri Lanka and Vietnam. It also remains a risk when refugees are returned to, or are kept in, transit countries from which they may be subject to chain *refoulement* (the subsequent return of refugees to the original country they were fleeing).

The *refoulement* of a refugee is prohibited under Article 33 of the Refugee Convention. If any individuals returned by Australia are at risk of torture, Australia's actions would also violate Article 3 of the Convention against Torture and Other Cruel, Inhuman or Degrading Treatment or Punishment (CAT). Furthermore, the return of a person to inhumane, degrading treatment, punishment, or to death is a violation of Articles 6 and 7 of the International Covenant on Civil and Political Rights (ICCPR).

ACCESS TO TERRITORY

International refugee and human rights law does not explicitly grant permission for refugees to enter a state's territory. However, there is a link between compliance with a state's negative obligation to prevent *refoulement* and the positive obligation to provide refugees access to the territory of a state. This is because a state's *non-refoulement* obligations do not end at its borders. A state, such as Australia, owes a *non-refoulement* obligation to anyone in its effective de jure or de facto control. Put simply, any refugee that is either directly or indirectly in Australia's control, such as individuals detained in Australia's extraterritorial processing centers or interdicted at sea, may be owed a *non-refoulement* obligation. Unless Australia provides protection to everyone that it has de jure or de facto control over, it must carry out fair and effective procedures to determine who is a refugee and is thus owed *non-refoulement* obligations, and who can be safely returned.

Hathaway argues that when there is a real risk of persecution due to a Refugee Convention ground, a duty of non-refoulement amounts to "a *de facto* duty to admit the refugee since admission is normally the only means of avoiding the alternative,

[63] Gammeltoft-Hansen, *Access to Asylum*, pp. 12–13.

[64] V. Moreno-Lax, "Must EU Borders Have Doors for Refugees? On the Compatibility of Schengen Visas and Carriers' Sanctions with EU Member States' Obligations to Provide International Protection to Refugees" (2008) 10(3) *European Journal of Migration and Law* 315–364, https://doi.org/10.1163/157181608X338180.

impermissible consequence of exposure to risk."[65] The Executive Committee of the United Nations High Commissioner for Refugees (UNHCR ExCom) agrees. In its 1997 Conclusions on Safeguarding Asylum, UNHCR Excom drew attention to the importance of the principle of refoulement and "the need to *admit refugees into the territories of States,* which includes no rejection at frontiers without fair and effective procedures for determining status and protection needs."[66] The UNHCR ExCom in its 1998 Conclusion reaffirmed this statement and again strongly deplored the refoulement of refugees.[67] In addition, in its Protection Policy Paper on Maritime Interception Operations, the UNHCR noted in 2010 that "claims for international protection made by intercepted persons are in principle to be processed in procedures within the territory of the intercepting State."[68] The paper explains that in-territory processing will generally be "the most practical means to provide access to reception facilities and to fair and efficient asylum procedures."[69]

Arbitrary Detention

Refoulement is not the only obligation that may be violated by Australia's current policies. As explained earlier, all refugees who arrive in or are intercepted while attempting to enter Australia can be transferred to and detained in Australia's extraterritorial detention facilities in Nauru and Papua New Guinea. Detention in these two countries is mandatory for people whose claims are being processed.

The Human Rights Committee has expressed the view that "detention should not continue beyond the period for which the State can provide appropriate justification," and that the factors necessitating detention must be "particular to the individual."[70] The ongoing detention of refugees transferred to Nauru and Papua New Guinea does not comply with this requirement. All individuals are detained regardless of their age, gender, nationality, or any other characteristic. The detention, therefore, is not particular to the individual circumstances of each person. It is thus likely that mandatory detention in Australia's extraterritorial centers violates the prohibition on arbitrary detention provided in Article 9(1) of the ICCPR.

---

[65] Hathaway, *The Rights of Refugees under International Law,* p. 301.

[66] *Conclusion No. 85: Conclusion on International Protection,* Executive Committee of the High Commissioner's Programme, U.N. Doc. A/53/12/Add.1 (October 9, 1998) (emphasis added).

[67] Ibid.

[68] United Nations High Commissioner for Refugees, *Protection Policy Paper: Maritime Interception Operations and the Processing of International Protection Claims* (November 2010), www.unhcr.org/refworld/docid/4cd12d3a2.html.

[69] Ibid.

[70] United Nations Human Rights Committee No. 560/1993, A v. *Australia,* U.N. Doc. CCPR/C/59/D/560/1993 (April 30, 1997), ¶ 9.2.

Poor Conditions of Detention

The poor conditions of detention centers also violate international law. The UNHCR has observed that asylum seekers in Nauru are kept in "cramped conditions, with very little privacy, in very hot conditions, with some asylum seekers sleeping on mattresses on the ground."[71] These inadequate conditions, which compromise the health of asylum seekers and refugees, are further exacerbated by:

- Lack of adequate medical facilities, including for heart conditions, dental issues, and, in one case, to address a metal plate embedded in one person's leg.
- Hygiene issues: many complained of skin conditions and other infections, including parasites and lice.
- Lack of a gynecologist for the women.
- Lack of access to x-rays and other medical equipment.
- Limited access to medication.[72]

Furthermore, as stated earlier, asylum seekers and refugees transferred by Australia to Nauru and Papua New Guinea have also been subject to both sexual and physical abuse.[73]

Article 10 of the ICCPR requires states to treat detainees with "humanity and with respect for the inherent dignity of the human person." The Human Rights Committee has stated that "States parties should ensure that the principle stipulated [under Article 10 of the ICCPR] is observed in all institutions and establishments within their jurisdiction where persons are being held."[74] The lack of medical care and cramped, hot conditions of detention are inconsistent with humanity and respect for the inherent dignity of the human person, and thus violate Article 10 of the ICCPR.

The conditions of detention may also violate Article 7 of the ICCPR, which prohibits cruel, inhuman, or degrading treatment. In General Comment No. 20, the Human Rights Committee states that, "[i]n the view of the Committee, States parties must not expose individuals to the danger of torture or cruel, inhuman or degrading treatment or punishment upon return to another country by way of their

---

[71] United Nations High Commissioner for Refugees, *UNHCR Monitoring Visit to the Republic of Nauru 7–9 October 2013*.

[72] Ibid.

[73] P. Farrell et al., "The Nauru Files: Cache of 2,000 Leaked Reports Reveal Scale of Abuse of Children in Australian Offshore Detention," *The Guardian*, August 10, 2016, www.theguardian .com/australia-news/2016/aug/10/the-nauru-files-2000-leaked-reports-reveal-scale-of-abuse-of-children-in-australian-offshore-detention.

[74] United Nations Human Rights Committee, *General Comment No. 21, Humane Treatment of People Deprived of Liberty* (April 10, 1992), p. 1, www.un.org/ga/search/view_doc.asp?symbol= HRI/GEN/1/Rev.1.

extradition, expulsion or refoulement."[75] The UN Special Rapporteur Against Torture has found that numerous aspects of Australia's policies in Papua New Guinea violate the right of detainees "to be free from torture or cruel, inhuman or degrading treatment."[76] This is in violation of Articles 1 and 16 of the CAT. The finding of torture or cruel, inhuman, or degrading treatment against vulnerable individuals who had sought Australia's protection highlights the brutality of Australia's border protection policies.

CONCLUSION

Australia has sought to control its borders by both air and sea by acting outside its territory. Sadly, this has come at a significant cost for the safety and security of vulnerable groups including refugees and has placed Australia in violation of its international obligations. The Australian prime minister has stated that Australia's border protection policies are "the best in the world."[77] Unfortunately, many world leaders, particularly in Europe, agree and are looking to emulate Australia's extra-territorial methods.[78]

Carrier sanctions, airline liaison officers, and the use of technology have limited the ability of protection seekers to come to Australia irregularly by plane while interdictions at sea, outside of Australian waters, have prevented the entry of those seeking protection by boat. Extraterritorial deterrence measures such as third country immigration detention has also acted as a discouragement to any refugees wishing to seek asylum in Australia by arriving by boat. Australia's actions have led to the refoulement of refugees, arbitrary detention, and poor conditions in detention. Such a regime cannot be "the best in the world" and must be dismantled immediately to ensure Australia's compliance with its international obligations.

---

[75] United Nations Human Rights Committee, *Compilation of General Comments and General Recommendations Adopted by Human Rights Treaty Bodies* (May 27, 2008), ¶ 9, www.ohchr .org/Documents/HRBodies/TB/HRI-GEN-1-REV-9-VOL-I_en.doc.

[76] United Nations Human Rights Council, *Report of the Special Rapporteur on Torture and Other Cruel, Inhuman or Degrading Treatment or Punishment, Juan E. Méndez (Addendum)* (March 5, 2015), www.un.org/ga/search/view_doc.asp?symbol=A%2FHRC%2F28%2F68%2FAdd.1&Su bmit=Search&Lang=E.

[77] P. Karp, "Turnbull Claims Australian Border Policies 'Best in World' Despite Widespread Criticism," *The Guardian*, September 17, 2016, www.theguardian.com/australia-news/2016/sep/ 18/malcolm-turnbull-australias-border-protection-policy-the-best-in-the-world.

[78] D. Ghezelbash, *Refuge Lost: Asylum Law in an Interdependent World*, Cambridge Asylum and Migration Studies (Cambridge: Cambridge University Press, 2018).

5

Protection through Revisionism?

UNHCR, *Statistical Reporting, and the Representation of Stateless People*

*Brad K. Blitz**

INTRODUCTION

One major problem complicating the task of effective humanitarian protection is the lack of quality data on the populations most affected. If protection agencies cannot identify those who need help, then their ambitions of assisting them are unlikely to be realized. This is especially relevant when considering "invisible," hard to reach, or historically marginalized groups for whom we have little baseline data and whose presence is a source of contention for national authorities.

Unfortunately, undercounting is not simply a matter for statisticians and social demographers. It is often a political matter. As Sarfaty writes, "numbers display governmentality because they serve as a technology of power that constitutes populations and makes individuals calculable and therefore governable – both by others and themselves."[1] *Who* is counted also tells us about governmental and institutional priorities and exposes biases about *what* counts, and how resources *should* be allocated. For example, voter registration may not include the total adult citizens because African Americans have been repeatedly denied the right to register to vote in some US states. Official processes may be exploited to discriminate against certain groups and published data may inaccurately reflect population trends.

The rationale for collecting data also reveals political and institutional priorities. National statistical offices play an essential role in governmental planning and are central to the state's claim to legitimacy. Similarly, international organizations, including the United Nations High Commissioner for Refugees (UNHCR), have

---

* The author would like to thank the editors, Molly Land, Kathy Libal, and Jillian Chambers, as well as Alessio D'Angelo, Jeff Crisp, Margaret Okole, and Don Kerwin for their helpful advice on earlier versions of this chapter. I am also grateful to Bronwen Manby for her helpful comments on this chapter.
[1] G. Sarfaty, "Regulating Through Numbers: A Case Study of Corporate Sustainability Reporting" (2013) 53 *Virginia Journal of International Law* 575–624 at 588.

turned to the collection of data in the name of enhancing accountability and improving operational delivery.[2] This includes gathering information to advance target-based agendas, such as the Sustainable Development Goals, and measure progress in meeting institutional priorities. Data collection is a tool of national and global governance.[3]

This chapter presents a critical account of how statelessness has been measured by the UNHCR and its partners. It examines how data have been collected and presented in official reports and joint advocacy initiatives to advance ambitious agendas, including UNHCR's #IBelong campaign, which seeks to end statelessness by 2024. Although UNHCR is mandated to collect data on people in need of protection,[4] and has for decades used statistical indicators to map refugee conditions, its focus regarding statelessness has been on measuring accession to international instruments and capturing the percentage of stateless people for whom nationality is granted or confirmed within a given year. While UNHCR has sometimes been accused of inflating refugee numbers,[5] in this chapter, I argue that UNHCR has actively sought to reduce the number of people counted as stateless.[6] I suggest that the process of undercounting is indicative of a revisionist turn in humanitarian management characterized by a fixation with narrow definitions and institutional priorities that demand "results," which has been enthusiastically supported by donor states, NGOs, and academics. My central claim is that the ways in which UNHCR data are presented reflect an increasingly top-down logic that ignores the lived experience of stateless people and undermines the provision of humanitarian protection to some who may need it.

The first part of this chapter explores the history of statelessness as a policy area within UNHCR. Developing Reichel's argument of "normative path dependency," I chronicle the evolution of UNHCR's embrace of statistical indicators and the introduction of results-based management approaches to support its Global Strategic Priorities.[7] I suggest that as the number of refugees appeared to be falling, UNHCR refocused on statelessness, mainstreaming this issue across the institution. The renewed interest in statelessness coincided with UNHCR's shift in favor of results-

---

[2] *See* E. Reichel, "Navigating between Refugee Protection and State Sovereignty: Legitimating the United Nations High Commissioner for Refugees," in K. Dingwerth et al. (eds.), *International Organizations under Pressure: Legitimating Global Governance in Challenging Times* (Oxford: Oxford University Press, 2019), pp. 195–231.

[3] *See* S. E. Merry, "Human Rights Monitoring and the Question of Indicators," in M. Goodale (ed.), *Human Rights at the Crossroads* (Oxford: Oxford University Press, 2013), pp. 140–150.

[4] Article 35(2) of the 1951 Convention Relating to the Status of Refugees obliges Contracting States to provide the United Nations High Commissioner for Refugees (UNHCR) with statistical data relating to the condition of refugees, the implementation of the Convention, and any laws and decrees relating to refugees upon request.

[5] *See* G. Kibreab, "Pulling the Wool over the Eyes of the Strangers: Refugee Deceit and Trickery in Institutionalized Settings" (2004) 17 *Journal of Refugee Studies* 1–26.

[6] *See* "About the #IBelong Campaign to End Statelessness," www.unhcr.org/ibelong/.

[7] Reichel, "Navigating between Refugee Protection and State Sovereignty."

based management tools, employing methodological approaches that put them at a considerable distance from the populations on whose behalf they claimed to be acting. They also set unrealistic targets. And as they worked to systematize their data, they reclassified those who no longer fell in neat categories and amalgamated them into other categories. Noting these failings, I conclude by recommending that rather than making humanitarian protection the servant of legal definitions or pursuing unattainable goals, relief agencies, donor governments, and researchers should recognize the lived experience of stateless people and embrace methodologically robust approaches to identification.

FROM REFUGEES TO STATELESS PERSONS: INSTITUTIONAL DEVELOPMENTS

Although the term "statelessness" is today treated as a social category in its own right, this is a relatively new trend. Statelessness was long considered a feature of forced displacement, and many of those who today we would describe as stateless were accepted as refugees by receiving states. This was especially true in Europe where the unraveling of the Austro-Hungarian, Russian, and Ottoman Empires gave rise to massive refugee flows. In the late nineteenth and early twentieth century, millions who fled had never enjoyed nationality to begin with, while others saw their nationality status canceled retrospectively or lost upon application for a second nationality, leaving them stateless in the interim.

In the United States, for example, foreign-born men seeking to acquire US nationality were required to file a declaration of intent, at which point they would be forced to renounce any allegiance to another power. Yet they would often wait more than five years before they formally became US citizens, which required a court hearing. As for married women, they were simply assigned their husband's nationality until the Cable Act of 1922.[8]

During the First World War and in the interwar period, states increasingly withdrew nationality to facilitate the expulsion of foreign-born groups. Torpey attributes this to the rise of the surveillance state and the use of immigration controls.[9] For example, France denationalized foreign-born residents in 1915, three years before the new Soviet and Turkish governments denationalized Russian, Armenian, and Hungarian refugees. In the lead up to the Second World War, Fascist parties introduced racial laws, most famously in Germany (1935), where overnight the Nuremberg Laws divided Germans into "full citizens" and "citizens without political rights."

Following the Second World War, in Europe, stateless individuals and refugees were understood as equivalent and largely interchangeable categories. It is therefore

---

[8] See The Cable Act 1922, ch. 411, 42 Stat. 1021 (also known as the "Married Women's Independent Nationality Act").

[9] J. Torpey, *The Invention of the Passport: Surveillance, Citizenship, and the State* (Cambridge: Cambridge University Press, 2000).

not surprising, given the expressly European context informing the design of the 1951 Convention on the Status of Refugees, that millions of stateless people saw their protection needs subsumed under the refugee regime. Although a new instrument was introduced specifically for stateless people, namely, the 1954 Convention Relating to the Status of Stateless Persons, few states were party to it. Moreover, the Convention itself established a narrow definition of statelessness. Under Article 1, it defined a "stateless person" as a person "who is not considered as a national by any State under the operation of its law."[10] This definition is used to describe those who are de jure stateless, in contrast to the vast majority of those who are de facto stateless or *effectively* stateless, that is, individuals who cannot obtain proof of their nationality, residency, or other means of qualifying for citizenship and are thus practically excluded from protection by the state.[11]

The 1954 Statelessness Convention was initially conceived as a protocol to be included as an addendum to the 1951 Refugee Convention. Both were developed from the premise that refugeehood and statelessness were temporary statuses and that states would eventually integrate the millions of people who fell within these categories. A second Convention on the Reduction of Statelessness was introduced in 1961 with provisions to disallow statelessness at birth and to avoid statelessness resulting from the loss, deprivation, or renunciation of nationality in later life, as well as statelessness resulting from state succession. Yet, this instrument also presented several limitations: most importantly, it defers to states and asserts that nationality shall be granted by "operation of law to a person born in the State's territory," where such persons would "otherwise be stateless."[12] One important failing of this convention is that it does not prohibit the possibility of revocation of nationality, nor does it retroactively grant citizenship to all currently stateless persons; hence, it only offers a partial remedy to the problem of statelessness.

Further geopolitical divisions during the Cold War, which largely prevented refugees from leaving the Soviet bloc, undermined any moves to establish an effective regime for stateless persons during that period. In the meantime, Palestinians, who were arguably among the most visible stateless groups, were also treated separately. Even though the 1961 Statelessness Convention provided for an international body that would serve to examine and assist individual claims,[13] the UN system was hampered by geopolitical and organizational tensions. In 1974, when the 1961 Statelessness Convention came into effect, UNHCR did not have the capacity to fulfill this role. Not only was the agency distracted by the surge in

---

[10]   United Nations Convention Relating to the Status of Stateless Persons, September 28, 1954, 360 U.N.T.S. 117.

[11]   The final act of the Convention includes a nonbinding recommendation that states should "consider sympathetically" the possibility of according de facto stateless persons the treatment that the Convention offers to de jure stateless people. For a historical overview, see C. A. Batchelor, "Stateless Persons: Some Gaps in International Protection" (1995) 7 *International Journal of Refugee Law* 232–259.

[12]   Convention on the Reduction of Statelessness, August 28, 1961, 989 U.N.T.S. 175.

[13]   Ibid.

refugees, especially in Asia, Latin America, and Africa, but until 2003, it was also operating under a temporary mandate renewable every five years.

Over the past fifteen years, UNHCR has sought to bring statelessness more prominently within its remit.[14] A background paper prepared by Hugh Massey in 2010 to identify UNHCR's responsibilities and set out the basis for more consistent operational definitions states that UNHCR "tended to assume that it had a mandate for de facto stateless persons who are not refugees just as much as it has a mandate for de jure stateless persons who are not refugees."[15] UNHCR now operates a statelessness unit that supports a range of field activities and, since 2006, has required its country offices to include stateless people in their reports. It has published papers on statelessness;[16] has assisted many countries with surveys, registration campaigns, and population censuses; and has also provided technical advice.

As the number of recognized refugees stabilized and then started to fall in the twenty-first century, interest in the phenomenon of statelessness rose, and UNHCR emerged as the most vocal advocate on this issue. One core responsibility of UNHCR is to promote legal reform to address gaps in nationality and related legislation, including pressing states to accede to the Statelessness Conventions. UNHCR points to some achievements here, recording that in 2020 some twelve countries took steps to remove gender discrimination from their nationality laws and forty-nine states acceded to the two conventions on statelessness.[17] In 2009, UNHCR published a policy paper to inform statelessness determination procedures and provide a mechanism for analyzing situations where persons are stateless or are at risk of becoming stateless.[18] It has since published handbooks and operational guides. UNHCR now routinely provides reports and recommendations for the Universal Periodic Review on the topic and covers statelessness in its Global Appeals and Global Reports. It has also published educational tools[19] and includes statelessness in its flagship report, *The State of the World's Refugees*.[20]

---

[14] See *Conclusion on Identification, Prevention and Reduction of Statelessness and Protection of Stateless Persons No. 106*, UNHCR ExCom., U.N. Doc. A/AC.96/1035 (October 6, 2006).

[15] *UNHCR and De Facto Statelessness*, Hugh Massey, LPPR/2010/01 (April 2010), www.refworld .org/docid/4bbf387d2.html, p. ii.

[16] See UNHCR, *Guidelines on Statelessness No. 3: The Status of Stateless Persons at the National Level*, HCR/GS/12/03 (July 17, 2012), www.refworld.org/docid/5005520f2.html.

[17] See "How UNHCR Helps Stateless People," www.unhcr.org/uk/how-unhcr-helps-stateless-people.html.

[18] UNHCR, "Statelessness: An Analytical Framework for Prevention, Reduction, and Protection," *Global Report 2018* (2019), www.refworld.org/docid/49a28afb2.html.

[19] UNHCR, *A Guide to Teaching on Statelessness* (September 2010), www.refworld.org/docid/ 4d7f5f982.html; UNHCR, *Self-Study Module on Statelessness* (October 1, 2012), www.refworld .org/docid/50b899602.html.

[20] UNHCR, *The State of the World's Refugees: In Search of Solidarity* (2012), www.refworld.org/ docid/5100fec32.html.

As the profile of statelessness within UNHCR increased, so too did budgets. There was a marked upturn in 2010 when UNHCR allocated US $38.5 million for its statelessness operations – approximately three times the expenditure on such activities just one year earlier.[21] Expenditure on this head has continued to rise. For 2021, $81.6 million has been allocated to UNHCR's statelessness program – 1 percent of the agency's overall budget.[22]

Accompanying this expansion has been a greater emphasis on targets. In the mid-1990s, on the heels of the Srebrenica massacre and genocide in Rwanda, the UNHCR was struck by several scandals that forced donors to question its accountability and effectiveness at supporting those in need of humanitarian protection. Since then, the UNHCR, like other humanitarian agencies, has worked to develop more coherent systems of accountability and has strived to recast its image to donors. To this end, it has enthusiastically embraced the use of standards and indicators. Most notably, the UNHCR was a founding member of the 1997 Sphere Project, which set out minimum standards to improve the quality of humanitarian responses. In 2002, UNHCR launched the "Standards and Indicators Initiative" to firm up assessment, planning, and implementation within the agency. The collection and presentation of statistical data was seen as promoting efficiency and measuring the effectiveness of projects in order to satisfy donors and other stakeholders. It also gave the impression of greater accountability, though as Dunlop argues, internally generated indicators may be less than objective and raise questions about who is collecting data, for whom, and who shapes the ways in which findings are presented.

> Regardless of whether the resulting data is released publicly or used internally to determine the effectiveness of programs, there may be incentives for collection officers to downplay or couch certain failures if they are perceived to reflect poorly on sectoral management.[23]

In 2004, UNHCR published a *Practical Guide to the Systematic Use of Standards and Indicators in UNHCR Operations*, which was followed by a comprehensive management and structural reform process two years later.[24]

Although the reform process was sparked by external events that had exposed the agency's failures, Reichel contends that internal factors, including a new institutional culture based on the need to show improvement for its legitimacy, set the

---

[21] *See* UNHCR, "Addressing Statelessness," *UNHCR Global Appeal 2010–11* (2010), www.unhcr .org/4b02c5e39.pdf, p. 42.

[22] *See* UNHCR Executive Committee, *Update on Budgets and Funding* (2019, 2020–2021), U.N. Doc. EC/71/SC/CRP.6 (February 20, 2020), www.unhcr.org/5e6a3c497.pdf.

[23] E. Dunlop, *Indications of Progress? Assessing the Use of Indicators in UNHCR Operations* (UNHCR, July 2011), www.refworld.org/docid/4e55ec4e2.html.

[24] *See* UNHCR Policy Development and Evaluation Service (PDES), *Measure for Measure: A Field-Based Snapshot of the Implementation of Results-Based Management in UNHCR*, U.N. Doc. PDES/2010/13 (November 2010), www.unhcr.org/4cf3ad8f9.pdf.

UNHCR on a managerialist path. She argues that a process of "discursive entrapment" accompanied by an "intellectual climate in which 'new public management' norms had gained clout, were equally relevant to determine the pace and course of the rise of managerial norms."[25]

Over the past fifteen years, UNHCR has moved to rely on a sophisticated results-based management approach in the planning, implementation, and assessment of its activities.[26] The approach, championed by the UN Development Group (UNDG),[27] now features in UNHCR's Results Framework, a log-frame-based tool that includes scores of indicators. This top-down orientation requires, for example, the introduction of "precise" and measurable criteria and "evidence of change."[28] Evaluations of UNHCR operations have repeatedly relied on such criteria.[29]

Statelessness features within UNHCR's Global Strategic Priorities, which include a range of legal and humanitarian objectives. Key measures are described as "impact indicators" and "engagement" and include: reforming of law and policy consistent with international standards on the prevention of statelessness, principally through accession to the two UN statelessness conventions, and achieving annual targets of individuals who will acquire nationality or have it confirmed.[30]

Although the results-based approach has made important contributions to UNHCR's work in its emphasis on transparency and benefits for budgetary planning in particular,[31] the new ways of measuring impact have shifted it away from the needs of the most vulnerable. Reichel goes so far as to suggest that the new managerialism has created a tension within the organization over its priorities to advance its humanitarian mission and the reality that it is increasingly beholden to states.[32] Arguably, the results-based approach has encouraged certain reductive practices, the effects of which have not been fully explored. In the case of statelessness, the imperative to present results, together with a narrow definition of who counts as stateless, has led the UNHCR to privilege certain statistical data sources over other information and in effect to round down a problem that they could not possibly estimate. The next section describes both of these shifts.

[25] Reichel, "Navigating between Refugee Protection and State Sovereignty," p. 229.

[26] Ibid.

[27] *See* UNDP, *Results-Based Management Handbook* (2011), www.ilo.org/public/english/bureau/program/dwcp/download/undg_rbm1011.pdf.

[28] *See* UNHCR, *Practical Guide to the Systematic Use of Standards & Indicators in UNHCR Operations* (2006), www.unhcr.org/uk/statistics/unhcrstats/40eaa9804/practical-guide-systematic-use-standards-indicators-unhcr-operations.html.

[29] *See, e.g.,* Oxford Policy Management, *Evaluation of UNHCR's Implementation of Three of Its Protection Strategies: The Global Education Strategy, the Updated SGBV Strategy, and the Child Protection Framework* (July 2017), www.unhcr.org/5a183d9c7.pdf.

[30] UNDP, *Results-Based Management Handbook*, p. 10.

[31] *See* PDES, *Measure for Measure*.

[32] Reichel, "Navigating between Refugee Protection and State Sovereignty."

UNHCR'S DATA ON STATELESS PEOPLE

The UNHCR currently reports that it has "data" on some 4,161,980 stateless people but admits that "the true global figure is estimated to be significantly higher."[33] It has also recently recognized limitations with its method of calculation:

> However, this [global] figure is not based on robust or transparent demographic methods and, as a result, its use to track progress on reducing statelessness and for policy, programming, or advocacy purposes is limited …. [M]ore is required to capacitate member states and coordinate data collection to estimate the number of stateless persons within their territory.[34]

Nonetheless, it claims to have reliable data for seventy-eight countries. These aforementioned claims warrant further examination.

Who Is Stateless? And Where Do They Live?

Until 2019, it was unclear if UNHCR's data only referred to de jure stateless people, those described as falling under their mandate, or if they also captured de facto stateless individuals and persons with indeterminate nationality.[35] While the term "de facto" no longer features prominently in UNHCR documents, UNHCR's website states that the agency is now considering both de jure stateless people and those with indeterminate nationality.[36] In its 2020 report to UNHCR Standing Committee, which reviews UNHCR's activities and programs, the agency recorded that it used mixed data types to estimate figures of stateless people but did not elaborate: "[The table] [r]efers to persons who are not considered as nationals by any State under the operation of its law …. but data from some countries may also include persons with undetermined nationality."[37]

Second, UNHCR's approach to working with data on those of "indeterminate nationality" introduces other practical considerations, including the presumption that states will provide accurate and impartial information and are prepared to recognize links to other countries. "UNHCR uses the working definition of a person who lacks proof of possession of any nationality and who at the same time has or is perceived as having links to a State other than the one he/she is living in."[38] Not only does this approach defer to states' cooperation, but it also discounts the possibility

---

[33] *See* UNHCR, *Global Trends: Forced Displacement in 2018*, www.unhcr.org/5d08d7ec7.pdf, p. 51.

[34] L. Chen et al., *UNHCR Statistical Reporting on Statelessness* (October 2019), www.unhcr.org/statistics/unhcrstats/5d9e182e7/unhcr-statistical-reporting-statelessness.html.

[35] UNHCR Executive Committee, *Update on Budgets and Funding* (2019, 2020–2021), p. 27.

[36] *See* UNHCR, "Refugee Data Finder – Methodology," www.unhcr.org/refugee-statistics/methodology/.

[37] UNHCR Executive Committee, *Update on Budgets and Funding* (2019, 2020–2021).

[38] Ibid.

that states may misuse data and personal information.[39] As noted elsewhere, there is a long history of states' culpability in the creation of stateless people.[40]

Third, while recognizing that "a formal definition of a person with undetermined nationality does not exist," UNHCR has changed its terms of measurement from one year to another: "UNHCR previously also reported on de facto stateless populations but discontinued doing so in mid-2019 based on an assessment that de facto statelessness was often incorrectly used to refer to people who meet the statelessness definition in the 1954 Convention and who should, therefore, be reported as such."[41] This inconsistency makes longitudinal and comparative analysis especially problematic.

Fourth, the presentation of figures raises additional queries about coverage. As the Center for Migration Studies (CMS) found in their 2020 study of statelessness in the United States, the net used by UNHCR misses a large number of people who are stateless or potentially at risk of statelessness. Rather, drawing upon different datasets, including the American Community Survey (ACS) data, they maintain that the population of stateless people is both more diverse and significantly larger than UNHCR assumes.[42] There is also a lack of published statistics for countries that have experienced major refugee flows and that have historically hosted stateless groups. Most importantly, there are no data for large refugee-hosting states and countries that have significant internal migration, such as Pakistan, South Africa, and Uganda. There is no information on other countries that previously were reported to have stateless populations such as Nepal, where the US government reported that an estimated six million individuals lacked citizenship documentation.[43] There are even gaps in reporting on states that have introduced statelessness determination procedures; there should be some reliable information, for example, for Switzerland. In other cases, these figures are bizarrely low.[44] For example, Egypt, a country with a population of more than 100 million, which has been home to

---

[39] *See* Economic Commission For Europe, *Difficult To Measure Census Topics: Measuring Statelessness through Population Census*, Conference of European Statisticians, U.N. Doc. ECE/CES/AC.6/2008/SP/5 (May 13, 2008), https://unstats.un.org/unsd/censuskb2o/Attachm ents/2008UNHCR_ECE-GUIDe59366dbdf874942bae645a8b8319128.pdf, p. 4.

[40] *See* B. K. Blitz and M. Lynch (eds.), *Statelessness and Citizenship: A Comparative Study on the Benefits of Nationality* (Cheltenham, UK: Edward Elgar Publishing, 2011).

[41] Ibid.

[42] The CMS authors argue that some 218,000 people are at risk of statelessness in the United States. *See* D. Kerwin, D. Alulema, M. Nicholson, and R. Warren, "Statelessness in the United States: A Study to Estimate and Profile the US Stateless Population" (2020) 8(2) *Journal on Migration and Human Security* 150–213.

[43] U.S. Department of State, *2019 Country Reports on Human Rights Practices: Nepal, Bureau of Democracy, Human Rights, and Labor* (2020), www.state.gov/reports/2019-country-reports-on-human-rights-practices/nepal/.

[44] The UNHCR tool, the "Refugee Data Finder," www.unhcr.org/refugee-statistics/download/? url=U3cg, provides "information on displaced and stateless populations, including their demographics. The database also reflects the different types of solutions for displaced populations."

more than 200,000 refugees, including generations of Palestinians, records having just five stateless people.[45]

Redefining Statelessness and Developing Data

With refugee numbers falling, UNHCR commissioned many studies on statelessness in which it prioritized de jure statelessness over other statuses:

> In practice, it may sometimes be difficult to distinguish between *de jure* and *de facto* statelessness. Because of these complexities, UNHCR would also recommend that censuses ordinarily be restricted to gathering information only about *de jure* stateless populations, and populations with undetermined nationality.[46]

In addition to the methodological challenges noted here, Massey's historical interpretation of the diplomatic discussions during the drafting of the 1954 Statelessness Convention led him to argue for a narrow definition that focused on de jure statelessness.[47] Massey calls attention to the Final Act of the 1951 Conference of Plenipotentiaries on the Status of Stateless Persons, which recommended limiting the scope of protection to only those "who have renounced that protection and whose reasons for doing so are considered valid by the foreign State."[48] Thus, the matter turns on state recognition of the individual's statelessness status. Massey then suggests that many of the areas one might consider to fall under the banner of de facto statelessness might be better covered under the Refugee Convention.[49] Furthermore, he notes that, as with refugee matters, the presumption is on the individual to demonstrate that they no longer have protection from their country of origin:

> As a rule, there should have been a request for, and a refusal of, protection before it can be established that a given nationality is ineffective. For example, Country A may make a finding that a particular individual is a national of Country B, and may seek to return that individual to Country B. Whether or not the individual is *de facto* stateless may depend on whether or not Country B is willing to cooperate in the process of identifying the individual's nationality and/or to permit his or her return.[50]

Based in part on Massey's paper, UNHCR developed a handbook to "advise on the modalities of creating statelessness determination procedures, including questions of evidence that arise in such mechanisms."[51] The handbook limited the recognition

---

[45] Ibid.
[46] Economic Commission for Europe, *Difficult to Measure Census Topics*, pp. 2–3.
[47] UNHCR, *UNHCR and* De Facto *Statelessness*, p. 27.
[48] Ibid., p. 18.
[49] Ibid., p. 30.
[50] Ibid., p. 74.
[51] UNHCR, *Handbook on Protection of Stateless Persons* (2014), www.refworld.org/pdfid/53b67
6aa4.pdf, p. 6.

of stateless persons to the definition in the 1954 Convention and focused on the obligations of States that are party to the Convention – again, the plight of de facto stateless persons was pushed to the margins. One consequence of UNHCR's advice in the handbook was that the authors of UNHCR-commissioned mapping studies did not try to estimate the number of that country's (i.e., the selected country included in the mapping studies) stateless population.[52]

One further dilemma, which arguably applies to all international agencies whose mandate relies on the implementation of international law, is the overt bias toward states – a tendency bolstered by the technocratic logic that further informed the work of UNHCR. Like other UN agencies that must present "results" to donors, over the past fifteen years UNHCR has been building up its statistical capacity, including most recently by establishing a joint data center with the World Bank.[53] In the 2005 Statistical Yearbook (published in 2007), for the first time the Agency set out its rationale for providing better statistical coverage: "In an effort to ensure evidence-based resource allocation and policy formulation, a variety of information sources are utilized to quantify and profile UNHCR's population of concern."[54] This ambition was reflected in its increased coverage of groups that had been under-reported. For example, while UNHCR's coverage of stateless people included just thirty states in 2004, by 2015, UNHCR was publishing data on seventy-nine states.[55]

Most important, UNHCR also started to explain its methodological processes for estimating people who fell under its mandate and then, like other agencies, sought to make its data more operational.[56] It offered more comprehensive definitions of the indicators used, the various categories of concern, and its main sources of data. In its notes to the published statistics, UNHCR provides some important small print. In the 2011 Global Appeal, UNHCR recorded that "the data are generally provided by governments, based on their own definitions and methods of data collection."[57] This statement was repeated to UNHCR's donors as recently as February 2020.[58] A close reading of the footnotes in UNHCR's principal publications records the methodological difficulties involved in data estimation and the challenges facing UNHCR and member states. For example, its 2020 report on its financial perform-ance lists the different approaches it has taken to produce data, which include relying on national estimates, excluding data, and adjusting based on censuses and

[52] Kerwin et al., "Statelessness in the United States."
[53] *See* Strategic Advisory Council, *Strategy for the Joint Data Center on Forced Displacement 2021–2023: Zero Draft* (August 27, 2020), www.jointdatacenter.org/wp-content/uploads/2020/08/ JDC-strategy_zero-draft_August-2020.pdf.
[54] UNHCR, *UNHCR Statistical Yearbook 2005* (Geneva: UNHCR, 2007), p. 19.
[55] *See* UNHCR, *2004 UNHCR Statistical Yearbook* (Geneva: UNHCR, 2005); UNHCR, *UNHCR Statistical Yearbook 2015* (Geneva: UNCHR, 2017).
[56] *See* UNHCR, *Guidance Document on Measuring Stateless Populations* (May 2011), www .refworld.org/docid/4f6887672.html.
[57] UNHCR, *Global Appeal 2010–11.*
[58] UNHCR Executive Committee, *Update on Budgets and Funding* (2019, 2020–2021), p. 30.

registers. In some cases, the information provided by national governments reflects a considered approach to estimation:

> The statelessness figure is based on a Government estimate of individuals who . . . migrated to Côte d'Ivoire ... and who did not establish their nationality at independence or before the nationality law changed in 1972. The estimate is derived in part from cases denied voter registration in 2010 because electoral authorities could not determine their nationality at the time .... The estimate does not include individuals of unknown parentage who were abandoned as children and who are not considered as nationals under Ivorian law.[59]

UNHCR also presented information in more user-friendly formats. Today, UNHCR's website includes a versatile data builder that allows users to select variables and indicators in order to construct detailed tables using composite data from UNHCR's operational and statistical activities, national sources, and other UN agencies and partners.

Amid claims of greater accuracy, UNHCR explicitly privileged certain types and sources of data.[60] Above all, it considered national censuses and population registers most useful, as Massey recommends:

> For such country-related information to be treated as accurate, it needs to be obtained from reliable and unbiased sources, preferably more than one. Thus, information sourced from State bodies directly involved in nationality mechanisms in the relevant State, or non-State actors which have built up expertise in monitoring or reviewing such matters, is preferred.[61]

There are several problems with this statement. First, it presumes that national censuses accurately record the status of individuals surveyed when, in practice, national censuses rely on self-completed questionnaires.[62] Moreover, some states do not have a central population registry.[63] Second, it fails to recognize how bias applies to all forms of data, including official information produced by state bodies. Third, it assumes that individuals have sufficient agency to obtain status and, equally important, that states will cooperate to recognize such claims. These challenges were acknowledged by the Conference of European Statisticians more than twelve years ago.

[59] Ibid., p. 31.
[60] The main sources include (1) UNHCR's statistical activities, which collate data from national sources and some UNHCR operations; (2) United Nations Relief and Works Agency for Palestine Refugees in the Near East (UNRWA), which provides information limited to registered Palestine refugees under UNRWA's mandate; (3) data provided by the Internal Displacement Monitoring Centre (IDMC), limited to people displaced within their country due to conflict or violence.
[61] UNHCR, *Handbook on Protection of Stateless Persons*, p. 33.
[62] Economic Commission for Europe, *Difficult to Measure Census Topics*, p. 5.
[63] *See* Kerwin et al., "Statelessness in the United States."

Moreover, in many countries, stateless persons live precariously on the margins of society because they lack identity documents, are illegally in the territory, or are subject to discrimination. They therefore may be reluctant to come forward to be counted, or to reveal their personal circumstances, because of concerns that such information may be used against them. Indeed, history shows that population data has even been misused in certain countries in the past to render certain groups stateless through denationalization.[64] Unfortunately, contrary to UNHCR's assumptions, testimonies of stateless people record that states have repeatedly dismissed these criticisms.

Here are two cases from the United Kingdom, a country that, both before and after the introduction of statelessness determination procedures, has proven reluctant to allow some long-standing citizenship claims deriving originally from the colonial period. There are six different classes of British nationality, offering more or fewer civil and political rights. In 1948, the United Kingdom introduced a new law to address its evolution from an imperial system to a commonwealth of independent states. The Commonwealth Heads of Government agreed that each member would adopt their own national citizenship, while the status of "British subject" would continue, as a supranational category.[65]

On January 1, 1949, the United Kingdom established the status of Citizen of the United Kingdom and Colonies (CUKC). Until the early 1960s, there was little difference in UK law between the rights of CUKCs and other British subjects, all of whom enjoyed the right to enter and remain in the United Kingdom for work or family life. However, in many parts of the Commonwealth, newly independent colonies introduced nationality provisions that withdrew CUKC status, unless the person had a connection to the United Kingdom or a remaining colony (e.g., through birth in the United Kingdom). There were some important exceptions. For example, CUKC status was not withdrawn from the Crown colonies of Penang and Malacca that were integrated into the Federation of Malaysia in 1957. Hence, hundreds of thousands continued to enjoy the dual status of CUKC *and* citizen of Malaysia.

Over the following fifty years, the UK government legislation reduced the rights of former imperial subjects and established a multitiered approach to UK citizenship, which over time disadvantaged those born outside the British Isles and gradually restricted the rights to enter, work, and settle in the United Kingdom to a minority of former subjects. Specifically, the 1971 Immigration Act introduced the concept of *patriality*, by which only British subjects with sufficiently strong links to the British Isles (e.g., being born in the islands or having a parent or a grandparent who was

---

[64] Ibid.

[65] The meaning of "British subject" changed radically in 1948. All those who were British subjects became CUKCs (Citizens of the United Kingdom and Colonies) in 1948; and the classification of British subject was then demoted to become an umbrella term used for everyone who had some sort of UK connection.

born there) had right of abode. The 1981 British Nationality Act further reduced the rights of former British subjects. Commonwealth nationals now enjoyed one of six categories of British nationality: British citizens, British Overseas Territories citizens, British Overseas citizens, British Nationals (Overseas), British subjects, and British protected persons. Today, only British citizens and certain Commonwealth citizens have the automatic right of abode in the United Kingdom.

Until the *Windrush* scandal of 2018,[66] when dozens of former British subjects who had arrived before 1973 were wrongly detained and deported to Caribbean countries, the controversies regarding British nationality statuses attracted little public attention. It was inconceivable that former British subjects, including those with the status of CUKC, might suffer from the loss of nationality on UK soil. Rather, statelessness was considered a distant and understudied problem, more applicable to the former colonies in the Global South. A handful of legal cases and press reporting on crimes involving nationals from former British colonies, however, served as a reminder that individuals present on UK territory might also be caught between nationality statuses. One notable case involved a group of individuals who were unable to rely on the UK government to determine their status.

In the summer of 2004, police and immigration officers arrested some refugee families in Oxford as part of "Operation Iowa."[67] The incident led to a criminal trial and inquiry that resulted in the cancellation of refugee status and withdrawal of state protection from the families, including the children. What complicated the matter was that the families concerned claimed not to be Pakistani, as reported, but from the disputed region of Kashmir, administered by India since 1954.

Even though the United Kingdom has extensive official channels to the governments of India and Pakistan, all three states refused to rule on the status of the families. The nationality struggles facing Kashmiris are well documented. Those affected include more than 100,000 Punjabi refugees who fled to Jammu and Kashmir from neighboring Sialkot (now in Pakistan) in 1947, and whose descendants have been denied Indian citizenship ever since.

The refugees who settled in Oxford claimed to be from Kashmir, although they had ties to Pakistan and their ancestral home was described as "Sialkot." Their specific nationality status was brought to light when they were taken to court, where their rights to remain in the United Kingdom were called into question. In the 2005 criminal case, *R* v. *Faruq and Others*[68] (Operation Iowa), the Crown Prosecution Service claimed that there had been a conspiracy to contravene the Immigration Act by bringing relatives into the United Kingdom under bogus pretenses and then falsely claiming asylum (on the grounds they were persecuted

---

[66] The name referred to the *Empire Windrush*, the ship that brought one of the first groups of West Indian migrants to the United Kingdom in 1948.

[67] See C. Sawyer and B. K. Blitz (eds.), *Statelessness in the European Union: Displaced, Undocumented, Unwanted* (Cambridge: Cambridge University Press, 2011).

[68] *R* v. *Faruq and Others* (Operation Iowa) (2005) (unreported).

in India as Kashmiri) as a prelude to falsely claiming benefits from government departments and local authorities. The Home Office revoked the status of several of the parties concerned, including the children of the families involved. It was argued that if the families had lied during their asylum application, then other information could no longer be considered credible, including the ages of some of the children. For more than a decade, the Kashmiri children lived without status, turning to charitable organizations and the goodwill of professionals to get by.

The story of Liew Teong Teh, a resident of the United Kingdom since 2001, presents a contrasting case where a law-abiding British Overseas Citizen (BOC) was rendered stateless, while the UK government proved unwilling to correct his status. Teh was born a BOC and citizen of Malaysia. After completing an MSc in Engineering at the University of Wolverhampton, he applied for indefinite leave to remain in 2005, under the impression he would be eligible for British citizenship based on his status. Following the advice of his lawyers, he renounced his Malaysian citizenship in 2006 and applied for leave to remain in the United Kingdom. In so doing, he became stateless. He recalls:

> I was shocked to discover that the legal advice I had been given was misleading and that renouncing my Malaysian citizenship violated the Home Office's Asylum and Immigration tribunal's own rules .... Even though I have proof that I was misled and given the wrong advice on relinquishing my Malaysian citizenship, neither the Malaysian High Commission or the Home Office will accept me as a citizen.[69]

Teh then applied for permission to remain in the United Kingdom as a stateless person under Part 14 of the Immigration Rules. He asked the Malaysian authorities to confirm that he had successfully renounced his citizenship of Malaysia, which they did in 2009. However, on two occasions, the Home Office refused his request and he was liable for removal. In 2013, the Home Office issued guidance relating to the removal of certain classes of British passport holders:[70]

> Removing British Protected person, BOTC, BNO, and BOC passport holders[:] Passport holders may be served with notice of illegal entry but removal is not straight-forward. The person concerned must apply for entry clearance to the appropriate Embassy or High Commission of the country to which he is to be removed. If entry clearance is issued, he may then be removed. If the Embassy or High Commission refuse the application and he can prove this by presenting a letter from them, leave to remain in the UK may be granted by Temporary Migration if further efforts to obtain re-admission to his country of origin are unlikely to prove successful.[71]

---

[69] J. Andersson, "Man Stuck in Limbo after Being Left Stateless for 15 Years," *inews* (July 22, 2020), https://inews.co.uk/news/man-limbo-stateless-15-years-home-office-mistake-558555.

[70] *See* Home Office, "Immigration Enforcement General Instructions" (December 10, 2013), https://assets.publishing.service.gov.uk/government/uploads/system/uploads/attachment_data/file/270023/chapter48.pdf#page=7.

[71] Ibid., p. 8.

The Home Office also issued specific guidance in the case of BOCs who were formerly citizens of Malaysia, like Teh, noting that the UK government was working with the Malaysian authorities to devise a scheme whereby they can be returned to Malaysia and reestablish Malaysian nationality from within Malaysia.[72]

One positive outcome from the discussions between the UK government and Malaysia was the decision to suspend removals,[73] even though it did nothing to advance Teh's request for nationality, which in turn would ground his right to remain in the United Kingdom permanently. After further refusals by the Home Office to recognize his status, Teh then sought to press the High Court for a judicial review of the Home Office's decision, and his petition was refused in 2017 in part because the UK government contested Teh's status as a stateless person because he holds British Overseas citizenship and is admissible to Malaysia.[74]

As of September 2020, Teh is no longer considered a national by Malaysia, nor of the United Kingdom, and remains in limbo. Teh's case bears many similarities to the plight of the Oxford-based Kashmiri families, where neither India nor Pakistan was prepared to address their claims. In their case, we see how historical antagonism between neighboring states can undermine the prospect of collaboration in determining "ineffective nationality," as Massey proposes.

These examples are far from exceptional. Across the globe, there are many ways in which states may obstruct individuals from securing recognition of their claims or affirming their status. Even more glaring is how some states have conspired to keep people in precarious situations. Thus, minorities in Assam are currently facing the threat of exclusion from the all-India National Register of Citizens. Although the government claims to be updating the register to prevent immigrants from Bangladesh settling in India, millions of long-term-settled residents have been caught up in this exercise in retrospective immigration control. When a draft register was released in 2018, an estimated 4.1 million people were left off the list. Although this number has come down to approximately two million, many remain at risk of statelessness since local authorities refuse to accept official documents such as school leaving certificates (known as migration certificates) as evidence of status.[75]

These case studies also challenge other methodological assumptions that underlie UNHCR's results framework, above all the belief that some of its indicators accurately reflect the outcomes they seek to measure. As Teh's case shows, the United Kingdom's accession to both UN statelessness conventions and its introduction of statelessness determination procedures does not mean that the United Kingdom has

---

[72] Ibid.
[73] Ibid.
[74] *Teh v. Secretary of State for the Home Department*, [2018] EWHC 1586 (Admin) (June 22, 2018).
[75] For a comprehensive list of those categories of people who qualify to be registered, see "What Is NRC? Here Is What You Need to Know," *India Today* (June 20, 2019), www.indiatoday.in/ information/story/what-is-nrc-here-is-what-you-need-to-know-1552817-2019-06-20.

resolved situations of statelessness. Rather, Teh's case demonstrates that legal reform – UNHCR's go-to solution – may not be sufficient.

COUNTING AND MISCOUNTING STATELESS PEOPLE

Within UNHCR, statistical reporting now focused on de jure statelessness, as recorded in the 2015 Statistical Yearbook.[76] No longer did UNHCR speak of de facto statelessness and those with indeterminate nationality. The figures presented, however, raised many questions about the methodologies used and the veracity of their sources. Until 2017, UNHCR's formal position was that there were an estimated ten million stateless people in the world.[77] This number had come down from twelve million over the previous five years, with little explanation. Even though UNHCR recognized that its estimates were provisional, it continued to rely on them, amalgamating data sources and rough estimates.

In addition to their program of identifying and estimating the global population of stateless people,[78] the logic of reporting, of focusing on more closely defined categories of stateless groups, and the wider mandate that seeks to reduce and prevent statelessness, gave rise to a new ambition: UNHCR was to end statelessness.

The Politicization of Data

With glossy photographs reminiscent of Benetton adverts, UNHCR launched a 2014 campaign, #IBelong, to end statelessness within a decade – this, although its reporting on statelessness was still a work in progress, and it did not have reliable baseline data on the scale of the problem. Benetton eventually appeared as UNHCR's formal partner, with its logo at the foot of UNHCR's website. UNHCR also set unrealistic targets, including the collection of ten million signatures from the public in support of ten actions deemed essential to end statelessness.[79] By August 2020, the #IBelong campaign had secured 98,296 signatures – just under one percent of its target – and was attracting fewer than twenty-five signatures a month.[80]

UNHCR published quarterly updates on the #IBelong campaign but, to date, there has been no independent assessment, no performance or output based evaluations, and no recognition that UNHCR and its partners are failing to meet their targets. Instead, UNHCR has called attention to the many recent *pledges* made by member states that include introducing statelessness determination procedures,

[76] UNHCR, *UNHCR Statistical Yearbook 2015*, p. 4.

[77] *See* UNHCR, *Global Trends: Forced Displacement in 2016* (June 19, 2017), www.unhcr.org/dach/wp-content/uploads/sites/27/2017/06/2016_Global_Trends_WEB-embargoed.pdf.

[78] UNHCR, *Global Action Plan to End Statelessness* (2014), www.refworld.org/docid/545b47d64.html.

[79] *See* UNHCR, "ibelong," www.unhcr.org/ibelong/.

[80] *See* UNHCR, "Sign the Open Letter," www.unhcr.org/ibelong/sign-the-open-letter/.

improving birth registration, and providing training.[81] What is more, UNHCR has also set itself further annual targets, including that 100,000 individuals will acquire nationality or have it confirmed by the end of 2020.[82]

Furthermore, although UNHCR has improved its data collection, the significant gaps in its coverage and quality of information presented undermine its advocacy efforts. UNHCR has not yet arrived at a consistent position on the inclusion of those who do not neatly fall within its mandate. There is a lack of disaggregation in the figures presented, which leaves UNHCR's data open to misinterpretation. It remains unclear if those with indeterminate status are truly considered stateless for the purposes of estimation.

Until recently, UNHCR gave the impression of an agency that was driving forward its ambitions blind to the aforementioned substantive methodological considerations. Official publications from 2019 now qualify that the data presented are incomplete, and on its website, there is an apologetic note which explains that it compiles data on two categories: stateless persons who meet the Convention definition (de jure), and persons with undetermined nationality, but that over the past decade these and the de facto category "have sometimes been applied inconsistently in different UNHCR country operations for the annual statistical reporting process."[83]

Despite these problems, the UNHCR continues to present as reliable the statistical information it has collected, which omits estimates from highly populated regions of the world where discrimination based on nationality, the denial of documents, and the refusal to accede to – and abide by – international legal instruments and standards are the norm. The same criticism could be leveled at UNHCR's most vocal advocates, which published simplistic accounts that reiterated the agency's claims and repeated its calculation errors,[84] though eventually they too started to raise questions.[85]

Operational Challenges and Methodological Solutions

This account illustrates just how difficult it is for humanitarian agencies, including UNHCR, to establish accurate figures. It also records how institutional preferences

[81] In the 2019 High-Level Segment on Statelessness during the Executive Committee gathering held on October 7, 2019, UNHCR reported that 252 of these pledges were delivered by States, 70 by civil society organizations, and 38 by international and regional organizations. *See* UNHCR, "Results of the High Level Segment on Statelessness," www.unhcr.org/ibelong/results-of-the-high-level-segment-on-statelessness/.

[82] UNHCR, "UNHCR in 2020," https://reporting.unhcr.org/sites/default/files/ga2020/pdf/Chapter_Overview.pdf.

[83] *See* UNHCR, "Measuring Forced Displacement and Statelessness," www.unhcr.org/refugee-statistics/methodology/.

[84] *See* Institute on Statelessness and Inclusion, *The World's Stateless*, https://files.institutesi.org/worldsstateless.pdf.

[85] Institute on Statelessness and Inclusion, "Statelessness in Numbers: 2019 – An Overview and Analysis of Global Statistics," https://files.institutesi.org/ISI_statistics_analysis_2019.pdf.

may be formed. In the cases discussed, we note how statist and technocratic biases have privileged national sources as "reliable," even as some states have engaged in efforts to redefine membership based on exclusive understandings of nationality. Such biases are not new: As Dunlop recorded almost ten years ago, the use of results-based management tools favored states over other beneficiaries, above all those who fell under its protection mandate.[86] In addition, UNHCR's tendency to limit reporting on statelessness to de jure stateless populations – until very recently – may have encouraged a process of methodological revisionism where the numbers of stateless people in need of protection were rounded down. Narrowing legal definitions logically leads to undercounting.

As argued earlier, it is potentially a fallacious assumption that individuals and groups that may be experiencing persecution from a particular state and may have had their nationality withdrawn should then have their claims affirmed by the state in question. It is perverse to suggest that such states might be called upon to record the presence of these stateless people and remedy their situation. Even when states have grappled with the issues of statelessness and demonstrated a commitment to examine claims, a heavy evidentiary burden still falls on individual applicants. Even though statelessness determination procedures were introduced in the United Kingdom in 2013, additional rules have been designed that disadvantage applicants. In 2019[87] and again in 2020, the UK Immigration Rules were amended to include further requirements, such as the obligation to obtain a residence permit in the United Kingdom. The new rules still require a stateless applicant to have "sought and failed to obtain or re-establish their nationality with the appropriate authorities of the relevant country."[88] As the case studies of the Kashmiri children and Teh record, seeking status on the basis of a claim to being stateless is far from straightforward.

How UNHCR identifies those under its statelessness mandate remains contentious. As recorded earlier, there was a tendency to take large numbers of people out of the category of statelessness by excluding de facto stateless individuals. Now, there is a shift to aggregate de jure and de facto stateless people as well as those with indeterminate nationality. While this might make reporting simpler, it does not inform our understanding of why these people are stateless and how their plight may be corrected.

There are many broader possible explanations for UNHCR's attachment to such practices, which complement Reichel's notion of normative path dependency

---

[86] Dunlop, *Indications of Progress.*

[87] *See* House of Commons, "Statement of Changes in Immigration Rules" (October 24, 2019), https://assets.publishing.service.gov.uk/government/uploads/system/uploads/attachment_data/file/841772/CCS001_CCS1019317048–001_Statement_of_changes_in_Immigration_Rules_Text.pdf.

[88] *See* "Immigration Rules Part 14: Stateless Persons" (June 4, 2020), www.gov.uk/guidance/immigration-rules/immigration-rules-part-14-stateless-persons.

discussed earlier. Sociologists have long sought to challenge the presentation of actors, including organizations, as rational and agentic; rather, they suggest that organizations operate in an environment constructed around social practices that give rise to institutional norms. One recurring theme is the notion of "institutional scripts."[89] Drawing upon Berger and Luckmann's phenomenological approach,[90] where the actor – be it an individual or organization – operates on a social stage and has a scripted identity that enacts a scripted action, for example, a role, Meyer argues that "actorhood" is also scripted by institutional structures. He claims that both actors (e.g., organizations) and actions (e.g., policies, decisions, innovations) have institutional scripts behind them: "The actor–action relation is a package, and as people and groups enter into particular forms of actorhood, the appropriate actions come along and are not usefully to be seen as choices and decisions."[91] Just as people fall into roles, so too do organizations.

In this chapter, we might consider UNHCR's reliance on statistical measures, its quest for indicators, and the use of results-based management as part of an institutional script. As Sarfaty argues, institutions draw their legitimacy from international legal instruments that rely on indicators to operationalize global norms and assess compliance. Indicators drive agendas – "what gets measured, gets done."[92] As UNHCR engaged in comprehensive management and structural reform, it followed the example of other UN agencies and turned to managerialist approaches that relied on the collection of measurable data to advance claims of greater accountability, efficiency, and effectiveness. One might argue that a restrictive understanding of UNHCR's 1951 mandate reduces the numbers of stateless people under its remit, and hence helps to demonstrate success and better positions the agency to meet its ambition of ending statelessness.

RECOMMENDATIONS

As the Conference of European Statisticians noted in 2008, UNHCR and its partners could improve the way they collect data on statelessness. There are some glimpses of progress, for example, in reporting on selected countries, where figures have been adjusted, as well as in recent conversations between UNHCR and critics who have presented compelling alternative methodologies, most notably the Center for Migration Studies (CMS).[93]

---

[89] J. W. Meyer, "World Society, Institutional Theories, and the Actor" (2010) 36 *Annual Review of Sociology* 1–20.

[90] P. L. Berger and T. Luckmann, *The Social Construction of Reality: A Treatise in the Sociology of Knowledge* (Garden City, NY: Anchor Books, 2010).

[91] J. W. Meyer, "Reflections on Institutional Theories of Organizations," in R. Greenwood, C. Oliver, R. Suddaby, and K. Sahlin (eds.), *The SAGE Handbook of Organizational Institutionalism* (London: SAGE Publications Ltd, 2008), p. 792.

[92] Sarfaty, "Regulating Through Numbers" at p. 588.

[93] Kerwin et al., "Statelessness in the United States."

Yet, to arrive at a better quality of data, the top-down approach of applying narrow legal definitions should be revisited. As noted earlier, most censuses rely on self-identification, while UNHCR's definition of who counts as a stateless person is determined by the definitions found in the 1954 Convention. In this context, the inclusion of questions on citizenship in national censuses is indicative of a broader problem. While capturing data on those who may be considered de jure stateless, the use of national censuses also offers an opportunity to clarify what is meant by "indeterminate nationality," and hence evidence of nationality and state recognition. Questions posed to respondents should, therefore, capture data on their access to rights, concomitant with definitions of citizenship. Although this approach takes us well beyond UNHCR's reach, it would nonetheless assist the agency to have more standardized definitions and to remove some of the exceptions as found in the small print of its official reports.

In terms of UNHCR's own reporting, as Kerwin et al. contend, the different ways in which statelessness arises require specific methodologies that cannot be applied across the board.[94] For example, if stateless people are located in a region that has witnessed succession or defederation, then that may encourage an investigation of rates of naturalization among de jure stateless people and the incorporation of those data in subsequent estimates. One might reasonably start by investigating de jure population estimates at the point when new nationality legislation is introduced. Equally, in countries that have introduced new nationality reforms, as in Madagascar where women may now pass on nationality to their children, it would be appropriate to adjust figures. In this instance, official demographic information would record that, under stable conditions, the numbers of stateless people would decline as children reach the age of majority. When adjusting population estimates, it is important to consider the interplay of other factors. If, as Balaton-Chrimes et al. observe, deprivation of nationality reduces the quality of health,[95] then this factor should be considered for its impact on life expectancy – though there are also conflicting studies that suggest limits to this approach.[96]

The relationship between migration and statelessness should also be interrogated on a country by country basis to assess the status of migrant populations whose nationality status may have lapsed during their time spent abroad and who may be at risk of statelessness. For example, Danish nationals born outside Denmark may lose their Danish nationality on attaining the age of twenty-two, unless they apply between the ages of twenty-one and twenty-two to retain it.[97] Other countries similarly place restrictions on foreign-born nationals living abroad. Such an

---

94 Ibid.
95 S. Balaton-Chrimes, B. K. Blitz, M. Lynch, and R. W. D. Lakshman, *The Cost of Statelessness: A Livelihoods Analysis* (Washington, DC: U.S. Department of State, 2011).
96 L. Liu and G. Singh, "Mortality Trends and Differentials by Nativity Status in the United States" (2018) 28 *European Journal of Public Health* 21, https://doi.org/10.1093/eurpub/cky047.008.
97 Ministry of Foreign Affairs of Denmark, "Danish Nationals Born Outside Denmark and the 22-Year Rule," 2020, https://storbritannien.um.dk/en/travel-and-residence/family-and-legal-matters/dual-and-multiple-nationality/danish-nationals-born-abroad/.

investigation requires contextual knowledge of the selected countries, the immigration histories of settled migrants, and up-to-date information on the country of origin of arriving migrants. It may require a mapping against the nationality laws of both countries of origin and destination for the selected migrant groups to determine their risk of losing nationality.

UNHCR could also take the bold step of affirming the status of certain groups as stateless persons, rather than bracket them off as people of "indeterminate nationality." This is not without precedent. Not only has UNHCR abandoned the use of some accepted categories, such as de facto stateless, but it has also created new ones. We note that while UNHCR recognizes that stateless people may also be refugees and should be included in their data on refugees, it has reported on more than one category and has equally created a formal category of stateless IDPs in the case of the Rohingya.[98]

The above recommendations may improve the ways in which UNHCR collects data. They may also help to advance the wider ambition of providing effective humanitarian protection and give greater meaning to its claims to support participation with beneficiaries, including stateless people. How UNHCR reports on those under its mandate has many knock-on effects, including cooperation with national governments and partner agencies that rely on their data, notably the International Organization for Migration and World Bank. Without accurate data on populations of concern for UNHCR, the task of identifying and allocating resources becomes considerably harder for them too.

CONCLUSION

When the international community addressed the plight of stateless people in the aftermath of the Second World War, statelessness was bolted onto the emerging refugee regime and only later emerged as an issue area in its own right.[99] Since then, statelessness has crept up the agenda and is now recognized as a global problem. Although UNHCR has included stateless people in its reporting for more than a decade, it began doing so without established definitions and lately has underestimated the scale of the problem.

For social scientists, this conclusion may not be surprising. As an international agency, UNHCR relies on the interpretation of international law and on this basis has experimented with the establishment of operational definitions. These definitions are neither sufficiently inclusive nor precise to capture the reality of a world where hundreds of millions of people are on the move, many without recognized status, and where others may be locked in discriminatory systems unable to enjoy such levels of mobility.

The absence of accurate data reduces the chances that UNHCR will be able to measure the effectiveness of its work and achieve its targets. As UNHCR recognizes,

---

[98] UNHCR, "Statelessness: An Analytical Framework".
[99] Batchelor, "Stateless Persons."

its own data are limited to under half the world's countries and to stateless people under its mandate. Hence, UNHCR's data are at best a rough projection of a much larger global problem.

UNHCR has argued that "the best way to address statelessness is to prevent it from occurring."[100] This is undeniably true, but it is not a simple task. As Brennan argues, in her discussion of feminist approaches to understanding statelessness, the battle lines are not simply ineffective laws but rather the wide-ranging structures that permit hierarchies, privilege, and domination.[101] As noted in this chapter, there are broader sociological explanations behind the use of narrow definitions and emphasis on statistical data and indicator-based frameworks that are found in many institutional scripts circulating among international organizations.[102] Controversially, we might add that the persistence of such scripts is fostered by patterns of recruitment within UNHCR and partner NGOs – legal experts untrained in social scientific study who have not questioned the prevailing orthodoxy.

UNHCR could start by reviewing its own biases, including a top-down logic that drives demand for "results." Equally, rather than exclude categories of stateless persons that are harder to identify, such as those who may have indeterminate status, it could further investigate their claims and grant them status, as it has done with Rohingya IDPs.[103] UNHCR and its partners would do well to constantly review the causes of statelessness, including the prospect of millions of people living in situations of protracted displacement as a result of the global crises mentioned, and use this information to inform their profiling and data collection. These recommendations require both greater contextual knowledge and familiarity with more sophisticated demographic methods. In this context, the creation of a Joint Data Center on Forced Displacement with the World Bank is encouraging, provided it includes stateless people within its remit and does not fall prey to the deficiencies of the aforementioned results-based approaches.[104] If the aim is to end statelessness by 2024, then it is urgent UNHCR and its partners address their limitations.

[100] UNHCR, "Statelessness: An Analytical Framework," p. 7.

[101] D. Brennan, "Statelessness and the Feminist Toolbox: Another Man-Made Problem with a Feminist Solution?" (2019) 24 *Tilburg Law Review* 170–181.

[102] Merry, "Human Rights Monitoring."

[103] *See* UNHCR, *Global Trends: Forced Displacement in 2018*, Annex Table 1, p. 67, n.29 ("The figure of persons of concern under the statelessness mandate relates to stateless persons in Rakhine state and persons of undetermined nationality residing in other states in Myanmar. The figure of stateless persons in Rakhine state has been estimated on the basis of the 2014 census report and 2017 General Administration Department (GAD) of Ministry of Home Affairs (MoHA) data. This figure exceptionally includes stateless IDPs who are also of concern under the statelessness mandate. This approach will not be replicated in the database and in the Excel version of this table and, therefore, figures may differ.").

[104] *See* Strategic Advisory Council, *Strategy for the Joint Data Center on Forced Displacement 2021–2023: Zero Draft.*

6

Reflections on Anti-immigration Narratives and the Establishment of Global Apartheid

Yajaira Ceciliano-Navarro, Tanya Golash-Boza, and
Luis Rubén González Márquez

APARTHEID IDEOLOGY: A PERSISTENT WORLD ORDER

Although Apartheid in South Africa was dismantled in 1994 in the aftermath of massive national demonstrations and international pressure, the ideology of apartheid persists on a global scale. The global apartheid paradigm helps to explain global trends in the distribution of wealth and rights according to place of birth, race, and ethnicity, where some groups face more movement restrictions and criminalization than others.[1] Some of the main principles of this paradigm are White racial superiority, persistent fear of national-identity loss, a desire to protect national territories, the war against immigrants, and the idea of free markets as the only avenue for prosperity.[2] Those who subscribe to this ideology resort to creating laws, norms, and institutions that allow them to restrict people's movements, which at the same time distributes resources and inequalities along racial lines. Individuals placed at the bottom of this hierarchy are usually people of color who have limited geographic mobility due to visa restrictions. These people are often unable to enjoy fundamental human rights, such as employment, education, and housing. In contrast, White people, who are a numerical minority in the world, are placed at the top of this

---

This chapter is a revised translation of Y. Ceciliano and T. Golash-Boza, "Reflexiones sobre el Apartheid Global y la Migración," in C. Sandoval García (ed.), *Puentes, no muros: contribuciones para una política progresista en migraciones* (México: Fundación Rosa Luxemburg and CLASCO, 2020), pp. 25–47.

[1] *See* N. Sharma, "Anti-Trafficking Rhetoric and the Making of a Global Apartheid" (2005) 17(3) *NWSA Journal* 88–111; H. Van Houtum, "Human Blacklisting: The Global Apartheid of the EU's External Border Regime" (2010) 28(6) *Environment and Planning D: Society and Space* 957–976.

[2] F. V. Harrison, "Global Apartheid, Foreign Policy, and Human Rights" (2002) 4(3) *Souls* 48–68; A. H. Richmond and K. Valtonen, "Global Apartheid: Refugees, Racism, and the New World Order" (1994) 14(6) *Refuge: Canada's Journal on Refugees* 25–28.

racial structure and enjoy the vast majority of existing wealth and privileges.[3] This racial hierarchy promotes a world order characterized by racism and ethnocentrism. It operates at political, social, and geographic levels, and violates norms of justice, basic needs, human rights, democracy, and racial equality.[4] The global apartheid ideology limits the opportunities of most people in the world.[5]

The global apartheid ideology is organized around narratives that criminalize immigrants and immigration. This criminalization justifies the establishment of different mechanisms that control and restrict immigrants' movements. People who have already crossed borders become vulnerable in diverse ways; due to fear, they do not access or request fundamental rights, and due to their status, they are more at risk for deportation. With restrictive immigration policies, unauthorized immigration tends to increase but the migratory process is more expensive and riskier. As if these immigration restrictions were not enough, this segregationist ideology also adopts subtle mechanisms of control, removal, and exploitation of migrants worldwide. These actions result in the preservation of wealth for a small minority.

The ideology of global apartheid fosters negative discourses and actions regarding the arrival of undocumented and poor immigrants from the Global South into the Global North. These actions can be described as a war against poor and undocumented immigrants.[6] Given these circumstances, freedom of movement has transformed into an expensive and unsafe process – a privilege but not a right. One of the novelties of how this ideology operates today has been defined by Harrison as *micro apartheid*, where new territories and regions exhibit subtle racial and ethnic segregation mechanisms.[7] In Europe, this trend continues to increase. France, Spain, and other European countries block the entrance of hundreds of migrants daily.[8] At the same time, countries such as Chile and Israel have been adopting more subtle mechanisms for immigrants' removal.[9] These "well-intentioned" mechanisms that help immigrants return to their home countries are part of this global trend. In this section, we analyze the modalities of reproduction of these discursive mechanisms and practices in different regions of the world.

---

[3] *See* M. Omi and H. Winant, *Racial Formation in the United States* (New York and London: Routledge, 2014); J. R. Feagin and K. Ducey, *Racist America: Roots, Current Realities, and Future Reparations* (New York and London: Routledge, 2018).

[4] G. Köhler, "The Three Meanings of Global Apartheid: Empirical, Normative, Existential" (1995) 20(3) *Alternatives* 403–413.

[5] Harrison, "Global Apartheid, Foreign Policy, and Human Rights."

[6] Van Houtum, "Human Blacklisting: The Global Apartheid of the EU's External Border Regime."

[7] Harrison, "Global Apartheid, Foreign Policy, and Human Rights."

[8] S. Alscher, "Knocking at the Doors of 'Fortress Europe': Migration and Border Control in Southern Spain and Eastern Poland," in Working Paper 126 (San Diego: The Center for Comparative Immigration Studies at University of California, San Diego, 2017).

[9] S. Willen, *Fighting for Dignity: Migrant Lives at Israel's Margins* (Philadelphia: University of Pennsylvania Press, 2019).

Narratives of Immigrants as a Threat and Criminalization
of Immigrants and Their Movements

To achieve the criminalization of migrants, governments, media, and anti-migrant groups resort to narratives that portray them as inferior, unassimilable, and a threat to the country's stability, national identity, labor markets, or national security.[10] The media shapes these public imaginaries, in which migrants are represented as violent and aggressive savages that must be stopped.[11] Sharma argues there is a growing perceived need to protect migrant-receiving nations from "dangerous aliens."[12] Once the portrayal of immigrants as a threat is invented, governments and other agents justify the creation of laws that prevent and punish immigrants' movements. The discursive representation of immigrants of color varies in different regions of the world, yet themes of immigrants as a problem and a threat are universally present. In the United States, for example, these populations have traditionally been depicted as a threat to national security and are considered violent and vicious.[13] Hooghe and Dassonneville state that narratives in the United States "focused on racist resentment toward ethnic minority groups," mostly with regard to Mexicans.[14] Otto Santa Ana argues that the United States' political narratives severely dehumanize immigrant workers.[15] This dehumanization includes animalizing immigrants, which means portraying them as wild animals or savages that must be hunted by potent border predators of the state. For instance, along the border regions of the United States and Mexico, it is common to use terms like coyotes to refer to smugglers and *pollos* (chickens) to describe undocumented immigrants.

Immigrants are considered a burden in other regions and are often used as scapegoats for internal social problems such as unemployment or security. In Europe, migrants have been used by some extreme right-wing parties, whose leaders take advantage of growing discontent toward immigration policies and the influx of refugees.[16] For these radical right-wing parties, immigrants threaten national identity

---

[10] M. Fennema, "Populist Parties of the Right," in J. Rydgren (ed.), *Movements of Exclusion: Radical Right-Wing Populism in the Western World* (New York: Nova Science Publishers, 2005), pp. 1–24; Richmond and Valtonen, "Global Apartheid: Refugees, Racism, and the New World Order."

[11] O. Santa Ana, "'Like an Animal I Was Treated': Anti-Immigrant Metaphor in US Public Discourse" (1999) 10(2) *Discourse & Society* 191–224.

[12] Sharma, "Anti-Trafficking Rhetoric and the Making of a Global Apartheid."

[13] L. Chavez, *The Latino Threat: Constructing Immigrants, Citizens, and the Nation* (Santa Clara, CA: Stanford University Press, 2013).

[14] R. Dassonneville and M. Hooghe "The Noise of the Vote Recall Question: The Validity of the Vote Recall Question in Panel Studies in Belgium, Germany, and the Netherlands" (2017) 29 (2) *International Journal of Public Opinion Research* 316–338.

[15] Santa Ana, "'Like an Animal I Was Treated': Anti-immigrant Metaphor in US Public Discourse."

[16] P. C. Gattinara, "Europeans, Shut the Borders! Anti-refugee Mobilisation in Italy and France," in D. Della Porta (ed.), *Solidarity Mobilizations in the "Refugee Crisis": Contentious Moves*

(the "necessary" ethnic homogeneity) and also increase "competition" with locals for limited resources such as employment. In Europe, these narratives also permeate mobilizations in response to the refugee crisis.[17] Richmond and Valtonen argue that wealthy and predominantly White countries have initiated a crusade to protect themselves from these perceived threats to safeguard their territories and privileged lifestyles.[18] These discourses emphasize feelings of insecurity around immigrants, specifically the perceived threat they pose to the economy, society, racial purity, and national identity.[19] For Fennema, one reason for the resurgence of these parties and narratives as well as their sympathizers is the growing perception of the dysfunction of national governments.[20] Decision-making is viewed as having been centralized at the level of international organizations. Thus, among the public, there is a strong belief that national governments have lost credibility, leadership, and control over their borders, and these new far-right parties advocate for recovering state control over their countries.[21]

These ideologies have gained strength for different reasons. According to Richmond and Valtonen, these ideas grow due to the nostalgia evoked by a "simple life" – the idea that, in the past, the inhabitants of wealthy countries felt safer in more ethnically or racially homogeneous places.[22] With the demographic transformations linked to global migration, these groups now feel that they are living in less secure and more "chaotic" conditions because of ethnic diversity. Other scholars posit that these criminalizing characterizations originate in fears over global terrorism that intensified after the attacks on New York and Washington, DC (9/11/01), Madrid (3/11/04), and London (7/7/05). From such a perspective, all immigrants of color from poor countries are a threat that must be stopped and punished.[23]

CONTROL AND RESTRICTION OF IMMIGRANTS' MOVEMENTS

Governments attending the call to defend their nations against a perceived immigration threat rely on a series of structures and institutions to operate. Restrictive immigration laws constitute one of the most effective instruments for global apartheid's organization and application.

(Basingstoke: Palgrave Macmillan 2018), pp. 271–297. Dassonneville and Hooghe, "The Noise of the Vote Recall Question"; Fennema, "Populist Parties of the Right."

[17] Gattinara, "Europeans, Shut the Borders! Anti-refugee Mobilisation in Italy and France."

[18] Richmond and Valtonen, "Global Apartheid: Refugees, Racism, and the New World Order."

[19] Rydgren, *Movements of Exclusion.*

[20] Fennema, "Populist Parties of the Right."

[21] Ibid.; C. M. Pied, "Ethnography and the Making of 'The People': Uncovering Conservative Populist Politics in the United States" (2019) 78(3) *American Journal of Economics and Sociology* 761–786.

[22] Richmond and Valtonen, "Global Apartheid: Refugees, Racism, and the New World Order."

[23] *See* Sharma, "Anti-trafficking Rhetoric and the Making of a Global Apartheid." *See also* Van Houtum, "Human Blacklisting: The Global Apartheid of the EU's External Border Regime."

Immigration Restriction and Immigrants' Control in the United States

The United States was a sovereign nation for more than a century before immigration became a political issue. The first major piece of legislation on immigration was the Chinese Exclusion Act of 1882. This Act set the bar for entry into the country and had an openly racist frame directed toward a specific group: Chinese workers. By excluding members of this group based on class and race, the Chinese Exclusion Act paved the way for the immigration policies of the twentieth century.[24] Although repealed in 1943, the judicial decisions derived from the Chinese Exclusion Act still shape current legal approaches to immigration. The second relevant moment in immigration legislation was the Asian Exclusion Act of 1924, which expanded the regulations of the Chinese Exclusion Act and prohibited most immigration from Asia into the United States.[25]

These restrictive laws were repealed in 1965 with the passage of the Hart-Celler Act, which set an annual quota of 20,000 immigrants from each country of the world. This act changed the face of migration to the United States – from primarily European to increasingly Asian and Latin American. In this context of multiethnic migration, the United States began to pass new laws restricting the rights of migrants. The 1996 Antiterrorism and Effective Death Penalty Act (AEDPA) and the Illegal Immigration Reform and Immigrant Responsibility Act (IIRIRA) eliminated judicial review for some deportation orders and established mandatory detention for a significant number of non-citizens.[26] They also allowed for the use of secret evidence in specific cases. Some of the most damaging consequences of these laws are the deportations of legal permanent residents. Under IIRIRA, if permanent legal residents are found guilty of "aggravated felonies," they face mandatory deportation. Relatively minor crimes such as shoplifting or drug possession could lead to mandatory deportation for long-term residents.[27]

After these laws were implemented, immigrants from Latin America and the Caribbean became more likely to be deported. The punitive and severe 1996 regulations disproportionately affect people of color. Kevin Johnson argues that, since the majority of immigrant populations living in the United States are minorities of color, the differential treatment toward non-citizens corresponds to legal practices that amount to racial discrimination.[28] These practices have created an environment of tension and fear within Latino communities.[29]

---

[24] Y. Le Espiritu, *Asian American Panethnicity: Bridging Institutions and Identities* (Philadelphia, PA: Temple University Press, 1992).

[25] Ibid.

[26] T. Golash-Boza, *Immigration Nation: Raids, Detentions, and Deportations in Post-9/11 America* (London and New York: Taylor & Francis, 2012).

[27] Ibid.

[28] K. Johnson, "Racial Profiling after September 11: The Department of Justice's 2003 Guidelines" (2004) 50 *Loyola Law Review* 67–87 at 67.

[29] M. H. Lopez and S. Minushkin, 2008 *National Survey of Latinos: Hispanic Voter Attitudes* (Washington, DC: Pew Hispanic Center, 2008).

The ideology of global apartheid was further strengthened with President Trump's election. He campaigned for the presidency primarily on the slogan "Build the Wall." Although there has long been a physical structure separating the United States from Mexico, this slogan itself is harmful to migrants as it implies that Mexicans pose a threat to the United States. On the campaign trail and as president, Trump has continued to take openly anti-immigrant positions. In several speeches, President Trump has portrayed immigrants as a threat by suggesting they are violent, criminal, and dangerous people.[30] These anti-immigrant narratives, accompanied by a series of legislative decrees have led to the removal of thousands of immigrants and the expansion of immigration bans to more countries.

US Immigration Policy and the Southern Border

The ideology of global apartheid was challenged by the recent "Migrant Caravan" (or "Caravan for Life"), which began in 2018 in San Pedro Sula, Honduras. This caravan was formed by Salvadoran, Honduran, and Guatemalan migrants who escaped the economic deprivation and violence of their countries. According to different reports, the caravan reached in some moments 17,000 people.[31] However, official data confirms that only five thousand of them reached the northern border of Mexico. On their way, Guatemala and Mexico closed their borders in response to pressure from the US government. However, this migratory event marked a milestone since it was not the traditional clandestine migration; the caravan was visible, massive, and filmed live in broad daylight. The caravan challenged and confronted classic actors in migration processes such as traffickers, governments, and NGOs. The migrant caravan reconfigured conventional ideas of clandestine migration. It also reconfigured territories, particularly for Mexico, which has traditionally been a migrant transit country and, on this occasion, became a "barred" country.[32]

Immigration Restriction and Control of Immigrants in Europe

European nations have also taken radical measures to keep people from poor countries out of their territories.[33] These measures have been supported by right-wing governments, parties, and anti-immigrant discourses favoring increased restrictions on African migrants. For van Houtum, this has been manifested significantly in the reinforcement of borders and territorial limits: "[T]he European Union (E.U.)

---

[30] Pied, "Ethnography and the Making of 'The People.'"

[31] A. Varela, "México, de "frontera vertical' a 'pais tapón.' Migrantes, deportados, retornados, desplazados internos y solicitantes de asilo en Mexico" (2019) 14(27) *Iberoforum. Revista de Ciencias Sociales de la Universidad Iberoamericana* 49–76.

[32] Ibid.

[33] J. Scott, "Hungarian Border Politics as an Anti-Politics of the European Union" (2020) 25(3) *Geopolitics* 658–677.

has composed a so-called 'white' Schengen list, and a 'black' Schengen list and the white list represents the countries whose citizens do not need to apply for a visa for a visitor transit in Schengen countries."[34] These lists indicate who is welcome (Whites) and who is not welcome (non-Whites) in Europe. This trend has continued in Europe after the migration crisis experienced in 2015. Many countries closed their borders in 2015 when more than a million migrants and refugees from Syria tried to reach the continent. Conflicts arose due to the different responses of each country to this migration crisis. While countries like Slovenia and Croatia closed their borders, others like Germany opened their borders and received a large number of refugees. Germany's attitude, described as generous, has been recognized internationally; however, it has sparked conflicts within the European community. Immigration is still a subject of controversy and contentious responses by European countries.[35]

Other expressions of this paradigm are present in different countries in Europe. For example, the migrant detention camp operating on the island of Lesvos, Greece, is a human rights crisis. Media have reported that thousands of migrants from various countries are stranded in Lesvos. Due to political decisions in different European countries, these migrants have been unable to continue their journey to Europe. The situation has become unsustainable not only for stranded migrants but also for the island's inhabitants.[36]

Denmark, a country where immigration was not previously present in the political agenda, has proposed similar initiatives designed to isolate immigrants.[37] Liberal parties have discussed sending "undesirable" immigrants to the small islet of Lindhom (in the Baltic Sea), with barely any infrastructure. According to a report by *El País*, these immigrants would be required by law to leave the Scandinavian Kingdom.[38] The Minister of Immigration, Inger Støjbeg, who is from the liberal party Venstre, declared on Facebook: "They are not welcome to Denmark and, they have to know it!"[39] As reported by *El País*, this is just one among more than one hundred measures the Danish government has taken against immigrants.[40] As van Houtum affirms, "with the construction of a gated island of wealth, and with the

---

[34] Van Houtum, "Human Blacklisting: The Global Apartheid of the EU's External Border Regime," p. 936.

[35] C. Kroet and B. Surk, "Slovenia, Croatia Close Borders to Migrants," *Politico*, March 9, 2016, www.politico.eu/article/slovenia-croatia-close-borders-to-migrants-refugees-serbia-macedonia-eu-deal-turkey/.

[36] A. Afouxenidis et al., "Dealing with a Humanitarian Crisis: Refugees on the Eastern EU Border of the Island of Lesvos" (2012)12(1) *Journal of Applied Security Research* 7–39.

[37] T. Bjørklund and G. A. Jørgen, "Anti-Immigration Parties in Denmark and Norway: The Progress Parties and the Danish People's Party," in M. Schain et al. (eds.), *Shadows over Europe: The Development and Impact of the Extreme Right in Western Europe* (New York: Palgrave Macmillan, 2002), pp. 107–136.

[38] B. Dominguez Cebrian, "Dinamarca: Una isla para desterrar inmigrantes," *El País*, January 17, 2019, https://elpais.com/internacional/2019/01/17/actualidad/1547719266_874449.html.

[39] Ibid.

[40] Ibid.

conscious denial of regular access to citizens from 135 countries, the E.U. widens the gap globally and regulates mortality of people on a global scale."[41] All these restrictions mean that immigrants are increasingly vulnerable during the migration process and also when they are in the destination country, as described in the next section.

THE CREATION OF MIGRANT VULNERABILITY

Restrictive border policies make migrants more vulnerable both during the migration process and after their arrival in the country of destination. In the context of extreme global inequality, migration is the best and perhaps even the only choice to achieve a decent standard of living for a wide range of groups.[42] Most people in impoverished conditions do not have the option of legally moving to a wealthier country. When they decide to migrate illegally, they become vulnerable to danger in the migration process as well as after arriving in the host country.

Vulnerability in the Immigration Process

When people choose to migrate despite legal restrictions against doing so, they are resisting "the territorial confining and material deprivations which the system of global apartheid imposes on them."[43] In this process, Spener argues, "migrants face a wide variety of forms of personal, structural and cultural violence."[44] For example, migrants from Senegal travel in rickety boats across the Strait of Gibraltar to enter Europe through Spain. As reported by the United Nations High Commissioner for Refugees (UNHCR), in 2016, more than 5,000 migrants died or disappeared in the Mediterranean Sea.[45] Other NGOs say the number of deaths could be more than 13,000.[46] Additionally, there is evidence of at least 20,000 people trying to reach Europe who died in the Mediterranean Sea in the past two decades; meanwhile, from 2000 to 2013, the number of immigrant deaths among those trying to reach Australia is approximately 1,500.[47]

---

[41] Van Houtum, "Human Blacklisting: The Global Apartheid of the EU's External Border Regime," p. 968.

[42] J. H. Carens, "Who Belongs? Theoretical and Legal Questions about Birthright Citizenship in the United States" (1987) 37 *University of Toronto Law Journal* 413–443 at 413.

[43] D. Spener, "El apartheid global, el coyotaje y el discurso de la migracion clandestina: Distinciones entre violencia personal, estructural y cultural" (2008) 10 *Migracion y desarrollo* 127–156.

[44] Ibid. at 138.

[45] United Nations High Commissioner for Refugees, *Global Trends: Forced Displacement in 2016* (Geneva: UNHCR 2016).

[46] Van Houtum, "Human Blacklisting: The Global Apartheid of the EU's External Border Regime."

[47] Köhler, "The Three Meanings of Global Apartheid: Empirical, Normative, Existential," pp. 403–413; J. M. Loyd, "Carceral Citizenship in an Age of Global Apartheid" (2011) 30(3) *Geography* 118–128.

In August 2010, Mexican authorities discovered the bodies of fifty-eight men and fourteen women who were murdered and piled in the small room of a ranch near the city of Matamoros, which borders the United States (in a dark irony, the city name literally means "kill moors"). The dead migrants included people from Brazil, Ecuador, Guatemala, and other countries. Although no one has been convicted for their murders, authorities suspect Los Zetas – a paramilitary criminal organization from Mexico – were the perpetrators. The murdered migrants probably refused to comply with the organization's demands to become hitmen and drug smugglers or could not afford an extortion payment. Human rights organizations estimated that 20,000 immigrants are kidnapped every year in the journey to the United States from Latin America.[48] A significant number of Guatemalan and Brazilian immigrants report that traveling through Mexico was the most dangerous part of their journey.[49] This journey is particularly unsafe for women and children: as published by Amnesty International, six of every ten Central American women and girls are victims of sexual violence during their journey through Mexico.[50] The range of risks involved in this stage of the journey is a direct consequence of restrictive migration policies.

Nevertheless, despite all the risks and the new scenarios of hypervigilance, immigrants continue their odyssey; as van Houtum states "they adapt to the new rules, invent personalities, disidentify themselves by throwing away their papers or even crudely erase their fingerprints, that is, immigrants multiply and constantly build in new liminal forms."[51]

Living under the Threat of Deportation

The vulnerabilities that migrants face occur throughout the migration process. However, once immigrants manage to reach their destination, they live under the threat of these deportation regimes. The fear under these immigration policies changes family and community dynamics. Immigrants and their families become more vulnerable due to the fear of deportation. Immigrant workers do not claim their labor rights and are, therefore, more exposed to labor exploitation. Likewise, families, for fear of leaving their homes, also see their health and education affected negatively.[52]

---

[48] S. Shetty, "Most Dangerous Journey: What Central America Migrants Face When They Try to Cross the Border," *Amnesty International*, 2014, www.amnestyusa.org/most-dangerous-journey-what-central-american-migrants-face-when-they-try-to-cross-the-border/.

[49] T. Golash-Boza, *Deported: Immigrant Policing, Disposable Labor and Global Capitalism* (New York: New York University Press, 2015).

[50] Shetty, "Most Dangerous Journey."

[51] Van Houtum, "Human Blacklisting: The Global Apartheid of the EU's External Border Regime" at 973.

[52] S. W. Henderson and C. D. Baily, "Parental Deportation, Families, and Mental Health" (2013) 52(5) *Journal of the American Academy of Child and Adolescent Psychiatry* 451–453; D. Becerra,

In Europe, by 2016, the number of unauthorized immigrants peaked at 4 million. Many of these immigrants are refugee asylum seekers who arrived during the immigration crisis in 2015.[53] This crisis led to a growing migration emergency in Europe, with an increase in border closures and surveillance of migrants' entry.[54] This crisis also led to an increasing number of deportations. Some countries have been accused of using racial profiling to identify unauthorized migrants. In the United States, the high numbers of unauthorized migrants (11 million), combined with anti-migrant narratives and restrictive immigration, have created the conditions of possibility for mass deportation.

The approval of the 1996 Antiterrorism and Effective Death Penalty Act and the Illegal Immigration Reform and Immigrant Responsibility Act in the United States facilitated mass deportation by allowing the government to remove individuals without judicial review. According to official statistics in the last three decades, the United States has deported more than 7 million people. Most of these people were men from Latin American countries, revealing raced and gendered patterns in mass deportation.[55] This deportation regime caused many harmful consequences for individuals, families, and communities.[56] For example, millions of children have been separated from their parents as a result of deportations. The mass deportation system in the United States is very particular, not only because it expresses specific elements of the apartheid ideology, but also because its laws have historically been racist and discriminatory. Furthermore, the United States deportation system is a paradigmatic case of the negative and unquantifiable consequences for deportees, their families, communities, and the countries to which they have been forced to return.[57]

Multiple sources report that Spain has deported an average of 20 immigrants per day since 2011 (a total of approximately 50,000), most of them Moroccans. Government agencies cite their "irregular" status in the Spanish territory as a reason for expelling migrants.[58] Meanwhile, France, a country with historically stable

---

"Anti-Immigration Policies and Fear of Deportation: A Human Rights Issue" (2016) 1(3) *Journal of Human Rights and Social Work* 109–119.

[53] P. Connor and J. S. Passel, "Europe's Unauthorized Immigrant Population Peaks in 2016, Then Levels Off," *Pew Research Center*, November 13, 2019, www.pewresearch.org/global/2019/11/13/europes-unauthorized-immigrant-population-peaks-in-2016-then-levels-off/.

[54] Ibid.

[55] T. Golash-Boza and P. Hondagneu-Sotelo, "Latino Immigrant Men and the Deportation Crisis: A Gendered Racial Removal Program" (2013) 11(3) *Latino Studies* 271–292.

[56] J. Dreby, "The Modern Deportation Regime and Mexican Families," in C. Menjivar and D. Kanstroom (eds.), *Constructing Immigrant "Illegality": Critiques, Experiences, and Responses* (New York and Cambridge: Cambridge University Press, 2013), pp. 181–202.

[57] M. S. Zatz and N. Rodriguez, *Dreams and Nightmares: Immigration Policy, Youth, and Families* (Berkeley: University of California Press, 2015).

[58] Redaccion, "Mas de 83.000 inmigrantes deportados de España desde 2011," *La Vanguardia*, July 23, 2017, www.lavanguardia.com/vida/20170723/4343380857/mas-de-83000-inmigrantes-deportados-de-espana-desde-2011.html.

relationships with Spain, has a policy of deporting migrants to regions outside the European Union, but also within it – mostly to Spain. Since no official physical boundaries separate the two nations, activists argue that France selects immigrants for deportation to Spain according to an ethnic profile. Between January and October 2018, France deported almost 10,000 immigrants to Spain.[59]

In Australia, like in the United States and Europe, deportations have also increased in the twenty-first century. Whereas only about 1,000 people were deported a year in the 1980s, by 2015, this number had risen to 10,000 per year. At the same time, there were about 13,000 people in immigration detention facilities in Australia in 2014, compared to fewer than 100 in 1990.[60] Many people deported from Australia during this time were residents who had not returned to their countries of birth in a long time. Immigration enforcement in Australia has thus imposed many mental, social, and economic dilemmas for deported people.[61]

Each of these actions in Europe, the United States, and Australia play a fundamental role in preserving global apartheid.[62] At the same time, they become binary decision-making mechanisms: to admit entrance through borders or not, to include or to exclude.[63] These actions show how the United States has recently reinforced the apartheid ideology with the border wall construction and everyday anti-immigrant discourses, and how European countries have adopted this doctrine to maintain racial segregation, particularly in its application to people of African and Middle Eastern origin.[64]

The Emergence of a Desperate, Disposable, and Cheap Labor Force

As a result of these restrictive immigration and deportation regimes, immigrants must choose between their confinement in poor countries and joining a desperate labor force in another country.[65] This situation turns out to be highly convenient for the global economy, which requires a workforce with these characteristics. These workers are incredibly vulnerable. Employers can easily fire them, cut their salaries and benefits, and prohibit them from forming unions, which precludes the possibility of strikes or negotiating labor standards. In this context, wealthy countries manage

---

[59] M. Gonzalez and M. Martin, "Francia devuelve a España a 1.000 inmigrantes irregulares cada mes," *El Pais*, November 5, 2018, https://elpais.com/politica/2018/11/02/actualidad/1541179682_837419.html.

[60] J. Walsh, "Report and Deport: Public Vigilance and Migration Policing in Australia" (May 2018) 24(2) *Theoretical criminology* 276–295.

[61] G. Nicholls, *Deported: A History of Forced Departures from Australia* (Sydney: University of New South Wales Press, 2007).

[62] Spener, "El apartheid global, el coyotaje y el discurso de la migracion clandestina."

[63] Richmond and Valtonen, "Global Apartheid: Refugees, Racism, and the New World Order."

[64] Ibid.

[65] H. Walia, "Transient Servitude: Migrant Labour in Canada and the Apartheid of Citizenship" (2010) 52(1) *Race & Class* 71–84 at 72.

to impose conditions that produce a population of vulnerable laborers. Wealthy countries are aware that, eventually, this workforce will be integrated into global exploitation circuits before and during their migration as well as after deportation. These trends have been reported in countries like Canada and Israel, and in the Latin American region where immigrants with or without work visas are likely to be exploited.[66] In Latin America, transnational service companies hire people who have been displaced by neoliberal policies or deportation since a substantial part of this population is fluent in the English language and has knowledge of North American culture.[67]

ESTABLISHMENT OF SUBTLE AND RACIST MECHANISMS OF CONTROL, REMOVAL, AND EXPLOITATION OF IMMIGRANTS

Segregationist ideology can operate through openly racist and exclusionary immigration laws. However, as mentioned at the beginning, the efficacy of these ideologies relies on the ability to recreate themselves in more subtle yet still racist methods of control, removal, or exploitation of migrants. Border closures for humanitarian or political purposes have been established in various regions of the world; detention centers for immigrants have also been part of this new global order. More subtle mechanisms such as "voluntary" return programs have been identified, where migrants are forced to return to their countries of birth regardless of the reasons they immigrated. Finally, and in an even more sophisticated way, temporary work programs in which migrants are invited to work under exploitative conditions have spread around the Global North.[68]

Border Closure for Political, Humanitarian, and Security Reasons

In 2015, Costa Rica witnessed the arrival of a large number of Cuban and African immigrants who were in transit to the United States; the situation became problematic when the Nicaraguan government decided to close its southern border. As a result, at least 5,000 Cubans and hundreds of Africans became stranded in Costa Rica. Nicaragua justified its actions by arguing that Costa Rica acted irresponsibly by allowing these people to pass through their borders. Nicaragua vigorously defends its territory against threats such as drug trafficking, gangs, and human trafficking.[69] However, these actions also led to the death of twelve African immigrants, who

---

[66] Willen, *Fighting for Dignity: Migrant Lives at Israel's Margins*; Walia, "Transient Servitude: Migrant Labour in Canada and the Apartheid of Citizenship" at 72; T. Golash-Boza, "'Negative Credentials', 'Foreign-Earned' Capital, and Call Centers: Guatemalan Deportees' Precarious Reintegration" (2016) 20(3–4) *Citizenship Studies* 326–341.

[67] Ibid.

[68] Willen, *Fighting for Dignity: Migrant Lives at Israel's Margins*; Walia, "Transient Servitude: Migrant Labour in Canada and the Apartheid of Citizenship."

[69] "Migrantes atrapados en muro de contencion de Nicaragua," *Instituto Humanitas Unisinos ADITAL*, February 16, 2018, www.ihu.unisinos.br/161-noticias/noticias-espanol/576117-migr antes-atrapados-en-muro-de-contencion-de-nicaragua.

drowned in 2016 while trying to cross Lake Cocibolca in Nicaragua, in their journey from Costa Rica to the United States.[70]

A similar situation has been suffered by hundreds of thousands of people who were forced to leave Venezuela in recent years due to the country's political crisis. According to the UNHCR, more than 3 million Venezuelans have been forced to flee from Venezuela in 2015. Many crossed the border into neighboring countries, but this unleashed a crisis in the region. In Ecuador, thousands of Venezuelans found themselves stranded when Ecuador decided to close the passage through Rumichaca International Bridge. According to reports, this forced an increase in the undocumented crossing that involved a perilous route for women and minors. International organizations have requested Ecuador to "refrain from actions like closing borders, restricting access for people who might need international protection, punishing irregular entry or presence, requiring official documents like passports and records of past criminal activity, and resorting to immigration detention and hate speech."[71]

In Europe, one typical example is the ongoing conflicts in the Island of Lesvos mentioned previously. These conflicts between countries and regions over migration policy lead to negative consequences for migrants and at the same for the inhabitants in these territories. For Harrison, these new territories of *micro apartheid* hold a liminal position in the global racial hierarchy, in which countries and regions ally themselves with the dominant White minority. These countries attempt to sandwich themselves "between the 'Civilized White' and the 'Barbarous Black' countries."[72]

"Voluntary" Return Programs Enacted by Racist Ideologies

In October 2018, the Chilean government set up a Plan of Humanitarian Return to return Haitians living in Chile to Haiti.[73] Given the reasons Haitians migrate, this voluntary return is more of a punishment than "help" from the Chilean government.[74] Undocumented Haitians living in the country were invited to sign a document requiring them to leave and not return to Chile for nine years. Scholars labeled these measures as racist due to their singular focus on Haitians – who are nearly all

---

[70] ACAN-EFE, "Sube a siete cifra de migrantes africanos ahogados," *El Nuevo Diario*, August 2, 2016, www.elnuevodiario.com.ni/nacionales/399925-sube-siete-cifra-migrantes-africanos-ahogados-coci/.

[71] Inter-American Commission of Human Rights, "IACHR Concerned about Ecuador's New Measures to Address Forced Migration of Venezuelans," *Organization of American States*, February 27, 2019, www.oas.org/en/iachr/media_center/PReleases/2019/047.asp.

[72] Harrison, "Global Apartheid, Foreign Policy, and Human Rights" at 56.

[73] M. Andrade Moreno, "Programas de retorno voluntario. El caso chileno" (2020) 77(169) *Estudios de Derecho* 87–117.

[74] Ibid.

Black.[75] In an interview with Widner Darcelin, spokesman of the Haitian Communities in Chile, he described this allegedly humanitarian program as a deportation program.[76] Salazar and Ramirez affirm that this program is entirely discriminatory since it fundamentally targets Haitians living under extreme poverty in Chile.[77] The Chilean government has justified these deportations by arguing that Haitians have not been able to overcome cultural barriers to integrate into Chilean mainstream culture.[78] According to this report, in the five months since the plan was implemented in October 2018, almost 700 Haitians signed a commitment to "voluntary" return.[79]

Some studies reported how the Israeli government had invited African immigrants to leave the country voluntarily, a policy that follows a similar segregationist logic, where it has offered African immigrants US $3,000 either to return to Africa or move to another country; if they refuse, they are threatened with the alternative of facing imprisonment.[80] From the government's perspective, this initiative turns the deportation of temporary or irregular migrants into a voluntary and humanitarian process of leaving the country. It excludes women, children, parents of dependent children, and slavery and human trafficking victims. However, this policy is intended to remove "infiltrating" groups from the territory, which, according to the Israeli government, entered without proper documentation.[81] Furthermore, the government has initiated an anti-immigrant campaign based on the idea that "migrants might threaten the Jewish character of Israel."[82] Although a significant number of these immigrants are fleeing violence and armed conflicts in their home countries, the government has categorized them as economic immigrants rather than refugees.

---

[75] P. K. Sánchez et al., "Haiti, New Immigrant Community in Chile" (2018) 89(2) *Revista Chilena de Pediatria* 278–283; N. Rojas Pedemonte et al., "Racismo y matrices de 'inclusion' de la migración haitiana en Chile: Elementos conceptuales y contextuales para la discusión" (2015) 42 *Polis. Revista Latinoamericana*, online: journals.openedition.org/polis/11341.

[76] "Comunidades Haitianas denuncian que el Gobierno de Chile realiza 'una deportacion encubierta,'" *Sputnik News*, November 7, 2018, https://mundo.sputniknews.com/america-latina/201811071083274157-una-deportacion-masiva-de-haitianos/.

[77] C. Salazar and N. Ramírez, "El racismo como politica de estado: La deportacion de haitianos en Chile" *El Desconcierto*, November 7, 2018, www.eldesconcierto.cl/2018/11/07/el-racismo-como-politica-de-estado-la-deportacion-de-haitianos-en-chile/.

[78] AFP, "Haitianos se acogen a plan de retorno voluntario," *Diario Libre*, November 4, 2018, www.diariolibre.com/actualidad/internacional/180-haitianos-se-acogen-a-plan-de-retorno-voluntario-desde-chile-JG11179671.

[79] Ibid.

[80] Y. A. Orgal et al., "Israel's 'Voluntary' Return Policy to Expel Refugees: The Illusion of Choice," in M. Van Risen et al. (eds.), *Mobile Africa: Human Trafficking and the Digital Divide* (Oxford: African Books Collective, 2019), p. 209.

[81] "Israel, African Migrants Told to Leave or Face Imprisonment," *BBC News*, January 2, 2018, www.bbc.com/news/world-middle-east-42541515.

[82] Ibid.

Free Trade Agreements

Another strategy for creating a disposable workforce has been through free trade agreements. These pacts create the conditions for thousands of people to lose their jobs in their home countries and force them to migrate without documentation to wealthy countries. Immigrants with undocumented status are easily exploited. In this regard, Harrison states that "this neoliberal regime – in which developed nations aid poorer nations on the condition that they restructure their economies and political systems to accommodate maximum wealth accumulation by multinational corporations – has arrived packaged as so-called free trade."[83]

Walia cites the North American Free Trade Agreement (NAFTA) as an example since it dramatically impoverished many Latin American countries.[84] In the case of Mexico, more than 15 million people fell into poverty, and more than 1 million were displaced. Many Mexicans were forced to leave their communities, and now work as undocumented immigrants in the agricultural sector of Canada. Willen provides examples of this cheap labor export trend in Israel, as well. The Israeli government recruited workers from Thailand, Romania, Turkey, and China, responding to employers' demands. These workers are very "attractive" since employers presumed these workers are politically neutral. These employers are also attracted by the flexibility in which these workers are hired, meaning there are few labor regulations – making it easier to exploit them.[85] Willen describes the circumstances in which these movements and hiring processes occur as a form of human trafficking.[86]

These examples show how apartheid ideology operates and how it achieves its objective of racial segregation.[87] People of color are either forced to remain in their countries of birth or suffer exploitation or even death if they attempt migration in search of better circumstances. These actions show covert racism, whereby governments justify their restrictive migration policies by claiming that immigrants are not capable of integrating and therefore are culturally incompatible with the native culture. In reality, these arguments are an expression of racial intolerance.[88]

Preserving Wealth among a Minority

The mechanisms discussed help maintain the global apartheid system by eliminating most non-White people from wealthy countries and confining them to much

---

[83] Harrison, "Global Apartheid, Foreign Policy, and Human Rights" at 48.

[84] Walia, "Transient Servitude: Migrant Labour in Canada and the Apartheid of Citizenship" at 72.

[85] Willen, *Fighting for Dignity: Migrant Lives at Israel's Margins*.

[86] Ibid.

[87] Harrison, "Global Apartheid, Foreign Policy, and Human Rights."

[88] Fennema, "Populist Parties of the Right."

poorer nations. Thus, they seek to guarantee that the vast majority of the world's wealth stays in the hands of a White minority.

For scholars like Feagin and Ducey, this form of global organization preserves the power and wealth of Whites by creating an unfair distribution of resources.[89] According to Titus, the practice of apartheid includes the idea – implicitly assumed or explicitly stated – that a particular group has more rights than others, for example, the presumption that American citizens have a right to access social security while Mexican immigrants do not.[90] Global apartheid involves a strong commitment to protecting and preserving the privileges of White people, which take the form of regulations, immigration laws, and work programs, among other measures. All these mechanisms permit the ideology to operate.

These immigration laws, work programs, and other types of regulations establish racial categories that justify the existence of privileged and unprivileged groups. This ideology separates who belongs to a determined territory and who ought to be removed from it, or conversely, who holds rights and who does not.[91] At present, there is a concern about the excessive growth of this doctrine, mainly because this ideology resorts to increasingly subtle mechanisms. These practices invigorate racial segregation.[92] For Feagin and Ducey, this trend is historically rooted in the aggressive exploitation of Native Americans and African slaves.[93] They argue that White elites have created all possible mechanisms to maintain this social order, from laws to specific institutions.[94] Although Feagin and Ducey's arguments apply primarily to the United States, these same ideologies can be found worldwide.

CONCLUSIONS

Today's model of global apartheid has shaped migratory policies globally. The rise of highly popular extreme right-wing parties in Europe and anti-immigrant discourses throughout the settler colonial states of the United States, Canada, Israel, and Australia are evidence of the consolidation and spread of this ideology.[95] In addition, we have seen increased evidence of *micro apartheids*, which configure segregation at a smaller scale and in a more subtle manner.[96] Cases of policies in Israel, Chile, and Ecuador that limit human mobility and institute racial segregation are some examples of this broader tendency.

[89] Feagin and Ducey, *Racist America: Roots, Current Realities, and Future Reparations.*
[90] A. Titus, *Unravelling Global Apartheid: An Overview of World Politics* (Cambridge: Polity Press, 1996).
[91] Omi and Winant, *Racial Formation in the United States.*
[92] Harrison, "Global Apartheid, Foreign Policy, and Human Rights."
[93] Feagin and Ducey, *Racist America: Roots, Current Realities, and Future Reparations.*
[94] Ibid.
[95] Van Houtum, "Human Blacklisting: The Global Apartheid of the EU's External Border Regime."
[96] Harrison, "Global Apartheid, Foreign Policy, and Human Rights."

Restrictions on immigration at the global and local levels reflect how the global apartheid ideology enacts and justifies its goals through a wide range of discursive tropes and mechanisms, grounded in new racism. The specifications of this process are the programs of temporary work, voluntary return programs, and an overwhelming number of requirements for legal migration. These measures all severely restrict the possibility of poor people of color around the world – limiting their options to improve their living conditions.

The core problem with this ideology is the idea that some groups deserve rights while others do not based on the place of birth.[97] During the apartheid regime in South Africa, resource distribution followed racial boundaries. Under global apartheid, privileges and resources are allocated based on national origin, which creates a racialized divide between Europe and Africa and between the United States and Latin America.

---

[97] Van Houtum, "Human Blacklisting: The Global Apartheid of the EU's External Border Regime."

PART II

Belonging across Borders

7

Imagining New Forms of Belonging

The Futurity of the Stateless

Eleni Coundouriotis

What is the futurity of statelessness? The answer to such a broad question lies partly in the types of stories we tell about the refugee experience and in how we connect past and future. If we claim rights for the stateless, we imagine a future time of statelessness that is something other than the present. To posit new forms of belonging, moreover, presupposes that we have a grasp of the old forms of belonging that failed and caused statelessness. Yet, the process is not simply mechanistic, a toggle from past to future. We cannot settle the past and move on but neither can we imagine futurity without an understanding of the past.

The imagination (through the arts but also through humanistic critical inquiry) provokes us to expand our thinking beyond the familiar. Thus, it can take on the task of interpolating a future for statelessness, of thinking outside the box, to address the rapidly expanding crisis of our epoch. This is a different remit than expecting literature to foster empathic engagement, although the two may not be incompatible. Furthermore, this imaginative discourse contrasts with social scientific descriptive discourses that too frequently diagnose the problem by looking only at what is already in place, suggesting a stalled temporality that reveals a dystopic world of more of the worst aspects of the same. Such descriptive discourses frequently fail to grasp the dynamics of historical change, of relating the past to the future in becoming. The future envisioned here is instead one that finds in statelessness some creative energy for new forms of belonging, even as a resolution to legal statelessness seems elusive. These new forms of belonging will invariably be tested and reconfigured repeatedly, yet they have the potential to move forward the search for a positive path out of the crisis of unbelonging.

Testimony, a complex practice of relating the past to the present, is a privileged discourse in the history of refugees that plays a key role in understanding statelessness as a lived experience. A key contention of this chapter is that testimony, despite what's understood as its retrospective structure, makes legible the futurity of statelessness. Broadly understood as a truthful, first-person account of what happened, testimony has a complex relationship with time. Moreover, it has unique narrative features: testimony is performative (a subject gives testimony), eruptive (its key episodes disrupt the exposition of events, coming to the surface of the narrative unexpectedly and with force), and repetitive (we require to hear it multiple times). The experience of statelessness holds on to what anthropologist Michel Agier calls the stages of "destruction" and "exodus."[1] The dislocation of the stateless originated in acute danger, which engulfed the places they called home.[2] Thus, stuck in limbo in spaces of precarious refuge, they repeatedly give testimony that addresses their past: their history of war, persecution, and forced displacement.

Testimony of these experiences can be hugely consequential in determining the future trajectory and legal status of displaced persons. Furthermore, such occasions for testimony are varied and far from uniform, putting different types of pressure on the accounts we hear. This uneven terrain where particular stories of refugee experience come into focus has the potential to capture aspirations for future belonging born of past trauma. The literary and humanistic endeavor fosters the imagination of what these budding forms of belonging might be. Consequently, this chapter offers reflections on how to create a sense of belonging for the stateless that keeps them in our purview as historical agents who can determine their actions and meaning. Whereas the legal definition of statelessness remains a key category, the chapter examines the experiential implications of statelessness, understanding these as a form of unbelonging. Testimony makes legible the futurity of statelessness and invites creative engagement to elaborate on new aspirations.

Refugee camps, in particular, become places where past and future confront each other. Scenes of testimony – occasions when stories of "exodus" are repeated in refugee camps or other places of refuge – come to characterize something about the new place.[3] Paradoxically, therefore, new aspirations can emerge from the hindsight of retrospective accounting. Such occasions to remember the story of flight for survival, moreover, recur over long periods, sometimes a lifetime, and might even be repeated by future generations. The persistent iterations of such stories over time accumulate to the point of cohering into a "common story" that binds a refugee community and gives it a "collective voice."[4] A new form of belonging suggests itself in the "collective voice."

What follows is an attempt to explore the possible shape of such new belonging and see how it acquires meaning in an evolving present shaped by memory. Instead of assuming that the past holds secrets we need to uncover but is otherwise finished, reading for the purpose of identifying a new belonging demands a greater effort at integrating the past into the present and future. The past is dynamic and, upon

---

[1] M. Agier, *On the Margins of the World* (Cambridge: Polity Press, 2008), p. 3.
[2] A. Betts and P. Collier, *Refuge: Transforming the Broken Refugee System* (Milton Keynes: Penguin, 2017), pp. 16–17.
[3] Agier, *On the Margins*, pp. 74–75.
[4] Ibid., pp. 75, 78.

repeated reexamination, yields new insight. Statelessness appears at different points in the timeline of testimony, which might extend over generations. The prolonged precarity of the stateless speaks to the urgency with which the new form of belonging surfaces. Statelessness can take on an existential dimension but, as a term, it refers to the legal definition and the loss of rights that go with it. The new forms of belonging redress the existential crisis, creating momentum and pressure to resolve the legal roadblocks to citizenship.

To elucidate this process of an emerging, cohering story that accounts for the past so as to make a claim for future belonging, I examine a historical example, the Armenian Genocide, and the work of Peter Balakian. Balakian not only makes the history of the genocide particularly legible but intuits the futurity of statelessness in his creative work, connecting past and present and offering an expansive view of humanity's becoming that refuses to other the victims of genocide. It is from this ethical claim on his readers that Balakian's work gains wide resonance in the literature on statelessness. I turn first to Balakian's use of history and examine his ambitious layering of time. After a discussion of the temporalities of witness and testimony, I examine how Balakian works with this distinction to make an argument about the futurity of statelessness that draws from the impact of his grandmother's testimony.

HISTORY AND BELONGING

Our question, therefore, is: What kind of belonging does an extended project of testimony over decades create for stateless persons? Refugees, according to Liisa Malkki, have a "passion for history."[5] The past matters a lot to them. Can history provide a compensatory space to restitute these subjects sufficiently so they can imagine a future? Agier speaks of a *cultural recognition* ("based on narration of the experiences of war, exodus, and refuge") that creates a new community to replace what is destroyed while remaining connected to the past.[6] It is the emphasis on the new that distinguishes this project from other formulations of the politics of memory. Such reconstitution of belonging acknowledges the past but is pragmatically anchored in the present. The "common story" of accumulated testimony actively renegotiates identity in the present and the emphasis on the new is most meaningful for imagining belonging.

There are challenges, however, on this path. The vocabulary of exile and exilic community (which makes reference to territory) has afforded one model of how to

---

[5] Liisa Malkki, "News from Nowhere: Mass Displacement and Globalized 'Problems of Organization'" (2002) 3(3) *Ethnography* 351–360 at 359.

[6] Agier, *On the Margins*, p. 74.

talk about displaced communities.[7] Shifting the emphasis away from territory, as I do here following Balakian, leaves one with a difficult history that is unanchored, disjointed from place. Place can only be evoked in the present or the aftermath. In the texture of the present, Balakian thus discovers a traveling memory: a displaced history that speaks in another land. His life-long endeavor to recover the history of the Armenian Genocide in memoir, biography, poetry, and forensic documentation explores the potential for a diachronic belonging – a belonging in time – that speaks to the futurity of the stateless. Balakian's practice is multifaceted and extends the work of testimony: it uses the present to find the past and bring it forward, making it matter in our current lives as we live them. Therefore, the effort reconfigures our belonging in the present through an awareness of the effects of past crimes against humanity. Through ongoing memory work, a new form of belonging is forged that extends our ethical awareness of the stateless in the present.

Moreover, because the Armenian Genocide was perpetrated within the context of a struggle over citizenship rights, it has particular relevance as an example of how to imagine the futurity of statelessness. The pressures of modernization in late Ottoman Turkey reached a climax in the Revolution of 1908, which sought to secularize the state and guarantee equal participation in civil and political life, as well as citizenship, to minority populations.[8] The revolutionary ideals did not hold, however, and a devastating reaction ensued, resulting in various episodes of mass displacements, mistreatment, and killings that culminated in the genocide a few years later. Importantly, Armenians expressed their allegiance to the revolutionary ideas of 1908 with passion and they understood the huge suffering that followed as the loss, or failure, of citizenship rights.[9]

Although the crisis was viewed internationally through the lens of humanitarianism, Balakian accounts for his grandmother's experience through the more robust legal framework of human rights, making her visible as a rights-claiming subject with an outlook to the future. Whereas some displaced Armenians were resettled in the Soviet Republic of Armenia after 1920, most of the displaced survivors came from Anatolia (Turkey) and became long-term refugees, residing in camps and other temporary refuges, until their legal circumstances were clarified.[10] The expectation of an Armenian homeland to settle the historical wrong was not fulfilled (the Soviet Republic did not become such a symbol). Hence this "common story" that struggled to become legible against denial and silence is also an important example of how history – as an ongoing process of constructing the story of the past – functions as a

---

[7]   See, for example, Lucy Stonebridge's discussion of the enduring influence of Edward W. Said's thought on exile in Lucy Stonebridge, *Placeless People: Writing, Rights and Refugees* (Oxford: Oxford University Press, 2018), pp. 30–32.

[8]   K. D. Watenpaugh, *Bread from Stones: The Middle East and the Making of Modern Humanitarianism* (Oakland: University of California Press, 2015), p. 70.

[9]   Ibid., pp. 71–73.

[10]   Ibid., p. 168.

multigenerational point of reference for a community. Balakian's oeuvre as a whole makes legible the complex belonging in a common story that is also specifically addressed to the United States (he speaks very self-consciously as an American) and illuminates the ethical stakes for Americans in belonging together with the stateless.

We can describe Balakian's work as a literature of witness structured in the form of a multigenerational dialogue. He calls his grandmother (who died when he was ten years old) his "beloved witness."[11] A survivor of the death marches of 1915, when the Ottoman Turkish army forcefully removed the Armenian population of Diarberkir and marched them into Syria, Nafina found temporary refuge in Aleppo. There she earned a living as a seamstress for five years until she entered a home to deliver a wedding dress and saw a carpet that had belonged to her family. She filed a suit, reclaimed the rug, sold it, and paid the passage to America for herself and her two young daughters.[12] In the United States, she remarried another Armenian refugee, had a daughter (Peter's mother) and lived a second life as part of an affluent, educated, and intellectually inclined family in the New Jersey suburbs of New York City. But her life was carefully circumscribed to remain within a comfort zone that kept the trauma of the past suppressed. She refused to leave the United States even to accompany the family on a trip to Paris. Only in the United States did she feel safe, far enough away from the historical forces that threatened her.

That Nafina might stand as a historical figure who brings the stateless closer to us today is evident from Silvia Salvatici's history of humanitarianism. Salvatici quotes extensively from Nafina's testimony in 1920, recorded in her claim for reparations from the Turkish government.[13] Salvatici structures her history around key moments of testimony (used as epigraphs throughout the book) by historical figures who are paradigm-setting voices of witness for humanitarianism. Nafina's emblematic status is apparent from her place in this series representing landmark events in the history of humanitarianism that include, in addition to the Armenian Genocide, the Crimean War, Biafra, the Rwanda Genocide, and other events. Nafina's testimony (from her claim for reparations and other documents I discuss below) appears first in Balakian's memoir of his own growing up into consciousness of the genocide, then molds into the common story of surviving the genocide. Salvatici draws together the testimony of an individual survivor with the horrors perpetrated and recasts them in a collective narrative that outlines a historical event on a larger canvas: "The adult men were killed *en masse* and then the women and children were led to the desert regions of Mesopotamia."[14]

Thus, Balakian can be said to launch his grandmother's significant testimony into the public domain where it becomes a flashpoint for a common story of the

[11] P. Balakian, *Black Dog of Fate: A Memoir* (New York: Basic Books, 2009), p. 195.

[12] Ibid., p. 190.

[13] S. Salvatici, *A History of Humanitarianism, 1755–1989: In the Name of Others*, trans. P. Sanders (Manchester: University of Manchester Press, 2019), pp. 101–102.

[14] Ibid., p. 101.

genocide. It behooves us, therefore, to pay close attention to his own method of assembling the material for his memoir and for his subsequent writing, where he consistently returns to the genocide and connects it to an ongoing project chronicling the traumatic events of his era (including 9/11 in his collection, *Ziggurat*).[15] Balakian's exploration of the history of the genocide contributed to his Pulitzer Prize-winning poetry collection *Ozone Journal* in which he weaves the work he did in forensic archaeology (uncovering the remains of those who perished in the death marches of 1915) with the memories of his own personal life crisis in 1980s New York: his growing estrangement from his wife and his cousin's suffering in the last stages of AIDS. New York, moreover, is filtered through a more recent past, the 1970s, when he had been happier. Adding yet another layer of time, the entire poem connects to environmental catastrophe and the thinning of the ozone layer, warning of total death from the sun's unfiltered rays: "no plankton, no world: who can take in the dread—."[16] This question ("who can take in the dread—"), which ends with a dash and not a question mark as if it is permanent and unresolved, takes us back to the predicament of those who witnessed mass extermination while anticipating their own deaths. The poet draws an analogy between ecocatastrophe and genocide laying that feeling of "dread" at our door as we confront the fear that we might succumb. And, whereas it is doubtful that we can live up to our moment, we feel the imperative to try and figure out how to do it.

What is most important to our concerns here is the pattern of Balakian's exposition, which overlays the present onto the past in order to demand of the reader an expanded awareness. He places the present danger of violent destruction in the reader's sight. It should not be enough to join the poet in a painful awareness of the enduring trauma of the Armenian Genocide simply as an exercise of humanistic reading. The common story we should reach for grapples with the reality of contemporary mass violence and displacement in continuity with the past, and all of it in the context of environmental catastrophe. The reader might already be primed to recognize ecological catastrophe as a crisis. Balakian then links this by analogy and poetic image to the plight of the stateless, making it hard to refuse the urgent predicament of the stateless in our contemporary moment. Moreover, we realize that if we do not broaden to an understanding of statelessness and precarity in the present, we risk the kind of complicity in silence similar to the one that impeded Balakian's effort to apprehend the full import of his family's history. As we learn from the text, the family's silence about the genocide kept the young Peter in ignorance until his college years. Reading the memoir, we come to an appreciation of Balakian's discovery of history and, as a result, cannot blind ourselves to a similar interconnectedness with world events in the present.

---

[15] P. Balakian, *Ziggurat* (Chicago: University of Chicago Press, 2010).
[16] P. Balakian, "Ozone Journal, #17," in *Ozone Journal* (Chicago: University of Chicago Press, 2015), p. 38.

Balakian brings to mind Dori Laub's highest sense of witness: the expectation that to witness is to have interruptive force and intercede with the truth to stop a particular action. Laub describes this interruptive witness as a "concurrent" witness that calls out the truth of an event as it is unfolding.[17] The injunction to interrupt is suggestive for the kind of witnessing that Balakian seeks and his belief that one must constantly renew the witnessing of past atrocity in order to forestall its repression in memory. His grandmother is his "beloved witness" in the sense that Peter, as her beloved claimed as an intimate extension of herself, must carry on her witness. The historical figure (his grandmother) leaves behind testimony that he uses as material to posit his writing as "concurrent witness" to his own time. Such witness accounts create an enormous and hard-to-fulfill expectation of authenticity. How do they manage these expectations? Within literary discourse, we find a partial answer in the figure of the poet, as Balakian understands well.

The special function of the poet to bestow authenticity to historical experience is well established. Turning to the opening of Anna Akhmatova's "Requiem,"[18] legal scholar and human rights practitioner Ron Dudai reminds us that the poet is asked to "describe this": the scene of women standing outside Leningrad prison as they wait for word about their imprisoned men.[19] Akhmatova's celebrated poem gives witness to the sufferings caused by Stalin's purges in the 1930s. For Dudai, it is significant that the poet is asked to "describe this" as opposed to being asked "to help." Description is intervention. To give voice to a collective experience demands a special skill but also a person with recognized authority to speak for the group and persuade the targeted audience of the authenticity of the experiences. These are the poet's burdens, and they clarify for us what Balakian tasks himself with. As Dudai explains, however, we have come to expect from human rights reports of abuses that description gains authority by being pared down, "allowing the facts to speak for themselves," and suppressing literary elements or overly narrative qualities.[20] In practice, we construct evidence rhetorically – evidence is not what is true but that which is used to persuade us of the truth.[21] Literature, therefore, can persuade by providing the context for recognition, and hence also for potentially new forms of belonging.

---

[17] S. Felman and D. Laub, *Testimony: Crises of Witnessing in Literature, Psychoanalysis, and History* (New York: Routledge, 1992), p. 84.

[18] A. Akhmatova, "Requiem," in S. Kunitz and M. Hayward (eds. and trans.), *Poems of Akhmatova* (Boston, MA: Little, Brown and Company, 1973), pp. 99–117.

[19] R. Dudai, "'Can You Describe This?' Human Rights Reports and What They Tell Us about the Human Rights Movement" in R. A. Wilson and R. D. Brown (eds.), *Humanitarianism and Suffering: The Mobilization of Empathy* (Cambridge: Cambridge University Press, 2008), pp. 245–246.

[20] Ibid., p. 249.

[21] T. Keenan, "Getting the Dead to Tell Me What Happened: Justice, Prosopopoeia, and Forensic Afterlives" in Forensic Architecture (ed.), *Forensis: The Architecture of Public Truth* (Berlin, Germany: Sternberg Press and Forensic Architecture, 2014), pp. 43–44.

Theories of testimony have explored the difficulties of bringing forth the outline of events suppressed by trauma. As Shoshana Felman puts it, traumatic events are "events in excess of our frames of reference" that are difficult to talk about.[22] The traumatic event is the lacuna around which an account of trauma's toll blossoms. Expanding on this idea, Laub calls our attention to the "historical gap" that separates the events recounted from the recounting, and the difficulty or near impossibility of transmitting testimony in real time.[23] As noted, he provocatively suggests that should "concurrent witnessing" be achieved, it would bring about an interruption of the event being witnessed. Although Laub presents this as unlikely, its possibility is the great hope for what a mission to give witness might accomplish for human rights: to intervene and interrupt the harm. Witnesses in real time can thus be agentic subjects at the scene of catastrophe. NGOs such as Doctors Without Borders have, in fact, made witnessing a foundational aspect of their practice.[24] By contrast to witnessing, testimony is the task of retrieving the contours of the event retrospectively through the obfuscations of trauma. This is a process that takes time.

In a sense, Balakian fuses the two temporalities that distinguish witness from testimony: he acts as a witness in the present by responding to his discovery of a historical testimony that has taken a considerable amount of time to surface. His involvement in forensic projects to find the remains of Armenian victims carries forward the relevance of his findings to his contemporary moment, as is evident in the poems of *Ozone Journal* that weave this search for remains into an account of the challenges of our time. Forensics shares some qualities of the interruptive witness. Balakian's poetic practice and its corollary in forensics suggest that the "common story" of the Armenian diaspora, to whose formation Balakian has contributed significantly, imagines a broader belonging in solidarity with the stateless today. This is more than what Agier calls the "existential community" shaped immediately after a catastrophe.[25] The pull of this new belonging pushes us all to act as interruptive witnesses to create a new futurity for the stateless. Whereas ultimately the goal is to resolve legally the condition of statelessness, the futurity alluded to here creates momentum toward recognition and, from there, legal and political change.

THE CLAIMS ON THE "BELOVED WITNESS"

In *Black Dog of Fate*, Balakian reverse-engineers the authenticity of his grandmother's testimony: the historical truth he discovers as an adult grows out of his affective attachment, which lends authenticity to Nafina's testimony. Moreover, his method of exposition demonstrates how the present opens up the past and is of the

---

[22] Felman and Laub, *Testimony*, p. 5.
[23] Ibid., p. 84.
[24] P. Redfield, *Life in Crisis: The Ethical Journey of Doctors without Borders* (Berkeley: University of California Press, 2013), p. 100.
[25] Agier, *On the Margins*, p. 74.

most consequence in shaping a future. Balakian's "epiphany," recounted as the discovery and retransmission of his grandmother's words, underscores the impact of Nafina's testimony.[26] Importantly, an even more traumatic testimony by his Aunt Dovey surfaces alongside Nafina's witness. Gaining confidence from Peter's recognition of Nafina's empowered stance (apparent in her claims for reparations), his aunt comes forth with her memories. This synergy between the two historical voices demonstrates how a context of multiple testimonies emerges over an extended timeline. Decades separate these two testimonial utterances. Dovey gives Balakian a first-person account of the signature atrocities of the Armenian genocide, including the death of men by crucifixion and mutilation and the burning alive of women, who were first forced to dance while being whipped and beaten in public.[27] This difficult narrative is presented to the reader only after Balakian's extensive and poignant account of his childhood bond with his grandmother when the genocide was never discussed and he had no understanding of it. His retrospective account of his own growing up is filled with a sense of belated recognition of the signs genocide left on his family. These flashes of recognition, anchored in quotidian details, lend authenticity to his grandmother's testimonial legacy and free his aunt to speak to him. As he notes in a poem: "memory was focus, detail, the thing—" observed in the ordinary world that surrounds us.[28]

In large part, what Balakian describes in his memoir are the effects of post-memory: the inherited trauma that survivors' families experience, resulting from the silences and the unspoken, unmourned past. The passage of time, deracination, and the loss of home together condition post-memory.[29] Balakian channeled this haunting into his poetry. What he didn't know he knew burst forth in an early poem, "The History of Armenia," composed when he guiltily skipped his grandmother's memorial service ten years after her death to spend the weekend with his girlfriend. The process of writing the poem exposed how relevant the affective history of the genocide had been to him. Writing "The History of Armenia" reconnected him to his grandmother: "I could bring the two of us together again and create what she had in her encoded way told me. I realized that she was my beloved witness, and I the receiver of her story."[30] Here he is both interpreting his grandmother's code to understand her *and* creating new meaning by recasting their relationship in the present.

Thus, *Black Dog of Fate* can be read as a tribute to Balakian's grandmother, but it is also most importantly a story of Balakian's discovery of the history of the genocide,

---

[26] R. P. Mosby, "The Voice of History: An Interview with Peter Balakian" (2001) 67(3) *New Letters* at 49.

[27] Balakian, *Black Dog*, pp. 222–225.

[28] P. Balakian, "Ozone Journal, #9," in *Ozone Journal*, p. 33.

[29] M. Hirsch, *Family Frames: Photography, Narrative and Postmemory* (Cambridge, MA: Harvard University Press, 1997), pp. 22–23.

[30] Balakian, *Black Dog*, p. 195.

and his push against denial and silence. It exemplifies how coming to grips with the past is an ongoing, difficult process that simultaneously mediates the relationship with the present. As Balakian's lived experience, the confrontation with the past is necessarily also part of the forward-moving temporality of his life into which he carries an expansive sense of the predicament of statelessness.

Moreover, the text obsessively records the importance of a sense of place in belonging. Regions, neighborhoods, streets, bus routes, construction sites, home interiors are all meticulously described. If these details evoke in Balakian's readers a rich recognition of a particular place and time in metropolitan New York, they then also suggest that the place left behind by his family by analogy must have had an enormous affective significance. Its memory is teased out in the food, language, folk stories, and religious ritual that surrounded the young Peter. Growing up, he navigated these with some selectivity: loving the food, being perplexed by much of the rest, and in a flashpoint of conflict with his father not recognizing what he had no way of knowing, "what the Turks did to us."[31]

Reading becomes instrumental in bringing the contours of the past into the present. During a summer job while he was in college, Balakian spends his free time reading *Ambassador Morgenthau's Story*,[32] which he pulled from his parents' bookshelf because he had been intrigued by its possibility and was now ready to read it.[33] Yielding to Morgenthau's witness from the times and quoting extensively from his book, Balakian takes his reader along in his discovery of the magnitude of the atrocities. This story of reading, in which we participate as Balakian's surrogates, mimics a structure of human rights storytelling that is, in fact, widespread. Adam Hochschild, for example, structured *King Leopold's Ghost*, his human rights history of the atrocities in the Belgian Congo, around similar scenes. Hochschild tells us, therefore, how Edmund Morel discovered the human rights abuses in the Congo by reading ships' manifests and puzzling over what information was missing.[34] The idea that reading leads to discovery of fact is a bit peculiar in these cases: the facts are rarely new, and thus can't be discovered in a strict sense. Even to say that this amounts to a personal discovery isn't quite accurate because by the time Balakian, for example, reads Morgenthau he already has by his own admission a basic frame for these events from fragmented information that has been passed down to him. So, what is the significance of this story of reading? How does it offer something new?

The power of reading is frequently discussed in terms of its affective influence. It cultivates human sympathy and sharpens our abilities as ethical thinkers. Both dimensions are at play here but we need to put our finger on something in addition:

---

[31] Ibid., p. 100.
[32] H. Morgenthau, *Ambassador Morgenthau's Story* (New York: Doubleday, Page and Company, 1918).
[33] Ibid., p. 153.
[34] A. Hochschild, *King Leopold's Ghost: A Story of Greed, Terror and Heroism in Colonial Africa* (New York: Mariner, 1999), pp. 178–189.

in this example, the activity of reading becomes the plot of a story that explains retrospectively the impact of a text. This is different from drawing attention to a reader's interpretation of the text. The story of reading dramatizes for us the experiential impact of reading, its transformative power, which, moreover, dramatizes the acquisition of a new understanding – deeper, more complex, more immediate – of past events. Stories of reading in a human rights context are about connecting with history in a way that rewrites its narrative.

The common story forged through the accumulated testimony of events of mass displacement can appear in creative work such as Balakian's where it ignites a larger public awareness of an important past history and makes us aware of our connection to mass violence in our own time. This discovery in a shared story of reading situates the text as a reference point for belonging. The question of temporality with which this chapter began is pivotal. New forms of belonging can potentially be capacious but they require a flexible temporality, one that accommodates the flashes of traumatic memory and the "dread" of impending catastrophe in the present.

Balakian first published his memoir in 1997, a year before Hochschild's history appeared and around the same time that there was a burst of literary works defining themselves in terms of human rights.[35] Generally speaking, the late 1990s was a period of intensified engagement of literature with human rights and we find this reflected in Balakian's text where on several occasions he is explicit about his framing. Describing his reaction to hearing the phrase "remember the starving Armenians" as a college student and realizing that it existed in the popular conscience but he had never heard it at home, Balakian remarks: "No one ever told me that the image of Armenians starving to death was, for Americans, a slogan for the most dramatic human rights issue of the day."[36] The starving Armenians are referred to in the historiography as subjects of humanitarian concern,[37] but Balakian suggests that humanitarian concern elided the main issue. Morgenthau's account instead gets it right. He describes a genocide before the paradigm-setting history of the Holocaust and the body of international human rights law that followed and made such a designation recognizable.[38]

Balakian's story of reading culminates in his recognition of his grandmother as a human rights claimant. He reproduces the legal documents that record his grandmother's claims for reparations from the Turkish government in 1920. This is not only a claim for reparation of property but a claim made on the basis of the violation of her physical integrity rights and the suffering caused. The document ends with this statement: "The Turkish government is responsible for the losses and injuries happened to [me], because I am a human being and a citizen of U.S.A., I am under

---

[35] James Dawes, *The Novel of Human Rights* (Cambridge, MA: Harvard University Press, 2018), p. 29.
[36] Balakian, *Black Dog*, p. 173.
[37] Watenpaugh, *Bread from Stones*, p. 33.
[38] Balakian, *Black Dog*, p. 138.

the support of human and international law."[39] Nafina intuits the language of human rights and claims a future. These documents reveal facts that Balakian was unaware of: that Nafina was an American citizen by marriage to an Armenian merchant who was a naturalized American (and not Balakian's grandfather) and who had returned to Diarbekir in 1915 and died during "our deportation." Poignantly, she states: "my husband Hagop Chilinguirian being dead on the way."[40] The documents also include the list of other relatives that perished and thus outline her and her brother's claim to the family property.

Most striking, however, is his grandmother's stance as a human rights claimant on the basis of United States citizenship by marriage: because I am "a citizen of U.S.A," she says signing from Aleppo, Syria, she has the "support of human and international law." Unusual as her circumstance was, it shows that without the good fortune of an American citizenship by marriage, she would have no grounds from which to make a legal claim. She is acutely aware of this privilege, announcing this citizenship as the basis of her claim, but also appears anxious that it will not be recognized. Nafina's answer to "Question 63" of the legal form (asking her to explain the circumstances of her loss of property) states that her husband's naturalization papers and passport were taken from him, and therefore she is not in possession of them. Teetering between statelessness and US citizenship as a refugee in Aleppo, Nafina persists in her claim. Thus, here too her thinking is proleptic. She intuits the logic of Hannah Arendt's famous "right to have rights:" without citizenship, one cannot claim rights, thus human rights are not universal but conditioned on a particular form of belonging, that of citizenship.[41]

Included in Nafina's legal testimony are also the devastating details that outline the truth of the death march. Such details situate Nafina in the particulars of an established history but reveal to Balakian a new person, his grandmother in a different life, on a death march, widowed and accompanied by two young daughters. She withholds the details of her husband's passing, saying only that the male deportees were killed "one by one" and that her husband "feeble and indisposed, being subjected to such conditions, and seeing our relatives killed unhumanely [sic], he could not support the life, and died."[42] Balakian quotes extensively from the document and intersperses these passages with fragments from the most intense memories he had of his grandmother, scenes he has already rendered for the reader in the book's eloquent, intensely affective opening chapters.

Reconciling the grandmother who doted on him and told him fantastic stories (including the one about Fate and the dead black dog) to the historical figure, Balakian bridges the two selves she had not been able to integrate in her own life.

[39] Ibid., p. 211.
[40] Ibid., pp. 202, 204.
[41] H. Arendt, *The Origins of Totalitarianism* (New York: Harvest Books, 1976), p. 296.
[42] Ibid., p. 210.

This harmonizing is at once a fiction and a history that occupies an expanded space created by the multilayered acts of retrospection. For the reader, it is less a matter of sympathy as it is of a deeper understanding of what we know. Such recognition can afford a sense of belonging, a response against the forces of silence.

The memoir exceeds Balakian's personal remembrance of growing up and becoming a poet in suburban New Jersey. This surfeit significance gains over time and literally expands the text itself. The tenth anniversary edition adds two new chapters that give an account of Balakian's travels to Turkey and Syria where he explores his grandmother's path from Diarbekir, to the death camps of Der Zor, and then to Aleppo. The added material shifts our impressions of his grandmother once more by recasting her as the figure of the person in flight, a figure that is an enduring preoccupation of human rights. The deployment of its symbolism for the stateless by Balakian, therefore, updates the human rights framing for his text from 1997 to 2007. At the same time, these two added chapters perhaps make Nafina more spectral. She is less present than she was in the memoir as originally published. The narrative of flight distances the reader as it is a well-worn convention. But Balakian's lens also widens and, taking in the places he visits, he addresses the magnitude of the historical event. Reexamining the past is always an incomplete task to be renewed over and over.

What literature and the arts offer to an exploration of statelessness goes beyond the documentary or the illustrative. Such works help us imagine the new by engaging history and its deep marks on our present condition. They afford a type of recognition cast as discovery that urges us to witness and hence interrupt the ways the past continues into the present. Through this witness, the stateless find new interlocutors with whom to claim belonging. The broadened sense of participation in history that Balakian instils in his readers links explicitly to an ethos of human rights: Everything is pegged on the idea that human rights give legibility to the type of responsible subjectivity that extends belonging to the stateless. Once again, this is in reference to a kind of "existential" belonging, as Agier puts it, in advance of a legal resolution, but it keeps such a resolution in mind. If reading affords a sense of place while maintaining the discomforting irresolution that accompanies the condition of statelessness, it may turn us outward to coalition building rather than inward to a sense of individual moral uplift. For the displaced, moreover, keeping alive an evolving sense of belonging – crucial for owning one's historical subjectivity – requires receptive interlocutors willing to engage one's story.

8

"Either I Close My Eyes or I Don't"

The Evolution of Rights in Encounters between Sovereign Power and "Rightless" Migrants

Daniel Kanstroom[*]

Around the world, harsh migration enforcement has sparked courageous humanitarian reactions. This, in turn, has led to hundreds of criminal prosecutions of aid workers, volunteers, ship captains, and many others.[1] As a major 2020 report by Amnesty International entitled "Punishing Compassion" noted, "In recent years, human rights defenders and civil society organizations that have helped refugees and migrants have been subjected to unfounded criminal proceedings, undue restrictions of their activities, intimidation, harassment, and smear campaigns in several European countries."[2]

Such prosecutions ostensibly seek to vindicate the power of governments to control nation state borders. But, in a number of recent high-profile cases, they seem, ironically, to have achieved the opposite: They have vindicated, reinvigorated – and even inspired new forms of – basic human rights. Indeed, it is noteworthy that the subtitle of the Amnesty Report was "Solidarity on Trial."[3] This chapter explores how this has been happening and what it may portend.

Let us start with a brief introduction to perhaps the most famous such recent case. In 2017, Cédric Herrou, a French olive farmer, was criminally tried for having assisted unauthorized migrants in France, near the Italian border. Herrou, who had been arrested numerous times before for similar offenses, was described as being

---

[*] Thanks to the excellent editors of this volume and to Julie Dahlstrom and Katie Young for reading earlier drafts of this chapter and offering helpful suggestions. Thanks to Dean Vincent Rougeau for research support.
[1] N. Archer et al., "Hundreds of Europeans 'Criminalised' for Helping Migrants," *Open Democracy*, May 18, 2019, www.opendemocracy.net/en/5050/hundreds-of-europeans-criminalised-for-helping-migrants-new-data-shows-as-far-right-aims-to-win-big-in-european-elections/; *see also* L. Vosyliūtė and C. Conte, *Crackdown on NGOs and Volunteers Helping Refugees and Other Migrants*, www.resoma.eu/node/194 (ReSOMA, June 2019).
[2] Amnesty International, *Punishing Compassion: Solidarity on Trial in Fortress Europe* (2020), www.amnesty.org/download/Documents/EUR0118282020ENGLISH.PDF.
[3] Ibid.

part of a quasi-clandestine resistance against the French government's inhumane response to the European migration and refugee "crisis" that began around 2015.[4] He became an inspirational figure in some quarters as his actions – and the French government's reactions – provoked controversy and soul-searching around the world. Indeed, a *New York Times* writer analogized Herrou's movement to the Underground Railroad.[5]

Perhaps more significant than his actions, Herrou's legal cases have been both complex and unusually resonant. After one arrest in 2016, prosecutors declined to pursue charges because they accepted that Herrou was acting for "humanitarian reasons."[6] As he became increasingly prominent and continued his work with undocumented migrants, however, political and social pressures built. He was rearrested and charged with serious offenses. Herrou was, to say the least, unrepentant. At one of his trials, he testified, "My inaction and my silence would make me an accomplice, I do not want to be an accomplice."[7] Eric Ciotti, president of the Alpes-Maritimes department and a member of Parliament, held a quite different view: "Who can say with certainty that of the hundreds of migrants that Mr. Herrou has proudly brought across the border, there isn't hidden among them, a future terrorist?"[8] Ciotti argued more generally, "At the very moment when we need strict controls, Mr. Herrou's ideological, premeditated actions are a major risk."[9]

Herrou described his motivation clearly. When asked by a judge, "Why do you do all this," he described French migration enforcement as "ignoble."[10] He evoked the deepest, most basic human rights and humanitarian principles: "There are people dying on the side of the road. It's not right. There are children who are not safe." The prosecutor, however, argued that Herrou had demonstrated a "manifest intention to violate the law …. One can criticize it," he continued, "but it's got to be applied."[11] As the prosecutor bemoaned, "This trial springs from a communications strategy for a cause that I totally respect …. But I am the prosecutor. I must defend the law."[12]

---

[4] A. Nossiter, "An Underground Railroad in France, Moving African Migrants," *New York Times*, October 5, 2016, www.nytimes.com/2016/10/05/world/europe/france-italy-migrants-smuggling .html.

[5] Ibid.

[6] Ibid.

[7] K. G. Brown, "France Prosecuting Citizens for 'Crimes of Solidarity,'" *Aljazeera*, January 25, 2017, www.aljazeera.com/indepth/features/2017/01/france-prosecuting-citizens-crimes-solidarity-170122064151841.html.

[8] Ibid.

[9] A. Nossiter, "A Smuggler's Defense: 'There Are People Dying,'" *New York Times*, January 6, 2017, www.nytimes.com/2017/01/05/world/europe/cedric-herrou-migrant-smuggler-trial-france .html.

[10] Ibid.

[11] Ibid.

[12] Ibid.

Similarly polarized arguments about migration enforcement and humanitarian aid have been taking place in other criminal courts around the world. Two German "rescue" ship captains, Carola Rackete and Pia Klemp, have faced criminal prosecutions for rescuing distressed migrants at sea and bringing them to Lampedusa, Italy. In 2017, Italy had enacted a restrictive and highly controversial "Code of Conduct" pertaining to such rescues.[13] Captain Rackete's case was dismissed, but Captain Klemp faced up to twenty years in prison.[14] Echoing other human rights activists, she has, with critical irony, referred to her prosecution as a "crime of solidarity."[15] In Arizona, the US government has repeatedly prosecuted Scott Daniel Warren, who was arrested and tried after allegedly providing food, water, beds, and clean clothes to undocumented immigrants near Arizona's Sonoran Desert. His first trial resulted in a hung jury; the second in an outright acquittal, much to the dismay of the prosecutors.[16]

Such tectonic tension between government sovereign power to enforce migration rules and humanitarian or moral principles is not new. Criminal prosecutions of this type typically implicate notions of criminal intent (*mens rea*) and construction of ambiguous statutory terms. They may also implicate the so-called rule of lenity (the principle that statutes ought to be construed narrowly against the government so that people have a clear idea of what sort of conduct is criminally impermissible) or, more basically, notions of "necessity" as a defense to criminal prosecution. But Herrou prevailed through a different, new, and potentially deeply influential strategy. "Remember the last word in the French Republic's motto, 'Liberté, Egalité, Fraternité,'" his lawyer argued. "They are saying M. Herrou is endangering the

---

[13] "Italy's Code of Conduct for NGOs Involved in Migrant Rescue: Text," *Euronews*, March 8, 2017, www.euronews.com/2017/08/03/text-of-italys-code-of-conduct-for-ngos-involved-in-migrant-rescue.

[14] L. Tondo and J. Le Blond, "Italian Judge Orders Release of Ship Captain Who Rescued Refugees," *The Guardian*, July 2, 2019, www.theguardian.com/world/2019/jul/02/more-than-1m-raised-for-rescue-ship-captain-carola-rackete-italy. On January 17, 2020, the Supreme Court of Cassation of Italy rejected an appeal filed by Italian prosecutors of the dismissal of charges against Carola Rackete. "Italy's Highest Court Rejects Charges against Rescue Ship Captain," *The Maritime Executive*, January 17, 2020, www.maritime-executive.com/article/sea-rescue-captain-cleared-of-charges-for-unauthorized-port-entry.

[15] D. Boffey and L. Tondo, "Captain of Migrant Rescue Ship Says Italy 'Criminalising Solidarity,'" *The Guardian*, June 15, 2019, www.theguardian.com/world/2019/jun/15/captain-of-migrant-rescue-ship-says-italy-criminalising-solidarity; *see also* "La solidarité, plus que jamais un delit?" *Délinquants solidaires*, January 2017, http://snpespjj-fsu.org/IMG/pdf/delinquants_solidaires_manifeste.pdf ("Bien sûr, la solidarité n'a jamais été inscrite dans aucun code comme un délit. Cependant, des militants associatifs qui ne font que venir en aide à des personnes en situation de très grande précarité, victimes de décisions dangereuses, violentes, voire inhumaines, se retrouvent aujourd'hui face à la justice."); Brown, "France Prosecuting Citizens." *See also* F. Pusterla, "Legal Perspectives on Solidarity Crimes in Italy" (2020) *International Migration*, https://onlinelibrary.wiley.com/doi/abs/10.1111/imig.12740.

[16] R. Devereaux, "Bodies in the Borderland," *The Intercept*, May 4, 2019, https://theintercept.com/2019/05/04/no-more-deaths-scott-warren-migrants-border-arizona/.

Republic. On the contrary, I think he is *defending* its values."[17] Herrou was convicted at trial. However, in a landmark decision, the French Constitutional Council overturned the verdict and held, for the first time, that *fraternity* is a principle with constitutional value: "The freedom to help others for a humanitarian purpose, regardless of the regularity of their stay on the national territory follows from this principle."[18] In related, if less constitutionally portentous formulations, Captains Klemp and Rackete appealed to the ideal of *solidarity* in their defense. Warren's attorney, in closing argument, intoned to the jury, "Being a good Samaritan is not against the law, following the golden rule is not a felony."[19]

This chapter considers certain basic human rights and politico-legal questions illustrated by these cases and others like them: What is the full extent of the "law?" What effects might such cases have on human rights law in general, and migrant rights more specifically?[20] It suggests that these prosecutions illustrate how human rights laws and principles are tested – and sometimes expanded – at the *intersections* of sovereign power, law, and compelling moral claims.

The analysis herein transcends previous initiatives designed to protect "human rights defenders."[21] As migration enforcement has taken increasingly harsh and life-threatening turns in recent decades, new principles are evolving and connecting in deep ways with extant and inchoate constitutional principles. The more vigorous governments become in harsh migration enforcement, the more such principles are invoked, and the greater power they may assume. This implicates deep questions of constitutional legitimacy and migrant rights as it also illustrates how rights develop and evolve. The process of creating rights is not primarily confined – as some interpreters of Hannah Arendt argue – to the *internal* processes of the nation-state. Nor is it intrinsically tied to the so-called right to have rights of those with membership in a political community. Rather, rights often arise from encounters between raw state sovereign power and ostensibly extralegal, humanitarian actions for those at the lowest ebb of their power and with the least legal status (what Agamben has

---

[17] Nossiter, "A Smuggler's Defense" (emphasis added).

[18] Conseil constitutionnel décision no. 2018-717/718 QPC, July 6, 2018, www.conseil-constitutio nnel.fr/en/decision/2018/2018717_718QPC.htm.

[19] P. Ingram, "Scott Warren Found Not Guilty by Jury in No More Deaths Case," *Tucson Sentinel*, November 20, 2019, www.tucsonsentinel.com/local/report/112019_warren_trial_day_ 6/scott-warren-found-not-guilty-by-jury-no-more-deaths-case/.

[20] *See generally* D. Kanstroom, "'Alien' Litigation as Polity-Participation: The Positive Power of a 'Voteless Class of Litigants'" (2012) 21(2) *William & Mary Bill of Rights Journal* 399, https:// scholarship.law.wm.edu/wmborj/vol21/iss2/5/.

[21] *See, e.g.*, Declaration on the Right and Responsibility of Individuals, Groups and Organs of Society to Promote and Protect Universally Recognized Human Rights and Fundamental Freedoms, March 8, 1999, U.N. Doc. A/RES/53/144. The Declaration has been said to have "shifted the understanding of the human rights project: from a task accomplished mainly through the international community and States, to one that belongs to every person and group within society." *Report of the Special Rapporteur on the Situation of Human Rights Defenders*, U.N. Doc. A/73/215 (July 23, 2018), https://undocs.org/en/A/73/215.

called "bare life").[22] Such encounters demand a coherent legal response, which may be developed, if imperfectly, through such notions as *fraternité* and solidarity. These principles may enhance more well-accepted rights formulations such as dignity and equality as they engage the border between those who lack rights and those who seek to protect lives.

Such an analysis also helps us to understand and critique more technical initiatives, such as the European Union's 2002 "Facilitation Directive" and the so-called Facilitators' Package, which requests that member states criminalize behaviors that "facilitate" irregular entry, transit, and stay, aiming toward a consistent approach.[23] However, as a study commissioned by the European Parliament concluded, the European Union has brought about "legislative ambiguity and legal uncertainty."[24] Fundamental questions remain unresolved. As Captain Klemp poignantly argued, "I refuse to believe that we live in a Europe where you have to go to jail for saving lives in need."[25]

HERROU: "THERE ARE PEOPLE DYING ON THE SIDE OF THE ROAD. IT'S NOT RIGHT."[26]

The so-called European migration or refugee "crisis" that began in 2015 spawned not only reactionary politics and harsh policies but also creative legal responses at the

---

[22] G. Agamben, *Homo Sacer: Sovereign Power and Bare Life* (Stanford, CA: Stanford University Press, 1998).

[23] In 2002, the EU adopted the "Facilitation Directive," which defines "facilitation of unauthorized entry, transit and stay." Council of the European Union, *Council Directive 2002/90/EC of 28 November 2002 defining the facilitation of unauthorized entry, transit and residence*, OJ L 328, https://eur-lex.europa.eu/legal-content/EN/ALL/?uri=CELEX%3A32002L0090 (December 5, 2002). An accompanying Council Framework Decision strengthened the penal framework to prevent such facilitation. Council of the European Union, *Council framework Decision of 28 November 2002 on the strengthening of the penal framework to prevent the facilitation of unauthorized entry, transit and residence*, 2002/946/JHA, OJ L 328 (December 5, 2001), https://eurlex.europa.eu/legal-content/EN/ALL/?uri=CELEX:32002F0946.

[24] Directorate-General for Internal Policies, Policy Department C: Citizens' Rights and Constitutional Affairs, *Fit for Purpose? The Facilitation Directive and Criminalisation of Humanitarian Assistance to Irregular Migrants*, (Brussels: European Parliament, 2016), p. 10, www.europarl.europa.eu/RegData/etudes/STUD/2016/536490/IPOL_STU(2016)536490_EN .pdf; Directorate-General for Internal Policies of the Union, Policy Department for Citizens' Rights and Constitutional Affairs, *Fit for Purpose? The Facilitation Directive and the Criminalisation of Humanitarian Assistance to Irregular Migrants: 2018 Update* (Brussels: European Parliament, 2018), www.europarl.europa.eu/RegData/etudes/STUD/2018/608838/ IPOL_STU(2018)608838_EN.pdf; *see also* Amnesty International, *Punishing Compassion*, p. 20.

[25] J. Beenen and V. Wulf, "I've Never Been to Sea for Fun," *Basler Zeitung*, www.bazonline.ch/ ich-war-noch-nie-zum-spass-auf-see/story/31855284.

[26] A. Nossiter, "Farmer on Trial Defends Smuggling Migrants: 'I Am a Frenchman,'" *New York Times*, January 5, 2017, www.nytimes.com/2017/01/05/world/europe/cedric-herrou-migrant-smu ggler-trial-france.html.

intersections of sovereign power and basic human rights.[27] For example, a reinstatement of migration controls at the French–Italian border in November 2016 made the Roya Valley a dangerous crossing point for migrants seeking to enter France. In addition to other methods of police intimidation, harassment, and investigation, French prosecutors, since at least 2016, have brought criminal charges against activists and volunteers who assist migrants and asylum seekers.[28] Although many prosecutions resulted only in suspended sentences, they took a significant toll on the accused and contributed to the creation of "a hostile environment for humanitarian work in the region."[29] Indeed, a recent study found that between 2015 and 2019, at least eighty-three people have been investigated or prosecuted in Europe for facilitating irregular entry and transit, and eighteen were investigated or prosecuted for facilitating the stay or residence of migrants and asylum seekers.[30]

Pursuant to the French *Code de l'entrée et du séjour des étrangers et du droit d'asile* (CESEDA), any person who, directly or indirectly, facilitates the illegal *entry, circulation, or residence* of a foreign national in France or on the territory of another contracting party of the Schengen Agreement shall be sentenced to five years' imprisonment with a fine of €30,000.[31] The statute has long contained two exemptions: certain close relatives of the foreign national,[32] and the facilitation of illegal residence ("irregular stay") of a foreigner when the alleged act does not give rise to any direct or indirect compensation and only entails providing legal advice, food, accommodation, or health care in order to ensure decent living conditions for

---

[27] The term "crisis," though clearly inapt in various ways, is used herein to describe European migration events since 2015 because it was a staple of media reporting at the time and since. *See* "Migrant Crisis: Migration to Europe Explained in Seven Charts," *BBC*, March 4, 2016, www .bbc.com/news/world-europe-34131911 ("More than a million migrants and refugees crossed into Europe in 2015, sparking a crisis as countries struggled to cope with the influx, and creating division in the EU over how best to deal with resettling people."). Moreover, there has been substantial debate about the usage of the term "migrant," which connotes voluntariness, versus "refugee," to describe the people seeking to enter Europe in recent years. *See, e.g.,* C. Ruz, "The Battle over the Words Used to Describe Migrants," *BBC*, August 28, 2015, www.bbc.com/ news/magazine-34061097.

[28] Human Rights Watch, *Subject to Whim: The Treatment of Unaccompanied Migrant Children in the French Hautes-Alps* (2019), pp. 68–72, www.hrw.org/sites/default/files/report_pdf/franc eo919_web_o.pdf.

[29] Ibid.

[30] Vosyliūtė and Conte, *Crackdown*, p. 25 ("[Fifty-seven] persons are prosecuted simultaneously on both the grounds of the facilitation of entry and stay of migrants and other grounds including membership of a criminal organisation, sabotage or waste management contracts."); *see also* L. Fekete, F. Webber, and A. Edmond-Pettitt, *Humanitarianism: The Unacceptable Face of Solidarity* (London: Institute of Race Relations, 2017).

[31] Code of Entry and Residence of Foreigner and Right of Asylum (CESEDA), art. L. 622-1 www .legifrance.gouv.fr/affichCode.do;jsessionid=06DA61E11833B73124F3B0AEDCFD23B7 .tplgfr34s_2?idSectionTA=LEGISCTA000006147789&cidTexte=LEGITEXT000006070158& dateTexte=20200728; *see also* Editorial, "Fraternité" (2019) 15 *European Constitutional Law Review* 183–193.

[32] CESEDA, art. L. 622-4, §§ 1–2.

foreigners, or any other assistance aimed at preserving their dignity or physical integrity.[33] However, neither the facilitation of illegal *entry* nor illegal *circulation* (internal movement or transportation) are covered by the statutory exemptions.

Herrou and Pierre-Alain Mannoni, a marine ecology research professor, were criminally prosecuted for assisting several illegal immigrants en route from Sudan and Eritrea via Italy. Herrou was already well known for this work. Mannoni was arrested after he picked up three Eritrean women who had just crossed into France, intending to give them a ride to Nice. He described having seen them suffering on the roadside: "They are afraid, they are cold, they are exhausted, they have bandages on their hands, on their legs."[34] Herrou and Mannoni were convicted and given suspended prison sentences of, respectively, four and two months for facilitating the entry and/or circulation of illegal immigrants in France. Both appealed to the *Cour de cassation*, the supreme civil and criminal court in France. Their respective counsel then raised a "QPC" (*question prioritaire deconstitutionnalité*)[35] disputing the compatibility of the criminal statute with the principle of fraternity, in addition to other arguments. The *Cour de cassation* referred that question to the *Conseil constitutionnel*.

In its now famous decision of July 6, 2018, the *Conseil* held that fraternity is in fact a principle endowed with constitutional value in France.[36] The *Conseil* then concluded that the freedom to help one another, for humanitarian reasons – *regardless of whether the assisted person is legally residing or not within the French territory* – follows from the principle of fraternity. The *Conseil* made clear, however, that such freedom does not guarantee a general and absolute right of entry to – or even residence – on French national territory. The *Conseil* said that the legislature has the responsibility to "strike a balance" between freedom and fraternity in the fight against illegal immigration and a different constitutional objective: that of safeguarding "public order."[37] Thus, the decision contained an innovative approach to individual constitutional rights even as it reinforced rather traditional notions of fundamental government sovereign power and public order.

The *Conseil* essentially narrowed the offense and broadened the exemption as a matter of constitutional principle. It concluded, rather technically, that the legislature had failed to strike an appropriate balance between fraternity and public order by limiting the scope of the exemption to providing assistance for irregular stay

---

[33] Ibid., § 3.

[34] Human Rights Watch, *Subject to Whim*, p. 68.

[35] The QPC is a 2008 constitutional reform, 1958 Const. art. 61-1, that allows plaintiffs to raise an issue relating to the compatibility of legislation with the rights and freedoms guaranteed by the Constitution.

[36] Consiel constitutionnel decision No. 2018-717/718, July 6, 2018. The *Conseil* cited Article 2 of the Constitution, which contains the triadic Republican maxim, the Preamble, and Article 72-3, which refer to "the common ideal of liberty, equality and fraternity" between the French Republic and its overseas territories and populations. Ibid. ¶ 7.

[37] Ibid., ¶ 13.

("illegal residence"). The facilitation of illegal circulation (movement) was worthy of inclusion as an exemption to render the legislation constitutionally sound.[38] Recognizing the limitations of its legitimate role, however, the *Conseil* postponed the implementation of parts of its ruling. The immediate abolition of the contested parts of the statute might have had "clearly excessive consequences," for example, the effect of extending the criminal exemptions established in Article L. 622-4 to actions that facilitate or attempt to facilitate illegal entry into French territory. Therefore, it was up to the Parliament to determine the modifications that must be made in order to remedy the ascertained unconstitutional aspects of the prosecution.[39]

Simply put, the *Conseil* was treading a fine line between announcing rights-based enforcement limitations and superseding the state's sovereign authority to control its external borders. Still, as of the day of the publication of its decision, Herrou would be exempt from prosecution for "humanitarian acts that aimed to facilitate the circulation of illegal immigrants when the latter is ancillary to their residence."[40] A key, if rather complicated, line was maintained: "The assistance provided to the foreign national for his or her circulation does not necessarily give rise, as a consequence thereof, to an unlawful situation, in contrast with the assistance provided for his or her entry."[41] In other words, according to the *Conseil*, facilitating unlawful presence that *has already been achieved* is different for constitutional fraternity purposes than is assistance that enables entry.

The French legislature, called upon to act, did so quickly. The extant exemption was largely rewritten. It now covers all acts facilitating illegal circulation or residence that do not give rise to any direct or indirect compensation and that consist of providing legal advice, linguistic or social assistance, or any other assistance with an exclusively humanitarian objective.[42] The criminal cases were then remanded. Herrou was not necessarily completely liberated, either from this case or from future similar prosecutions. Indeed, the practical reach of the *Conseil* decision was, as noted, quite narrow. A key issue will now be "facilitation of entry." This remains an offense in France, whether or not motivated by humanitarian purpose.

Still, the Herrou decision has major implications. The substantive reliance on the fraternity principle – as a constitutional provision with real bite – may justifiably be called a milestone in French jurisprudence.[43] Indeed, the resonance of this case has led some to refer to the "Pandora's box" of fraternity as a fundamental rights

---

[38] Ibid., ¶¶ 13–15.
[39] Ibid., ¶ 23
[40] Ibid., ¶ 13.
[41] Ibid., ¶¶ 12, 24.
[42] *See* Art. 38 of Law No. 2018-778 of September 10, 2018 for contained immigration, an effective right to asylum and successful integration; Editorial, "Fraternité" at 4.
[43] Editorial, "Fraternité" at 5.

principle.⁴⁴ Moreover, the assertion by the *Conseil* of such broad interpretive and constitutional review power is a form of judicial authority that raises profound separation of powers questions. This is especially true in the legal realms of immigration and asylum, where deference to the government is typically strong.

To appreciate these phenomena more generally, let us now consider analogous cases in other legal systems: those of Captains Rackete and Klemp in Italy and of Scott Warren in the United States.

THE RESCUE CAPTAINS, RACKETE AND KLEMP: THE "CRIME OF SOLIDARITY"

The French *Conseil*'s affirmation of strong deference to government power at the border – an exception to its elaboration of the *fraternité* principle – is echoed in all legal systems. It has had particularly powerful consequences in Italy, where thousands of desperate migrants have faced death on the Mediterranean for many years.

From 2014 to 2018, more than 600,000 migrants attempted the perilous crossing from North Africa to Europe.⁴⁵ More than 10,000 people drowned.⁴⁶ In addition to government and EU-led rescue missions – many of which were widely criticized by human rights groups – European NGOs began to charter ships to monitor the waters off Libya, rescuing migrants and transporting them to Sicily.⁴⁷ This led Matteo Salvini, Italy's hardline, anti-immigrant interior minister, leader of the ultranationalist Lega (League) party, to close Italian waters to NGO rescue ships.⁴⁸ Malta soon followed suit. Several such boats were stranded at sea for weeks. Salvini, motivated by anti-immigrant sentiment and also concerned that France and other EU countries had not assumed what he saw as their share of the "burden," said: "We will use every lawful means to stop an outlaw ship, which puts dozens of migrants at risk for a dirty political game."⁴⁹ His understanding of the word "lawful" was soon to be tested.

---

⁴⁴ *See* G. Canivet, "La fraternité dans le droit constitutionnel français," in *Conférence en l'honneur de Charles Doherty Gonthier*, May 20–21, 2011, www.conseil-constitutionnel.fr/la-fraternite-dans-le-droit-constitutionnel-francais; *see also* Editorial, "Fraternité" at 5.

⁴⁵ C. Stephen, "Italy Bars Two More Refugee Ships from Ports," *The Guardian*, June 16, 2018, www.theguardian.com/world/2018/jun/16/italy-bars-two-more-refugee-ships-from-ports.

⁴⁶ *See* "Tracking Deaths Along Migratory Routes," *Missing Migrants*, https://missingmigrants.iom.int/region/mediterranean.

⁴⁷ Human Rights Watch, *EU/Italy/Libya: Disputes over Rescues Put Lives at Risk*, www.refworld.org/docid/5b646a9f4.html (2018).

⁴⁸ Stephen, "Italy Bars Two More Refugee Ships." The Lega governed Italy until September 2019 in a coalition with the antiestablishment Five Star Movement (M5S).

⁴⁹ L. Tondo, "Migrant Rescue Ship Defies Salvini's Ban to Enter Italian Port," *The Guardian*, June 26, 2019, www.theguardian.com/world/2019/jun/26/ngo-boat-carrying-migrants-defies-matteo-salvini-veto-lampedusa-italy.

In June 2019, following a grim, two-week standoff with Italian authorities, the Sea-Watch 3 docked at the Sicilian island of Lampedusa with forty-two rescued migrants on board.[50] One of the rescued migrants, a man from Ivory Coast, said in a video, "We can't hold on any longer. It's like we're in a prison because we are deprived of everything. Help us, think of us."[51] The captain, Carola Rackete, had knowingly defied Salvini's ban. In a video, Rackete said: "I know this is risky and that I will probably lose the boat, but the 42 shipwrecked on board are exhausted. I will bring them to safety."

Sea-Watch 3 declined to bring the migrants to Tripoli, as Italy had demanded. "Libya is not a safe country," said spokesperson Giorgia Linardi. "Forcibly taking rescued people back to a war-torn country, having them imprisoned and tortured, is a crime that we will never commit."[52] Salvini, however, called the Sea-Watch 3 "an outlaw ship." By early evening, the ship was about two to three nautical miles away from Lampedusa when it was boarded by Italian financial police. A Sea-Watch 3 spokesperson, Ruben Neugebauer, said: "We are waiting for Italian authorities now. There is not much more we can do. We will not run away."

Rackete was charged with criminal offenses, but the charges were dismissed in July 2019. Judge Alessandra Vella, among other concerns, opined that the crew's actions were justified under the circumstances "in the performance of duty" and found that neither Libya nor Tunisia were safe ports. The judge further concluded that Salvini's decree should not apply to rescue operations, but only to human trafficking. Salvini, unrepentant, said that Captain Rackete would be expelled to Germany because she was "dangerous for national security."[53]

In a related case, Pia Klemp, the captain of the *Iuventa*, another rescue vessel, was accused with nine others of aiding and abetting illegal migration in relation to their role in seeking to rescue people in danger after fleeing Libya. The charges carry a prison term of up to twenty years or a €15,000 fine for each person illegally brought to Italy.[54] This grim test of will, power, and principle shows little signs of definitive resolution. However, it has become clear that criminal law has become a fulcrum upon which to balance larger political and rights principles. A petition in support of Captain Klemp and her crew, signed by some 71,000 people, intones: "If the crew were convicted, it would be the end of humanity in Europe."[55] A court in Sicily

[50] Ibid.

[51] Sea-Watch International (@seawatch_intl), *Twitter* (June 24, 2019), https://twitter.com/sea watch_intl/status/1143251415374225409.

[52] Ibid.

[53] Sea-Watch International (@seawatch_intl), *Twitter* (July 2, 2019), https://twitter.com/seawatch_ intl/status/1146178020664889345.

[54] Boffey and Tondo, "Captain of Migrant Rescue Ship."

[55] *See* "Stop the Prosecution of Those Who Are Saving Lives in the Mediterranean Sea," *Change. org*, www.change.org/p/we-demand-impunity-for-saving-lives-at-the-mediterran-sea-freepia.

ruled in January 2019 that Salvini himself could be charged with kidnapping after he prevented refugees from disembarking from an Italian coast guard ship in August. "I confess," Salvini taunted back, "there is no need for a trial. It's true, I did it and I'd do it again."[56]

In June 2019, Italy's government closed Italian ports to migrant rescue ships and threatened fines of up to €50,000 and impounding of the vessel.[57] Claudia Lodesani, president of Médecins Sans Frontières in Italy, said: "The new decree is threatening legal principles and the duty of saving lives. It is like fining ambulances for carrying patients to hospital."[58] Carlotta Sami, the spokesperson for the United Nations High Commissioner for Refugees (UNHCR), said: "If we do not intervene soon, there will be a sea of blood."[59] In September 2019, a new agreement was reached pursuant to which Germany and France would take in 25 percent each of the migrants onboard another rescue ship, the *Ocean Viking*. Other EU states, including Italy, would process the others. Following a meeting with the European Council president, Donald Tusk, in Brussels, Conte said EU member states that refused to share the burden of the arrival of migrants should face financial penalties. Salvini, though out of power, was unwavering: "The new government has opened again its seaports to migrants," Salvini said, "The new ministers must hate our country. Italy is back to being Europe's refugee camp."[60]

Meanwhile, although the number of desperate migrants seeking to cross the Mediterranean has decreased recently, it is clear that risks have remained severe.[61] As the UNHCR notes, "it is likely that reductions to search and rescue capacity coupled with an uncoordinated and unpredictable response to disembarkation led to an increased death rate as people continued to flee their countries due to conflict, human rights violations, persecution, and poverty."[62]

---

[56] E. Schumacher, "Italy: Court Rules Far-Right Leader Salvini Can Be Charged with Kidnapping," *DW*, January 24, 2019, www.dw.com/en/italy-court-rules-far-right-leader-salvini-can-be-charged-with-kidnapping/a-47224819.

[57] L. Tondo, "Italy Adopts Decree that Could Fine Migrant Rescuers up to €50,000," *The Guardian*, June 15, 2019, www.theguardian.com/world/2019/jun/15/italy-adopts-decree-that-could-fine-migrant-rescue-ngo-aid-up-to-50000.

[58] Ibid.

[59] Ibid.

[60] L. Tondo, "Italy's New Government Says Migrants Can Disembark from Rescue Boat," *The Guardian*, September 14, 2019, www.theguardian.com/world/2019/sep/14/italys-new-government-says-migrants-can-disembark-from-rescue-boat.

[61] C. Mainwaring, "At Europe's Edge: Migration and Crisis in the Mediterranean," *Border Criminologies*, October 14, 2019, www.law.ox.ac.uk/research-subject-groups/centre-criminology/centreborder-criminologies/blog/2019/10/europes-edge; *see also* "Mediterranean Migrant Arrivals Reach 76,558 in 2019; Deaths Reach 1,071," *IOM*, November 10, 2019, www.iom.int/news/mediterranean-migrant-arrivals-reach-76558-2019-deaths-reach-1071.

[62] UNHCR, *Desperate Journeys: Refugees and Migrants Arriving in Europe and at Europe's Borders, January–December 2018* (2019), https://data2.unhcr.org/en/documents/download/67712#_ga=2.70740368.1640035127.1578321369-48067902.1578321369.

WARREN: WATER IN THE DESERT

The government failed in its attempt to criminalize basic human kindness.[63]

At least 7,000 migrants who have tried to cross the parched lands of the southern United States near the Mexican border since the 1990s have died doing so.[64] The deaths are a terrible consequence of "prevention through deterrence," a border control strategy first developed during the Clinton administration.[65] The Border Patrol built barriers in traditional entry points near urban areas such as El Paso to push border crossers out into more remote and dangerous terrain. Doris Meissner, then-Commissioner of the Immigration and Naturalization Service (which at the time included the Border Patrol), later described the plan in remarkably optimistic terms, suggesting that policymakers believed that once people saw how perilous the new routes were, they would stop trying. As Meissner put it in 2019, "The deaths weren't contemplated. Obviously, one can't be anything but regretful about the deaths."[66] As a 1994 Border Patrol memorandum had put it, however, the essential idea from the beginning was to disrupt traditional entry and smuggling routes so that "illegal traffic will be deterred or forced over *more hostile terrain, less suited for crossing and more suited for enforcement.*"[67] The planners knew that those who were thus compelled to avoid traditional routes could "find themselves in mortal danger." Indeed, the Border Patrol cruelly envisioned that "violence will increase as effects of the strategy are felt."[68]

The human costs of this strategy soon became horribly clear. By 1998, the Border Patrol launched the "Border Safety Initiative," a set of measures to warn migrants about risks, rescue those in trouble, and quantify border-crossing deaths. But the initiative left it up to leaders in each of the Border Patrol's nine Southwest border sectors to decide which bodies to count and how. By the mid-2000s, the rising death toll continued to raise hard questions. In a 2006 report, grimly entitled, "Border-Crossing Deaths Have Doubled Since 1995," the Government Accountability Office found that the Border Patrol had consistently understated the numbers of deaths.[69] Moreover, federal authorities had failed to ask local law enforcement agencies,

---

[63] J. Augilera, "Humanitarian Scott Warren Found Not Guilty after Retrial for Helping Migrants at Mexican Border," *Time*, November 21, 2019, https://time.com/5732485/scott-warren-trial-not-guilty/.

[64] B. Ortega, "Border Patrol Failed to Count Hundreds of Migrant Deaths on US Soil," *CNN*, May 15, 2018, www.cnn.com/2018/05/14/us/border-patrol-migrant-death-count-invs/index.html.

[65] U.S. Border Patrol, *Border Patrol Strategic Plan 1994 and Beyond* (1994), https://assets.documentcloud.org/documents/5987025/Border-Patrol-Strategic-Plan-1994-and-Beyond.pdf.

[66] Ibid.

[67] Ibid.

[68] Ibid.

[69] U.S. Government Accountability Office, *Illegal Immigration: Border-Crossing Deaths Have Doubled since 1995; Border Patrol's Efforts to Prevent Deaths Have Not Been Fully Evaluated* (August 2006), www.gao.gov/new.items/d06770.pdf.

coroner's offices, and others about cases. Still, diversion to hostile terrain has been a major part of US policy now for a quarter century.

Scott Warren, when arrested, was a thirty-seven-year-old geographer and a volunteer with No More Deaths (aka No Más Muertes), an aid group that leaves water and food for migrants who seek to cross the deadly Sonoran Desert. This group, along with others, was inspired by the so-called Sanctuary Movement of the late 1980s.[70] As described by one of the Sanctuary Movement's leaders, Reverend John Fife of the Southside United Presbyterian Church in Tucson, No More Deaths left water and provided medical aid. But it also documented abuses on the border, as "the most aggressive organization to challenge Border Patrol violations of human rights." Fife noted, "If you look at the founding principles of the Sanctuary Movement and No More Deaths, they're the same: 'civil initiative.'" As he elaborated, "if government isn't fulfilling its obligations, it's up to civil society members to step in."[71] As one local activist put it,

> When you think of how tiny our town is, and when you think of the number of bodies that were recovered last year – like 58 or 60 bodies that were recovered here – I can't imagine that happening in any town in our country and not having people be up in arms … you have to do something. You don't want to be a cemetery. These are human lives.[72]

Warren was arrested by Border Patrol agents on January 17, 2018.[73] No More Deaths had just published a report that had implicated the Border Patrol in the destruction of thousands of gallons of water left for migrants in the desert.[74] As one reporter noted, it now seemed that the Border Patrol was "punching back."[75] The agents caught Warren with two Central American migrants. Warren told the agents that he had given the migrants shelter, food, and first aid. All of this seemed to the agents to clearly violate US law, which bars "harboring" and "transporting" unauthorized migrants. The Border Patrol and prosecutors – unmoved by Warren's humanitarian motives – argued that he was assisting the migrants to evade custody. He was charged with two counts of harboring undocumented immigrants and one count of conspiracy to harbor and transport. He faced some twenty years in prison. Also, in a particularly bizarre exercise of state power, Warren, along with nine other volunteers, faced federal charges of littering for leaving water on the Cabeza Prieta National Wildlife Refuge.[76]

---

[70] This movement, some of whose members had been convicted at that time, also inspired civil legal action that led to the creation of Temporary Protected Status in US law. Ibid.
[71] Ibid.
[72] Ibid.
[73] Devereaux, "Bodies in the Borderland."
[74] Ibid.
[75] Ibid.
[76] Ibid.

At Warren's first trial in June 2019, the jury failed to reach a verdict.[77] The government quickly sought a retrial, although it dropped the conspiracy charge. After a six-day retrial in Tucson, Arizona, in November 2019, the jury found Warren not guilty after about two hours of deliberation. Reports from the trial and conversations with jurors might seem to indicate that Warren's case was quite different from those of Herrou and the captains. His lawyers did not mount an explicit "necessity defense" (i.e., arguing that Warren should not be criminally punished for avoiding a greater harm to others). Nor did they expressly argue for jury nullification to override the letter of the law in the pursuit of abstract ideals of higher justice. Warren's lawyers simply argued that the government had not proven criminal intent, something that was surely rather nebulous under these circumstances. The government had devoted enormous resources to investigation and surveillance. They had evidence. Warren, for example, was observed with the migrants pointing northward. Prosecutors argued that this meant he was guiding the migrants away from the border and deeper into the United States. But Warren testified that he was merely showing them local mountains.[78] He said that the only available highway ran between them. If they needed rescue, that's where they should go. But if they strayed outside of those mountains, they would find an active US bombing range and deadly desert.[79]

How should a jury decide such questions? One can hear the echoes of Warren's humanitarian motives and sense the larger debates about harm and justice in every facet of the case. Warren testified that the work he and others do is similar to that of the International Red Cross: neutral provision of aid amidst humanitarian crisis. From this, one gleans a hint of necessity and nullification. Such work, he said, is legal. The jury accepted this, apparently completely. One juror reportedly said, "He

---

[77] This was not the first encounter between No More Deaths and federal law enforcement. *See* ibid. In 2005, volunteers Shanti Sellz and Daniel Strauss were arrested and charged with multiple felony smuggling and conspiracy counts, after driving three seriously ill migrants to John Fife's church for medical care. "Volunteers Fight Arrests for Aiding Illegals," *Associated Press*, April 2, 2006, www.deseret.com/2006/4/2/19946256/volunteers-fight-arrests-for-aiding-ille gals. US District Judge Raner C. Collins dismissed the charges on the grounds that the volunteers had followed a protocol that they understood to be in line with the law, with full knowledge of the Border Patrol. D. Grossman, "'No More Deaths' Volunteer Charges Tossed," *Arizona Daily Star*, September 2, 2006, https://tucson.com/news/local/border/no-more-deaths-volunteer-charges-tossed/article_86d4dcod-ddf7-5b9c-9f8e-e5303d83edb2.html. In 2008, Daniel J. Millis, caught with other volunteers in an SUV loaded with water jugs on the Buenos Aires National Wildlife Refuge, was convicted of littering. He had been found guilty of "Disposal of Waste" pursuant to 50 C.F.R. § 27.94(a). His conviction was overturned by a 2-to-1 vote at the Ninth Circuit. The judges found that the term "garbage" in the regulation under which Millis was prosecuted is ambiguous, and applied the "rule of lenity" to vacate the conviction. *United States v. Millis*, 621 F.3d 914, 918 (9th Cir. 2010); *see generally*, K. Campbell, "Humanitarian Aid Is Never a Crime? The Politics of Immigration Enforcement and the Provision of Sanctuary" (2012) 63 *Syracuse Law Review* 71.

[78] Devereaux, "Bodies in the Borderland."

[79] Ibid.

seemed like a humanitarian that was just trying to help. He seemed very kind and not like he was trying to harbor somebody or do anything illegal at all."[80] As another juror put it, nullification of the law was not necessary: "There was just too much of a lack of evidence to convict," he said. "I think we can all agree, it was the intent . . . ." But a third juror chimed in after the trial: "I think we all agreed," she said, "what he and these people do is fantastic."[81]

In the end, Warren's jury – through their interpretation of his intent – policed the border between law and deep values. The prosecutor, a US attorney, did not see it this way. After the not guilty verdict, he promised that in future cases his office "won't distinguish between whether somebody is trafficking or harboring for money or whether they're doing it out of, you know, what I would say is a misguided sense of social justice or belief in open borders or whatever."[82] One of Warren's lawyers, Amy Knight, was offended by the word "misguided," seeing it as "a value judgment, not a legal judgment." As she paraphrased the instructions that had been given to the jury, "If you're doing it out of a sense of social justice, then you don't intend to violate the law."[83]

THE POTENTIAL POWER AND LIMITATIONS OF FRATERNITY

I speak an open and disengaged language, dictated by no passion but that of humanity . . . my country is the world, and my religion is to do good.[84]

The cases of Cédric Herrou, Captains Rackete and Klemp, and Scott Warren clearly involve distinct, technical legal questions and different sociopolitical backdrops. However, the fundamental issues they present have much in common, whether understood through the lens of fraternity, solidarity, necessity, or more general implicit values of justice and fairness that always guide interpretations of facts and law. These questions, most simply put, are:

1. What legal principles may be invoked when humanitarian actions impede or conflict with government power over "unauthorized" migrants?
2. Where do such principles come from and how do they evolve?

The idea that a particular doctrinal formulation is all one might need to inspire judges and legislatures to humanize border practices and to protect the fundamental rights of migrants is of course a form of magical thinking that must be resisted. Still,

---

[80] Ibid.
[81] Ibid.
[82] Ibid.
[83] Ibid.
[84] T. Paine, *The Rights of Man* (Ware: Wordsworth Editions Ltd., 1996), part II, p. 181.

the potential of power of fraternity, compared to solidarity, necessity, equality or even dignity, is worth considering.

Fraternity

Although the roots of fraternity as a philosophical principle may be traced back through antiquity, its resonant strength – and certain historically well-known and ideological objections to it – may be most directly traced back to its origins as a motto of the French Revolution.[85] Though its evolution as a politico-legal concept in France was rather slow and tentative, it was eventually incorporated into the 1958 Constitution.

Though some suggest – following Diderot – that fraternity may be largely a euphemism for the ostensibly broader concept of "humanity," fraternity is a narrower ideal that, in some respects, may paradoxically be a stronger source of obligation than humanity to those who arrive from outside of a particular civil society.[86]

Some, however, view fraternity as a rather limited, highly interpersonal concept. Wilson Carey McWilliams, for example, in a 1973 book entitled *The Idea of Fraternity in America*, saw fraternity as "a bond based on intense interpersonal affection." It was thus "limited in the number of persons and in the social space to which it can be extended." Moreover, it "implies a necessary tension with loyalty to society at large."[87] But this seems a rather parsimonious approach when compared to obligations that go beyond charity and beyond narrow conceptions of interpersonal relations or community.[88] Since the Enlightenment, fraternity has often been said to transcend a "feeling of a community and the demand for communion."[89] Rather, it "postulated an order based on the equality of men."[90] Whether that order – what Robespierre once called *les doux noeuds de la fraternité* ("the sweet knots of brotherhood") – is confined to the "Fatherland" or extends beyond that to a global community of values has always been an important if implicit question at the heart of the fraternity principle.[91]

---

[85] C. D. Gonthier, "Liberty, Equality, Fraternity: The Forgotten Leg of the Trilogy, or Fraternity: The Unspoken Third Pillar of Democracy" (2000) 45(3) *McGill Law Journal* 567–589 at 570.

[86] Ibid. It may certainly be stronger once they have become, in any way, a part of the fraternal community. But even before that universal "brotherhood" seems a stronger principle than simply being members of the same species.

[87] W. C. McWilliams, *The Idea of Fraternity in America* (Berkeley: University of California Press, 1973), p. 7.

[88] P. Vernière, *"L'idée d'humanité au XVIII siècle"* in *Lumières ou clair-obscur?* (Paris: Presses universitaires de France, 1987), p. 186 aux pp. 187–188 (quoted in Gonthier, "Liberty, Equality, Fraternity" at 571).

[89] Ibid.

[90] Ibid.

[91] J. Boulad-Ayoub, *Contre nous de la tyrannie. . .: Des relations idéologiques entre Lumières et Révolution* (Quebec: Hurtubise HMH, 1989), p. 58.

More recent invocations have sought to situate fraternity within broader theories of justice, fairness, equality, and liberty.[92] As former Canadian Supreme Court Justice Charles Gonthier wrote, fraternity advances core values that relate to *forming a community*.[93] It is in this sense a dynamic, evolutionary, aspirational, and idealized concept. Its related values, which he termed "interrelated threads weaving the cloth of fraternity," include empathy, cooperation, commitment, responsibility, fairness, trust, and equity.[94] If the essence of fraternity is based on membership in a community, however, it is puzzling how it could ground a theory of rights to outsiders, or "others." McWilliams' argument that fraternity "is limited in the number of persons and in the social space to which it can be extended" could thus be a significant limitation.[95] The broader view, as Pope Francis recently explained, is much more powerful: "Universal fraternity and social friendship are … two inseparable and equally vital poles in every society."[96] Fraternity, understood in this way, is "born not only of a climate of respect for individual liberties, or even of a certain administratively guaranteed equality. Fraternity necessarily calls for something greater, which in turn enhances freedom and equality."[97] Social friendship and universal fraternity both "necessarily call for an acknowledgement of *the worth of every human person*, always and everywhere."[98] Most relevant for our purposes: "No one, then, can remain excluded because of his or her place of birth, much less because of privileges enjoyed by others who were born in lands of greater opportunity. The limits and borders of individual states cannot stand in the way of this …."[99] As Justice Gonthier noted, "fraternity may be universal in its object," but it has specific applications.[100] Broad universal values of fraternity may, for example, be seen – in a relevant analogy to the Herrou matter – in the rather narrowly fraternal Quebec Charter of Human Rights and Freedoms, which contains a unique Good Samaritan provision.[101]

---

[92] *See e.g.*, J. Rawls, *A Theory of Justice* (Cambridge, MA: Harvard University Press, 1971), p. 105.

[93] Gonthier, "Liberty, Equality, Fraternity" at p. 570.

[94] Ibid.

[95] McWilliams, *The Idea of Fraternity in America*, p. 7.

[96] Encyclical Letter *Fratelli Tutti* of the Holy Father Francis on Fraternity and Social Friendship, October 3, 2020, Par. 142, http://w2.vatican.va/content/francesco/en/encyclicals/documents/pap a-francesco_20201003_enciclica-fratelli-tutti.html.

[97] Ibid., ¶ 103.

[98] Ibid., ¶ 106.

[99] Ibid., ¶ 121.

[100] Gonthier, "Liberty, Equality, Fraternity" at p. 575.

[101] Section 2 reads:
  Every human being whose life is in peril has a right to assistance.
    Every person must come to the aid of anyone whose life is in peril, either personally or calling for aid, by giving him the necessary and immediate physical assistance, unless it involves danger to himself or a third person, or he has another valid reason.
  Quebec Charter of Human Rights and Freedoms, chp. 6, § 2, June 27, 1975, http://legisquebec .gouv.qc.ca/en/showdoc/cs/c-12.

If fraternity were to be limited only to Good Samaritan ideals, however, then it would seem to amount to little more than charity, a relatively uncontroversial notion that does not imply much in the way of rights. The Herrou case, however, implies that fraternity is potentially more resonant and powerful than this. And for this reason, it has provoked historically well-known objections. Conservatives have long recoiled at the abstract ideal of love of "mankind," particularly when clothed in the language of brotherhood. James Fitzjames Stephen, for example, in his 1873 critique of the neo-utilitarian philosophy of John Stuart Mill in *Liberty, Equality, Fraternity*, offered a stinging rejoinder to proponents of universal fraternity. Though admitting as "common ground" that "upon some terms and to some extent it is desirable that men should wish well to and should help each other," Stephen expressed a feeling of disgust ... for expressions of general philanthropy" that he saw as "an insulting intrusion."[102]

The potential power of fraternity as a legal concept derives from the fact that it does not *necessarily* demand a clear choice between a cosmopolitan view of rights and a Burkean idea of rights as "a patrimony derived from ... forefathers."[103] Fraternity imbues charity with implications of universal obligation. This accounts for its invocation as the spiritual admonition in the very first article Universal Declaration of Human Rights: "All human beings are born free and equal in dignity and rights. They are endowed with reason and conscience and should act towards one another in a spirit of brotherhood."[104] In its recognition of the constitutional principle of fraternity in the Herrou matter, the *Conseil constitutionnel* thus articulated a humanistic, universal interpretation ideal deeply related to the Declaration and to Kant's duty of "hospitality."[105]

Scott Warren's lawyer argued to the jury, "Being a good samaritan [sic] is not against the law, following the golden rule is not a felony."[106] One could perhaps view this as an implicit invocation of fraternity. But it is a narrower argument against proof of alleged criminal intent. The potential power of fraternity is stronger: as a constitutional principle, it *could* – as some legal commentators have advocated – override government attempts to criminalize all sorts of arguably socially just behaviors.[107] This is especially powerful in migration cases where the principle

---

[102] J. Fitzjames Stephan, *Liberty, Equality, Fraternity* (London: H. Elder & Co., 1874), p. 106.

[103] E. Burke, *Reflections on the Revolution in France: A Critical Edition* (J. C. D. Clark ed., Stanford, CA: Stanford University Press, 2001).

[104] Universal Declaration of Human Rights, December 10, 1948, United Nations General Assembly Res. 217A(III), pmbl.

[105] I. Kant, *Perpetual Peace and Other Essays on Politics, History and Morals* (T. Humphrey, trans., Hackett: 1983), pp. 118–120.

[106] Ingram, "Scott Warren Found Not Guilty."

[107] *See* Gonthier, "Liberty, Equality, Fraternity" at 570; *see also* G. Canivet, "La fraternité"; J. C. Colliard, "Liberté, égalité, fraternité," in *L'État de droit: mélanges en l'honneur de Guy Braibant* (Dalloz, 1996), pp. 100–101, www.worldcat.org/title/etat-de-droit-melanges-en-lhon neur-de-guy-braibant/oclc/247045796/editions?referer=di&editionsView=true; M. Borgetto,

has a dual dimension: "a collective one based on solidarity and an individual one based on tolerance."[108]

Solidarity

Solidarity, too, may have this dual dimension. Solidarity has typically been viewed as an internal value *within* communities.[109] However, it also may apply – like humanity and fraternity – to global issues. As Pope Francis has put it, "No one can remain insensitive to the inequalities that persist in the world."[110] He then called for "a valuable lesson in solidarity, a word that is too often forgotten or silenced because it is uncomfortable," as he appealed to "those in possession of greater resources, to public authorities and to all people of good will who are working for social justice: never tire of working for a more just world, marked by greater solidarity."[111] Other exponents of the Catholic social teaching ideal of solidarity similarly emphasize the relationship between fraternity and solidarity. Pope Benedict XVI once noted that "As society becomes ever more globalized, it makes us neighbours but does not make us brothers."[112] On this view, solidarity is "simply the demand of fraternity, that we treat each other as brothers and sisters."[113] The Catechism of the Catholic Church thus emphasizes solidarity "among nations *and peoples*. International solidarity is a requirement of the moral order; world peace depends in part upon this."[114]

"La notion de fraternité en droit public français. Le passé, le présent et l'avenir de la solidarité" (1993) 48(1) *Revue internationale de droit comparé* 215–217.

[108] C. Dadomo, "'Liberty, Equality, Fraternity': The French Constitutional Court Confirms the Constitutional Status and Force of the Principle of Fraternity," *EU Law and Policy*, September 21, 2018, https://eulawpol57.wordpress.com/2018/09/21/liberty-equality-fraternity-the-french-con stitutional-court-confirms-the-constitutional-status-and-force-of-the-principle-of-fraternity/ ("By ruling that 'fraternity is a constitutional principle from which ensues the freedom to assist others for humanitarian reasons without consideration as to whether the assisted person is legally residing or not within the French territory' (paras 7 and 8 of the ruling), the Constitutional Court not only stresses the humanitarian dimension of acts of assistance but also provides the freedom to assist a general scope of application irrespective of whether the assisted person has a legal right or not to reside in France.").

[109] *See e.g.*, P. Kropotkin, *Mutual Aid: A Factor of Evolution* (New York: McClure Phillips & Co., 1902); E. Durkheim, *The Division of Labor in Society* (George Simpson, trans., New York: The Free Press, 1947).

[110] Address of Pope Francis, *Visit to the Community of Varginha (Maguinhos): Apostolstic Journey to Rio de Janeiro on the Occasion of the XXVIII World Youth Day*, July 25, 2013, www.vatican .va/content/francesco/en/speeches/2013/july/documents/papa-francesco_20130725_gmg-comu nita-varginha.html.

[111] Ibid.

[112] Pope Benedict XVI, Encyclical Letter *Caritas in Veritate*, June 29, 2009, www.vatican.va/ content/benedict-xvi/en/encyclicals/documents/hf_ben-xvi_enc_20090629_caritas-in-veritate .html.

[113] Ibid.

[114] Pope John Paul II, *Catechism of the Catholic Church* (1992), part 3, § 1, chapter 2, art. 3, www .vatican.va/archive/ccc_css/archive/catechism/p3s1c2a3.htm (emphasis added).

It is noteworthy that activists such as Cédric Herrou and Captains Rackete and Klemp sometimes refer, ironically, to the crimes with which they have been charged as crimes of solidarity.[115] This reflects how solidarity operates both as a normative principle and as legal doctrine in Europe. Article 2 of the 1993 Treaty on European Union (TEU) lists values that are common to the member states.[116] It then states that these values are common in a society in which "pluralism, non-discrimination, tolerance, justice, solidarity and equality between women and men prevail."[117] The EU Charter of Fundamental Rights lists solidarity more prominently and specifically as a value. Chapter IV of the Charter, "Solidarity" (which precedes the chapter on "Citizens' Rights"), lists rights of workers, prohibits child labor, protects family rights (including protections against dismissal due to maternal and guaranteeing parental leaves), social security, health care, access to "services of general economic interest," environmental protection, and consumer protection.[118] Thus, solidarity appears in the European Union as a "vector of concrete social rights . . . aimed at the *protection* of individuals as such or in their economic capacity."[119]

Solidarity, like some narrow visions of fraternity, may also work as an exclusionary principle. This can be seen in situations where solidarity is not viewed as a universal construct, but is limited to particular communities. Article 67 § 2 of the Treaty on the Functioning of the European Union, for example, mandates a common policy on asylum, immigration, and external border control, which is based on *solidarity between member states* but which is simply "fair" toward third-country nationals.[120]

Necessity

The lawyers in Warren's case and those planning the defense of Pia Klemp also rely on the defense of necessity. This defense, a form of justification, has been most simply defined as "the assertion that conduct promotes some value higher than the value of literal compliance with the law."[121] Others have called it the choice of "the

---

[115] *See also*, L. Fekete, "Europe: Crimes of Solidarity" (2009) 50(4) *Race and Class* 83–97; M. Tazzioli, "Crimes of Solidarity: Migration and Containment through Rescue" (2018) 2.01(2) *Radical Philosophy* 1–10, www.radicalphilosophy.com/commentary/crimes-of-solidarity#:~:text= Crimes%20of%20solidarity%20put%20in,migrants'%20acts%20of%20spatial%20disobedience .andtext=In%20this%20way%2C%20crimes%20of,crisis'%20and%20'security.

[116] Treaty on the European Union, November 1, 1993, www.refworld.org/docid/3ae6b39218.html ("[H]uman dignity, freedom, democracy, equality, the rule of law and respect for human rights, including the rights of persons belonging to minorities.").

[117] Consolidated Version of the Treaty on European Union, December 13, 2007, 2008/C 115/01, www.refworld.org/docid/4b179f222.html.

[118] Charter of Fundamental Rights of the European Union, December 18, 2000, 2000/C 364/01, www.europarl.europa.eu/charter/pdf/text_en.pdf.

[119] Editorial, "Fraternité" at 2.

[120] Treaty on the Functioning of the European Union, 2012/C 326/01, tit. V, chapter 1, art. 67, § 2, https://eur-lex.europa.eu/legal-content/EN/TXT/?uri=CELEX%3A12012E%2FTXT.

[121] G. Williams, *The Criminal Law* § 229 (2nd ed., London: Stevens & Sons, 1953).

lesser evil.”[122] It is obviously related to broader concepts within the Anglo-American adversarial system, such as jury nullification, and to related defenses such as "excuse.”[123] But there is a basic distinction between an excuse and a justification: that between being "forgivably wrong" versus being *right*. Thus, a person who claims justification does not seek pardon, nor argue for mitigation or excuse. Justification implies that there is no need for forgiveness.[124]

Though its roots in Anglo-American law are complex and interwoven with various semantic formulations, the basic idea of necessity has long resided at the intersection between positive law and moral principle.[125] Sir James Fitzjames Stephen, in his 1883 treatise, referred to the necessity defense as "one of the curiosities of law," and a subject on which the law of England was "so vague that if cases raising the question should ever occur the judges would practically be able to lay down any rule which they considered expedient.”[126] One might well ponder whether this renders necessity too vague to be a meaningful *legal* principle, perhaps more a matter of discretion than law.[127] In fact, necessity has sometimes been used as an epithet against judges themselves. A nineteenth-century Texas Justice of the Peace was reportedly known as "Old Necessity" because he knew so little about the law. Deadwood judge, W. R. Keithly, apparently had the same moniker during the Gold Rush.[128] Others, however, have historically sided with Sir Walter Scott that although the law of necessity "is not well furnished with precise rules … necessity creates the law; it supersedes rules; and whatever is reasonable and just in such circumstances is likewise legal.”[129]

The way in which the necessity principle has informed the development of international law illustrates its potential limitations.[130] Robert Phillimore cites

---

[122] E. Arnolds and N. Garland, "The Defense of Necessity in Criminal Law: The Right to Choose the Lesser Evil" (1975) 65(3) *Journal of Criminal Law and Criminology* 289–301, https://scholarlycommons.law.northwestern.edu/cgi/viewcontent.cgi?article=5903&context=jclc.

[123] *See* ibid. ("To justify does not mean to excuse; justification is a circumstance which actually exists and which makes harmful conduct proper and noncriminal, while excuse is a circumstance which excuses the actor from criminal liability even though the actor was technically not justified in doing what he did.") (citing *Final Report of the National Commission on Reform of Federal Criminal Laws*, § 601 (1971)).

[124] Ibid., p. 290.

[125] For a general overview, see A. Brudner, "A Theory of Necessity" (1987) 7(3) *Oxford Journal of Legal Studies* 339–368.

[126] J. Fitzjames Stephen, *A History of the Criminal Law of England* (London: Macmillan & Co, 1883), vol. II, p. 108.

[127] *See* D. Kanstroom, "Surrounding the Hole in the Doughnut: Discretion and Deference in U.S. Immigration Law" (1997) 71 *Tulane Law Review* 703–818.

[128] J. Agnew, *Crime, Justice and Retribution in the American West 1850–1900* (Jefferson, NC: McFarland & Company, 2017), p. 180.

[129] *The Gratitudine*, 3 Rob. Adm. R. 240 (1801); R. A. Anderson (ed.), *Wharton's Criminal Law*, 5 vols. (12th ed., Rochester, NY: Lawyer's Cooperative Publishing, 1957), vol 1, chapter 3, part 7, sub. 126.

[130] R. Phillimore, *Commentaries upon International Law* (London: Hodges, Foster & Co., 1871), vol 2.

Lord Stowell, who opined that "a clear necessity will be a sufficient justification of everything that is done fairly and with good faith under it."[131]

One's potential admiration for Cédric Herrou or Captains Rackete and Klemp should not obscure the difficulties inherent in the defense of necessity, however. Its invocation is always – indeed inevitably – highly controversial.[132] It arose famously in nineteenth-century cases of cannibalism among those adrift on the high seas. The British Home Office[133] and judges reportedly worried that if yielding to temptation were sanctioned, necessity might become "the legal cloak for unbridled passion and atrocious crime."[134] Perhaps the most salient example of this is that necessity was invoked as a defense to prosecution by the defendants at Nuremberg, whose counsel argued that a necessity defense "must also be considered one of the fundamental principles of the criminal law of all civilized nations."[135]

THE (RE-)BIRTH OF RIGHTS THROUGH FRATERNITY, SOLIDARITY, AND NECESSITY

Hannah Arendt famously (and chillingly) noted the failures of abstract human rights principles to protect "national minorities" and stateless people prior to the Second World War: "The world found nothing sacred in the abstract nakedness of being human."[136] Arendt reasoned that, to have meaningful rights, individuals must be more than mere human beings; they must be members of a political community. She called this right the "right to have rights." As she wrote in *The Origins of Totalitarianism*: "We became aware of the existence of a right to have rights [to live in a framework where one is judged by one's actions and opinions] and a right to belong to some kind of organized community, only when millions of people emerged who had lost and could not regain these rights."[137]

---

[131] Ibid., p. 110.

[132] The phrase "Neede hath no law," an English version of the Latin proverb, *necessitas non habet legem*, has been traced as far back as the fourteenth-century work, "Piers Plowman." J. Simpson and J. Speake (eds.), *The Oxford Dictionary of Proverbs* (5th ed., Oxford, UK and New York: Oxford University Press, 2008) www.oxfordreference.com/view/10.1093/acref/9780199539536 .001.0001/acref-9780199539536-e-1526; *see generally* H. Potter, *Law, Liberty, and the Constitution: A Brief History of the Common Law* (Woodbridge, UK: Boydell Press, 2015), p. 241.

[133] The Home Office is a ministerial department of Her Majesty's Government of the United Kingdom, responsible for immigration, security, and law and order. "Home Office," *Government of the United Kingdom*, www.gov.uk/government/organisations/home-office.

[134] Ibid.; *see also Regina v. Dudley and Stephens*, 14 QBD 273 (1884).

[135] *Trials of War Criminals before the Nuremberg Military Tribunals* (Washington, DC: United States Government Printing Office, 1952) vol. 8, pp. 986–987, www.loc.gov/rr/frd/Military_Law/pdf/NT_war-criminals_Vol-VIII.pdf.

[136] H. Arendt, *The Origins of Totalitarianism* (New York: Harcourt Books, 1994), p. 299; *see also* S. DeGooyer et al., *The Right to Have Rights* (London: Verso, 2018).

[137] Arendt, *The Origins of Totalitarianism*, p. 294.

The cases of Herrou, Warren, and Captains Rackete and Klemp challenge this rather circumscribed formulation. They offer powerful examples of how encounters at or near the borders of the "organized community" between potentially "rightless" outsiders and state agents cannot be completely insulated from legally salient human rights claims. Rights norms grounded in fraternity, solidarity, and necessity are, to be sure, complex and nuanced. They arise in technically detailed ways at particular points of legal processes. Moreover, one might object that, in all of the cases discussed herein, they have been successfully deployed *not* by migrants themselves but derivatively by those who sought to aid them. This is an important objection. But it does not disprove my main thesis. Logically, one cannot make sense of fraternity, solidarity, or even necessity without acknowledging that the migrants themselves must be understood to have certain basic human rights, too, albeit in a perhaps rather nascent form. As evolving legal principles, they are thus firmer, more distinct, more crystalized, more enforceable, and more a part of law itself than, for example, an aspirational ideal such as charity.

To be sure, this is a challenge for human rights theories in general. As Jacques Rancière has noted, echoing Arendt: "the Rights of Man turned out to be the rights of the rightless, of the populations hunted out of their homes and land and threatened by ethnic slaughter. They appeared more and more as the rights of the victims, the rights of those who were unable to enact any rights or even any claim in their name."[138] The effects of this, as well illustrated by the cases described herein, are problematic in many ways. For one thing, as Rancière highlights, "eventually their rights had to be upheld by others, at the cost of shattering the edifice of International Rights, in the name of a new right to 'humanitarian interference.'"[139] This raises the old concern of Arendt that "the 'man' of the Rights of Man was a mere abstraction because the only real rights were the rights of citizens, the rights attached to a national community as such."[140]

But a deeper analysis of such ostensibly humanitarian cases offers a more optimistic rights vision. Fraternity, for example, is a dialogical concept. It implies certain human rights that go beyond those of Herrou to be kind, as it were, to any living creature. While the *Conseil* was at pains not to create an explicit right to *enter* France, the extension of what one might call derivative constitutional fraternity rights to those on French soil without legal status is a conceptual step forward from the EU ideals of solidarity and surely a more powerful rights principle than using necessity merely as a defense.

Moments such as the encounters between Herrou, Warren, Captains Rackete and Klemp, and state agents are significant because they also involve the presence of

---

[138] J. Rancière, "Who Is the Subject of the Rights of Man?" (2004) 103(2) *South Atlantic Quarterly* 297–298.

[139] Ibid. at 298.

[140] Ibid.

other human beings, *the migrants themselves*, who have *definable* – and perhaps someday *enforceable* – rights claims. Thus, justice and rights are much more than "a negotiation between the conflicting rights of members of a community."[141] These encounters illustrate a profound negotiation *between* the rights of members of a community and the rights of those who are *not* members of that, or perhaps of *any* legally cognizable, community.[142]

Legal challenges by, on behalf of, or in relation to unauthorized migrants are often seen by governments as an impediment or an annoyance, if not part of a crime. Others view such claims more positively, but still in an impoverished way – as, at best, a humanitarian corrective against occasional harsh practices. But such invocations of evolving legal principle are much more than this. As the Herrou case demonstrates quite clearly, they are part of the dynamic process of mediating the inevitable tension between majoritarian, "sovereign" power and the rights aspects of law. Indeed, this is a component of the essential revitalizing project of both constitutional democracy and of international human rights law. As Bonnie Honig has suggested, we should reframe the traditional question: "How should 'we' solve the problem of foreignness?"[143] That question inevitably leads us to ask what "we" should do about "them." A more intriguing and useful inquiry is: "What problems does foreignness solve for us?"[144] The most important such problem is how – in a real, tangible way – to implement Martha Nussbaum's admonition that, "[w]e should recognize humanity wherever it occurs, and give its fundamental ingredients, reason and moral capacity, our first allegiance and respect."[145]

In sum, noncitizens, especially the unauthorized and ostensibly "rightless," are uniquely positioned to challenge, to critique, and to improve the meaning of law in constitutional democracies and of international human rights. This is both despite and because of the threats and disadvantages they experience. Through the legal system, noncitizens are a crucial part of a "circular process that recursively feeds back" into engagement and debate.[146] Since legitimate lawmaking both responds to and generates communicative power from, as it were, below, noncitizens play a central role in translating communicative power into administrative power and law.

---

[141] S. Degooyer and A. Hunt, "The Right to Have Rights," *Public Books*, May 5, 2018, www
.publicbooks.org/the-right-to-have-rights/.

[142] Ibid.

[143] B. Honig, *Democracy and the Foreigner* (Princeton, NJ: Princeton University Press, 2001), p. 4.

[144] Ibid.

[145] M. C. Nussbaum, "Patriotism and Cosmopolitanism," *Boston Review*, October 1, 1994, http://
bostonreview.net/BR19.5/nussbaum.php.

[146] J. Habermas, *Between Facts and Norms: Contributions to a Discourse Theory of Law and Democracy* (William Rehg, trans., Cambridge, MA: MIT Press, 1996), p. 130; *see also* Kanstroom, "Alien' Litigation as Polity-Participation."

The reactions of the French Parliament to the *Conseil* decision in the Herrou case illustrate this phenomenon well. Although the cases described in this chapter offer only moderate cause for optimism in terms of a more robust and comprehensive corpus of rights for migrants, the evolution of principles such as fraternity and solidarity may yet benefit not only "them," but all of us, together.

9

Do Non-citizens Have a Right to Have Economic Rights?

Locke, Smith, Hayek, and Arendt on Economic Rights

Serena Parekh

Many chapters in this book have examined the rights of non-citizens and what it might take to more fully realize these rights. In this chapter, I explore the topic of the economic rights of non-citizens through the lens of the history of philosophy. I make two different but interconnected arguments in this chapter, one that relates directly to the economic rights of non-citizens and one that relates more indirectly. In the first part of the chapter, I examine the claims made by John Locke, Adam Smith, and Friedrich von Hayek that a well-regulated market, supplemented by robust government support, is necessary for the realization of basic economic rights. To be sure, these writers do not use the term "economic rights." They do, however, argue for what we in the twenty-first century consider to be economic rights: the right to unionize, to a living wage, to subsistence rights, to education, to labor rights such as safe working conditions, to adequate housing, and to social security. All three put forth views on the role of the state in guiding markets so that people are able to access these rights and the importance of government intervention when markets fail.

These arguments are important to highlight because they are often neglected in favor of their claims about free or unregulated capitalism. For example, many are familiar with Adam Smith's idea that a free market requires limited government interference – the "invisible hand" of the market must be allowed to govern supply and demand. Yet he also believed that governments must, to some extent, regulate markets to ensure they are fair, do not produce too much inequality, and allow people to access what they need for a life of dignity. In other words, a "free" market must be carefully regulated for the sake of what we call economic rights. The purpose of this part of the chapter is to stress that in its theoretical foundations, economic rights required a particular relationship between markets and the state: markets must be allowed to work, but they must be regulated in ways that result in economic rights; when this does not happen, the state must directly step in to provide these basic rights. The work of Locke, Smith, and Hayek shows that, contra free-market or libertarian thinkers, the government is essential for economic rights. Recognizing how economic rights can be realized – that we should pay attention both to how markets are structured and how governments supplement them – is a crucial foundation for understanding the economic rights of non-citizens.

Though the views of Locke, Smith, and Hayek are important in understanding how economic rights can be realized and the role the state should play in this, they do not directly address what this might mean for non-citizens. Though the term "non-citizens" usually refers to residents of a country who do not have citizenship, I will be using it here mainly to refer to people who are present in a country without legal authorization, such as undocumented immigrants, as well as people who may be legally permitted in the country but are not permitted to participate legally in the economy, such as refugees living in refugee camps. Because Locke, Smith, and Hayek were not thinking about how non-citizens living in their countries might realize their economic rights, I suggest in the next section that their views must be supplemented by the work of Hannah Arendt and her concept of the *right to have rights*.

Arendt argued that most of what we considered human rights were really civil rights since they relied on a state to enforce them and states only cared about the rights of its citizens. In her view, what human beings needed was a *right to have rights*, which she understood as the right to belong to some kind of political community that recognized you as a member. However, Arendt was not thinking of economic rights specifically. What was on the forefront of Arendt's mind when writing *The Origins of Totalitarianism* were the civil and political rights that had been denied to millions before and during the Holocaust, the rights to political participation, to legal standing, and to security of the person in particular.[1] These are the rights that permit human beings to *act* as political agents, which for Arendt was the capacity to begin something new that reveals ourselves to the world. *Work* and *labor*, the activities through which we build a world and sustain life – what we would consider economic activities – already occupied a privileged place in the modern world.[2] Indeed, Arendt worried that humans had already been reduced to *homo economicus*, to exclusively economic beings, to the neglect of the life of action. As such, economic rights did not seem to need their own protection.

I want to suggest, nonetheless, that her argument can be extended to economic rights because it is clear in the twenty-first century that being human is not enough to have one's economic rights protected. Many non-citizens who are able to find work are often exploited and face poor working conditions. For those who cannot find work, and often even for those who can, poverty is the likely outcome, and this includes lack of access to basic health care and education for their children. Others,

---

[1] H. Arendt, *Origins of Totalitarianism* (2nd ed., New York: Harcourt, 1978).
[2] Her discussion of these topics can be found in H. Arendt, *The Human Condition* (Chicago: University of Chicago Press, 2nd ed., 1998).

like refugees, who are not able to work in camps, remain dependent on international aid that is often inadequate and prevents them from accessing an adequate standard of living. Non-citizens need a right to have economic rights, that is, a right to belong to an economic community. Ensuring the economic belonging of non-citizens, even when states deny citizenship to them, is essential in order to help protect their other rights. How might non-citizens gain the right to have economic rights? That is, how might they be included in the economic life of a country?

I conclude by discussing the example of refugees in the Global South. Refugees in the Global South, most of whom will remain refugees for over a decade, are denied economic rights such as the right to work and the right to adequate subsistence. They are not permitted to become citizens because they are considered to be living in host countries only temporarily, so citizenship is simply not a way for them to gain access to their economic rights. I argue that we can and should be supporting economic belonging in refugee camps. This may take various forms – temporary work permits, public–private partnerships, etc. – but the goal is ultimately to focus on economic belonging as a way to promote the economic rights of non-citizens rather than keeping them dependent on aid that is largely insufficient. Ultimately, what I show in this chapter is that economic rights, especially those of non-citizens, require well-regulated markets and robust government support, as well as a *right to have economic rights*, a right that can be envisioned as a right to economic belonging and inclusion.

At the outset, let me address two potential objections to my view and methodology. First, an objection. Why not just focus on citizenship? If non-citizens were granted citizenship, they would then be allowed to participate legally in the economy and receive welfare benefits. Why is economic belonging, independent of citizenship, necessary? In some cases, citizenship is enough for both sets of rights, but not always. As an example, we can look at formerly incarcerated people in the United States, who are often systematically disadvantaged in their ability to access economic rights[3]. This is a case of citizenship not being sufficient for economic rights to be realized. In other cases, non-citizens are highly unlikely to ever be granted citizenship as a way to access rights. Some refugees may never be granted citizenship in their host countries but are in desperate need of economic rights given that they are likely to remain refugees for years, perhaps decades.[4] It is imperative to think of ways that we may increase their economic belonging, even when states deny them citizenship. Domestic work permits, regional travel and work schemes, and public–private partnerships between relatively wealthy Western states and states that host refugees are some ways scholars have put forth that would allow refugees to

[3]   *See* M. Alexander, *The New Jim Crow: Mass Incarceration in the Age of Colorblindness* (New York: The New Press, 2012).

[4]   *See* A. Betts and P. Collier, *Refuge: Rethinking Refugee Policy in a Changing World* (New York: Oxford University Press, 2017); S. Parekh, *No Refuge: Ethics and the Global Refugee Crisis* (New York: Oxford University Press, 2020).

better access their economic rights while they remain refugees[5] These, in my view, are forms of economic belonging that should be encouraged.

Second, why look at the history of philosophy? I acknowledge that much excellent scholarship has been done around economic rights and their realization in recent decades.[6] Many of the chapters in this book look at empirical obstacles to the realization of human rights for non-citizens. This chapter aims to supplement those approaches by providing a more abstract view of the issues under consideration in this book. The aim of this chapter is to provide a theoretical way of framing some of the challenges involved with helping non-citizens access their basic economic rights.

THE STATE AND THE MARKET: JOHN LOCKE

John Locke was one of the first philosophers to think about the role of the market (or the economy) in promoting economic rights. Yet this was not the primary question he sought to answer in his main work of political philosophy, *The Second Treatise of Government*. Here he sought to understand why we should follow the rules of a state without relying on a theistic foundation. To do this, he postulated that we have *natural rights*, and ultimately, these are what the government must protect if it is to be a legitimate government. Locke ultimately determined that the government must also institute and protect a *market* in order to protect one of our natural rights, the right to property. As such, Locke is among the first theorists to analyze the relationship between the government and the economy.

Locke theorizes a complex relationship between the "natural rights" to life, liberty, and property that all human beings are born with; the market; and the state. He suggests that a market, and not merely a government, is essential to realizing and protecting our rights. In his view, the economy is essential for our right to subsistence and consequently our right to life. For Locke, our right to subsistence does not come directly from the government, unlike the rights to life and liberty, but from the government protecting private property rights and a flourishing market.

In his *Second Treatise on Government*, Locke set out to understand why citizens should accept the authority of the state in the absence of a God-given mandate to do so. His way of explaining this is to ask people to imagine what life is like in a "state of nature," a world that has no government to enforce or create laws.[7] In the state of

---

[5] *See* Betts and Collier, *Refuge*; Airbel Impact Lab, "Alex Aleinikoff on Displaced: Creating a New Refugee Regime," *Medium*, May 1, 2018, https://medium.com/airbel/alex-aleinikoff-on-displaced-creating-a-new-refugee-regime-d541e06cf57e.

[6] For example, *see* S. Hertel and L. Minkler, *Economic Rights: Conceptual, Measurement and Policy Issues* (Cambridge: Cambridge University Press, 2007); S. Fukuda-Parr, T. Lawson-Remer, and S. Randolph, *Fulfilling Social and Economic Rights* (Oxford: Oxford University Press, 2015).

[7] J. Locke, *Second Treatise of Government* (1689), p. 4, www.earlymoderntexts.com.

nature, he imagines human nature as basically good and theorizes that all human beings have natural rights, including the right to life, liberty, and property. The right to life means that we cannot kill others or ourselves. Our right to liberty means that we are free to do whatever we want as long as we do not infringe on the right to life or liberty of others. Though the state of nature is initially peaceful, occasionally our rights are violated and we are allowed to punish others who violate our natural rights. But Locke thinks we are bad judges of those who hurt us and in punishing are likely to overdo it. As a result, the state of nature will turn into a state of war in which we are never truly free. This motivates us to form a social contract with a government. We agree to give up our right to liberty and our right to enforce the law of nature for the sake of security and protection. He concludes that the basis of government is the consent of the people and a legitimate government is one that rules for the sake of protecting natural rights. A state must protect life and liberty through the creation and enforcement of laws equally across all people.

If our natural rights to life and liberty are protected via the social contract, what about our natural right to property? The existence of private property is a puzzle for Locke. His starting premise is that God gave the earth and its bounty to all people in common. How then can an individual privately own a part of it? If individuals are not able to legitimately own property, this means that a monarch is able to take property and possessions at will and interfere with the private lives of individuals, something Locke is keen to avoid. The key to unlocking the puzzle for Locke is his assertion that our bodies are our property, and when we mix the labor of our bodies with something found in nature, it becomes our private property. This is why property is a natural right; it emerges when what is naturally ours, the labor of our bodies, mixes with nature held in common.

Private property and the right to subsistence go hand in hand, and the right to the latter gives rise to the right to the former. Locke writes, "men, once they are born, have a right to survive and thus a right to food and drink and other things as nature provides for their subsistence."[8] In order for nature to provide for our subsistence, we must mix our labor with nature and create private property. The role of the government, then, is not so much to provide our subsistence right, but to protect private property so that we can access subsistence rights through our labor.

But in the state of nature, that is, before a government is established, private property is only legitimate when two conditions apply. First, I can take as my private property only what I can use before it spoils or goes rotten. If I pick more than I can eat, this would deny others a right to their subsistence and infringe on their right to life. Second, there must be "enough and as good" left for others for similar reasons.[9] That is, even if I could eat everything I pick before it goes bad, I am still required to leave enough for others to subsist on. But Locke is not worried that this will be a

[8]   Ibid., p. 10.
[9]   Ibid., p. 11.

problem because he imagines nature as plentiful and boundless: "there is land enough in the world to suffice twice as many people as there are."[10] Though these conditions place limits on what one can accumulate, ultimately, the invention of money as a system of exchange allows for unlimited accumulation and the creation of inequality.

The primary question Locke set out to answer in the *Second Treatise* is why we should accept the authority of a state. His answer is that we should give our tacit consent to a government because it is essential for the protection of our natural rights. Put in terms of human rights, the state becomes necessary to protect our civil and political rights, our rights to freedom, security, and autonomy. However, the state is also necessary for our economic rights, including the right to subsistence, insofar as the state is necessary for the protection of the system of currency and private property that allows economic rights to be sustained. "For in governments, the laws regulate the right of property."[11] The state continues to gain its legitimacy through protecting not only life and liberty, but the system of private property and currency known as the market. Our right to life, which requires a right to subsistence, requires the creation and protection of a market.

To see how novel this was for its day, we can compare it to the Greek sense of economics (*oikos nomikos*). For the Greeks, economics meant household management and survival, what had to be taken care of so a person could be free to leave the private realm and go out into the public.[12] For Locke, the government is needed for the sake of increasing and accumulating wealth for the sake of furthering subsistence. The state then is necessary not only for security (as it was for Thomas Hobbes, for example) or human flourishing (the ancient Greek view), but because it is necessary for capitalism and the accumulation of wealth. This accumulation is now seen as necessary for other basic rights to be met, such as the right to subsistence. Wealth and inequality are now consistent with human rights and, in a sense, a requirement of justice. After Locke, markets become a focus of other political thinkers.

ADAM SMITH: "FREE" MARKET AND ECONOMIC RIGHTS

Human rights depend on markets for Adam Smith as well, though for him, the role of the government in helping markets to flourish was more complex than for Locke. For Locke, as we noted earlier, markets were a device that were necessary to preserve our right to property and ultimately to subsistence and life. But for Smith, the market has its own inherent moral value and is not merely a device used to

---

[10] Ibid., p. 14.
[11] Ibid., p. 18.
[12] *See* C. Lord (ed.), *Aristotle's Politics* (2nd ed., Chicago: University of Chicago Press, 2013); Arendt, *The Human Condition*.

accumulate wealth. Its moral value comes from the fact that free market capitalism, unlike feudalism, allowed individuals to engage with each on the basis of equality. We are all equally buyers or sellers, engaging with each other out of our desire to pursue our own self-interest. Everyone equally has the ability to control their lives in this way. In a market, workers have the freedom to change jobs, organize to demand better conditions and wages, and, in this respect, are able to exercise more agency over their lives. Markets fundamentally further equality in another way as well. When properly regulated, markets can help eliminate the kind of dehumanizing poverty that was created under feudalism and that sustained fundamentally unequal social relations. By generating wealth, people in all sectors of society, including the poor, benefit. This is important for Smith because poverty implies not only a lack of necessities, but a lack of the things needed for dignity and respect. To put it in contemporary terms, human dignity requires the realization of economic rights.

What role should the government play in supporting the moral value of markets, that is, the ability of markets to permit individuals to engage with each on the basis of equality for Smith? He is often seen as the father of laissez-faire economics, the view that the government should stay out of the economy. Smith argued that the "invisible hand," the unobservable market force that determines the supply and demand of goods, should be allowed to work in peace without interference from the government.[13] He is associated with the idea that the rational self-interest of individuals, not government policy, should drive the economy. Producers make what people want in adequate quantities, thereby satisfying people's preferences in an efficient manner. The government's job, according to this logic, is to stay out of the market and focus on ensuring peace and security. On this view, it would seem that though it must protect civil and political rights, the government has little role to play in furthering the economic rights of its citizens, other than to not get in the way of market forces.

Such an interpretation of Smith, while common, is nonetheless incomplete. For Smith, while it is true that the government should not fix prices, impose tariffs on imported goods, and should limit taxation so that it is not overly burdensome, it does have a role to play in ensuring that a market can deliver the goods needed by people in a relatively fair way. The government must ensure that conditions of fairness prevail so that feudal relations, characterized by the oppression of workers, do not return. As Debra Satz puts it, "Rather than propounding a doctrine of spontaneous order, Smith continually stressed that markets can function as vehicles of freedom and efficiency only under very definite institutional arrangements."[14] In other words, the market only functions efficiently and is able to achieve the moral goals Smith believes it would – reduction in poverty, equal standing for laborers and

---

[13] A. Smith, *The Theory of Moral Sentiments* (1759), p. 249, www.earlymoderntexts.com.
[14] D. Satz, "Liberalism, Economic Freedom, and the Limits of Markets" (2007) 24(1) *Social Philosophy and Policy* 120–140 at 134.

management, freedom to change jobs when necessary, dignity of choosing and purchasing goods – when the government sets the conditions for it to do this.

Take labor markets. Smith believed that a free market for labor, where people could sell their labor power in exchange for a wage, was best for laborers as well as factory owners. This is because laborers have freedom to choose their job and leave if they are treated badly, a freedom they sorely lacked under feudalism. But in order for labor markets to produce workers that can negotiate on fair terms, they must be skilled, and in order for them to be skilled, the government must provide free public education. Without education, workers are liable to be exploited by their employers. As such, public education was important to make sure that workers were not dominated by the wealthy. But public education was not only important for the individual worker. It supported all of society because an educated, competitive labor force means a stronger economy. The "free" market would not be free without the provision of public education by the government.

Another example of the government setting conditions for a "free" market can be found regarding wages. It surprises many to note that the father of laissez-faire economics supported a government-set minimum wage but Smith did so for two reasons. First, there is an economic necessity: "A man must always live by his work, and his wages must at least be sufficient to maintain him. They must even upon most occasions be somewhat more; otherwise it would be impossible for him to bring up a family, and the race of such workmen could not last beyond the first generation."[15] Without a fair minimum wage, there wouldn't be another generation of workers to keep the economy going. Second, there is a moral reason. Smith is aware that factory owners would drive wages as low as possible and workers, having few other options, would be powerless to challenge this. This would essentially mean a return to feudal relations of dependence and servitude, thus eliminating one of the major advantages of capitalism.

Without a minimum wage, the right to unionize, and public education, there is a risk of creating an impoverished working class. This is bad because of the social exclusion and lack of dignity that comes with poverty:

> The poor man, on the contrary, is ashamed of his poverty. He feels that it either places him out of the sight of mankind, or, that if they take any notice of him, they have, however, scarce any fellow-feeling with the misery and distress which he suffers ... The poor man goes out and comes in unheeded, and when in the midst of a crowd is in the same obscurity as if shut up in his own hovel.[16]

It is imperative, for Smith, that poverty be avoided and the free market structured in such a way that "servants, laborers and workmen," who make up the majority of people in society, have access to the necessities of life. Indeed, he famously wrote:

---

[15] Smith, *Theory of Moral Sentiments*, pp. 57–58.
[16] A. Smith, *An Inquiry into the Nature and Causes of the Wealth of Nations* (1776), p. 33, www .earlymoderntexts.com.

"No society can surely be flourishing and happy, of which the far greater part of the members are poor and miserable."[17] To reiterate, this is because poverty was closely tied to dignity for Smith. This is why he considered necessities to be "not only the commodities which are indispensably necessary for the support of life, but whatever the custom of the country renders it indecent for creditable people, even of the lowest order, to be without."[18] Necessities are social in nature and included in his time things such as linen shirts and leather shoes. These are things that in his day were required to be treated with dignity, "the lack of which would be taken to indicate the disgraceful degree of poverty which (it is presumed) nobody can fall into without extreme bad conduct."[19] For Smith, poverty and a lack of access to economic and subsistence rights constitutes a deep moral harm, one which makes the proper functioning of an economy so important.

In short, for Smith, like Locke, an effective economy is necessary for economic and subsistence rights, the lack of which result in a denial of dignity. The government must make sure workers are educated and not impoverished, two conditions that we later come to recognize as basic rights: the right to education and the right to subsistence. Though Smith thought many economic functions were better left unregulated, he insisted that the market could fulfill its moral role and relieve people of dehumanizing poverty only when the government played a large role in setting the conditions for this to happen.

FRIEDRICH VON HAYEK: CAPITALISM AND ECONOMIC SECURITY

Political economists who come after Smith, such as Friedrich von Hayek in the twentieth century, would argue that Smith was right that market capitalism was the only mode of human exchange that was able to provide basic economic rights. Hayek stressed that in addition to this, markets were the only method of economic distribution that preserved liberty in the sense of freedom of choice, the kind of freedom most valued in liberal societies. For Hayek, like Smith and Locke, though economic rights require market capitalism, the state also has a role to play in ensuring that the market is able to deliver these goods, though he understood this role in a very different way. I emphasize this here because Hayek is often considered one of the fathers of unregulated, free market capitalism. Yet, even he held that the government must play a role in ensuring basic economic rights.

Like Smith, Hayek believed that economic rights are best sustained through a robust economy where the government created conditions of fairness. Competition is the best way to guide economic activity because it does not require coercive intervention by the state. But it does require the state to play a role. Like Smith, he

---

[17] Ibid., p. 235.
[18] Smith, *Theory of Moral Sentiments*, p. 676.
[19] Ibid.

believed that the government has to intervene for the sake of workers and to make competition effective. In his view, the government should intervene to "limit working hours, to require certain sanitary arrangements, to provide an extensive system of social services" as well as "to prevent fraud and deception, to break up monopolies."[20] These government interventions are for the sake of maximizing competition and hence economic efficiency and freedom of choice.

Hayek differs from Locke and Smith, though, in one important way. He acknowledges a limitation of capitalism: Capitalism cannot provide robust economic security. According to Hayek, there are two kinds of economic security that might be achieved through government intervention: limited security, a "minimum sustenance for all," and absolute security, "a given standard of life."[21] The former kind of security would ensure a basic level of subsistence, while the latter would require that the government provide a job and income. He believed that absolute security was incompatible with capitalism, democracy, and freedom because it would require denying the freedom of individuals to choose their profession based on a given wage and the ability to change jobs. However, limited security is compatible with capitalism. He writes, "There is no reason why in a society which has reached the general level of wealth which ours has attained the first kind of security should not be guaranteed to all without endangering general freedom."[22] He includes among the basic goods a state should guarantee food, shelter, and clothing, sufficient to preserve health, along with a system of social insurance against the "common hazards of life."[23] He saw these as ways of preserving individual freedom. As long as an economy allowed for competition, wages and positions were not fixed, Hayek is happy to declare: "Let a uniform minimum be secured to everybody by all means."[24] In short, for Hayek, though capitalism is the only system able to ensure liberty and freedom of choice, economic rights can still be provided by the government when they fail to emerge from the system.

In short, what we see from this cursory survey of the history of philosophy is an acknowledgment that economic rights require a market, but a market regulated in certain important ways. For the most part the government is less the direct source of economic rights and more the facilitator of the conditions that allow people to realize their economic rights. However, even for the most seminal free-market economists like Smith and Hayek, when markets are not able to provide basic economic rights and economic security, the government must provide them directly.

[20] F. von Hayek, *The Road to Serfdom* (1945), p. 38, www.iea.org.uk/sites/default/files/publica tions/files/upldbook43pdf.pdf.

[21] Ibid., p. 58.

[22] Ibid., p. 59.

[23] Ibid.

[24] Ibid., p. 61.

But what about non-citizens? Of course non-citizens, as much as citizens, require a well-regulated market supplemented by the government, but this is not enough. In many cases, non-citizens, especially those without legal authorization, are not permitted to participate legally in the labor market, and when they participate informally, are exploited and often unable to meet basic economic needs. They are rarely entitled to government welfare benefits that would allow them to access their basic economic rights.

It is for this reason that I turn to the seminal thinker of the rights of non-citizens, Hannah Arendt. For her, human rights could not be grounded in human dignity or our common humanity, as many believed. She insisted that human beings need to belong to some kind of organized political community that is willing to recognize you as a member. She called this the *right to have rights*. As I show in the next section, we can use her analysis to supplement the views of Locke, Smith, and Hayek discussed earlier. I argue that in addition to a well-regulated market supplemented with government support, non-citizens require a right to have economic rights, or a right to economic *belonging*.

ARENDT ON THE RIGHT TO HAVE RIGHTS

Hannah Arendt observed that states have a difficult time protecting the human rights of non-citizens, such as refugees and stateless people.[25] This was no accident or matter of incompetence. This was due, in her view, to a flaw in the way that human rights were understood. Human rights were supposed to be grounded in our humanity or human nature, but in practice, they turned out to be dependent on citizenship. Without citizenship, states were virtually unable to protect non-citizen residents. Furthermore, international organizations that existed in the first half of the twentieth century were equally unable to provide the kind of rights protection non-citizens needed. People in this situation – no longer able to access the protection of their home state and denied protection in their state of residence – were fundamentally *rightless* in her view. To be rightless for Arendt means that there is no political institution that can protect you as a matter of *right*. For her, "the loss of national rights was identical with the loss of human rights."[26] Elsewhere she writes, "the rights of man, supposedly inalienable, proved to be unenforceable – even in countries whose constitutions were based upon them – whenever people appeared who were no longer citizens of any sovereign state."[27] Instead, the rightless are forced to rely on charity:

---

[25] For a longer discussion of Hannah Arendt's view of human rights, see S. Parekh, *Hannah Arendt and the Challenge of Modernity: A Phenomenology of Human Rights* (New York: Routledge, 2007).

[26] Arendt, *Origins of Totalitarianism*, p. 292.

[27] Ibid., p. 293.

The prolongation of their lives is due to charity and not to right, for no law exists which could force the nations to feed them, their freedom of movement, if they have it at all, gives them no right to residence which even the jailed criminal enjoys as a matter of course; and their freedom of opinion is a fool's freedom, for nothing they think matters anyhow.[28]

In other words, for non-citizens like refugees, human rights cannot be protected as a matter of right but are, at best, granted as a matter of charity.

She called this flaw in our understanding of human rights, that human rights are not grounded in our humanity and cannot be claimed unless people are recognized as part of a political community, one of the cruelest ironies of the twentieth century:

No paradox of contemporary politics is filled with more poignant irony than the discrepancy between the efforts of well-meaning idealists who stubbornly insist on regarding as "inalienable" those human rights, which are enjoyed only by citizens of the most prosperous and civilized countries, and the situation of the rightless themselves.[29]

To put it bluntly, non-citizens who are not part of a political community effectively do not have human rights.

The reason behind this is not merely structural – that states were not yet equipped with the legal or political tools to enforce human rights for non-citizens. Rather, it is metaphysical and rooted in concepts of human dignity and human nature. Since Locke, theorists have asserted that our natural or human rights are rooted in some feature of our humanity. But in Arendt's view, human beings do not recognize each other merely as humans or because of some feature that we all share in common. For her, there was a deep hypocrisy in the idea that the human being in and of itself, is valuable, sacred, or worthy of special treatment. In fact, "It seems that a man who is nothing but a man," writes Arendt, "has lost the very qualities which make it possible for other people to treat him as a fellow-man."[30] Being seen as "nothing but a man" means that you can be easily discarded. Indeed, "the world found nothing sacred in the abstract nakedness of being human."[31]

If humanity is not sufficient to ground human rights, what is? In her view, non-citizens must be recognized as political agents, that is, as individuals with the power to act, to work together with others in speech and action. This can only happen when they are recognized as belonging to a political community. What the rightless have lost when they lose their citizenship is something more fundamental than their human rights: they have lost "the right to have rights." She writes:

---

[28] Ibid., p. 296.
[29] Ibid., p. 279.
[30] Ibid., p. 300.
[31] Ibid., p. 299.

We become aware of the existence of a right to have rights (and this means to live in a framework where one is judged by one's actions and opinions) and a right to belong to some kind of organized community ... only when millions of people emerged who had lost and could not regain these rights because of the new global political situation.[32]

For Arendt, what the loss of human rights deprives us of is a *place in the world that makes opinions significant and actions effective*. People outside a political community are deprived, not of the freedom to do what they want but ability to act in meaningful ways with others for a collective purpose. They lose not the right to think what they want but the right to have their opinions considered seriously by others and taken into consideration. In other words, it is not that a person *can* no longer speak or act, but rather, they are no longer *judged* according to their words and deeds but instead according to what is "merely given" about their existence – the fact that they are human beings in general. Speech and action are *intersubjective*, they require the presence and *recognition* of others.[33] Politically speaking, without the right to have rights, words, opinions, and actions do not "matter," in the sense that they are not acknowledged or valued by others. As a result, the rightless person does not matter either.

What does it take to realize the right to have rights? For Arendt, this is not just a matter of citizenship. For her what is important is *belonging* to an "organized community" that is willing to include and recognize you. Citizenship is not the only way to include someone in a political community, though it is certainly the most obvious. An "organized political community" can take many shapes. The sine qua non is that the political community recognizes you via your words and deeds, the features of individual life that make us most human. For Arendt, like Aristotle, what it means to be political or live in a political community is to make decisions through words and persuasion, not through force or violence. It is not merely that we have the ability to speak, but that we can engage in a way of life in which speech makes sense.

As I have argued elsewhere, central to Arendt's view on human rights is that they are fundamentally established through intersubjective commitment.[34] She writes:

We are not born equal; we become equal as members of a group on the strength of our decision to guarantee ourselves mutually equal rights. Our political life rests on the assumption that we can produce equality through organization, because man can act in and change and build a common world, together with his equals and only with his equals.[35]

---

[32] Ibid., p. 297.
[33] Parekh, *Hannah Arendt and the Challenge of Modernity*.
[34] Ibid., chapter 1.
[35] Arendt, *Origins of Totalitarianism*, p. 301.

In short, it is a political decision to create the conditions that allow equality and human rights. She rejects normative foundations and instead insists that human rights are an ongoing struggle that we must commit to over and over again. The first commitment is including those who lack citizenship into some kind of political community.

I am inclined to agree with Arendt that it is belonging in this meaningful way, and not just citizenship, that is so critical for human rights. Though citizenship is important, people need to be recognized as individuals and have the conditions of their agency protected, conditions that allow them to speak and act in meaningful ways. Recognition of identity is as important as the political rights and economic benefits that come with citizenship. While there remains some debate over whether or not she is correct or in fact that international institutions and international law are adequate to protect the human rights of non-citizens in the absence of state protection, many have recognized the importance of Arendt's argument.[36] Political belonging matters for human rights.

What about economic rights? As I mentioned at the beginning of this chapter, Arendt did not seem to have in mind economic rights like the right to work or to basic subsistence. Yet I suggest in the next section that it is possible to extend her argument on the right to have rights to economic rights. There is a parallel between Arendt's analysis of political rights requiring political belonging with economic rights. I show that economic rights require economic belonging, and this can in some situations be provided more easily than citizenship.

A RIGHT TO ECONOMIC BELONGING?

What would a right to economic belonging entail in the twenty-first century? To answer this question, I examine one of the quintessential groups of non-citizens: refugees. Currently, there are more than 20 million refugees, the majority of whom live informally in cities in the Global South. The rest live in UN-run refugee camps. In both situations, refugees are deprived of many human rights, including their basic economic rights, especially the right to work and the right to an adequate standard of living.[37] This is all the more important because of the duration of refugee situations: people are likely to remain refugees for around seventeen years and spend about ten years in a refugee camp.[38] Most refugees are not allowed to integrate into their host states and, as such, have limited access to citizenship rights. By most accounts, host countries do not seem interested in granting refugees citizenship at any point in the

---

[36] See A. Gündoğdu, *Rightlessness in the Age of Rights: Hannah Arendt and the Contemporary Struggle of Migrants* (Oxford: Oxford University Press, 2014).

[37] Parekh, *No Refuge.*

[38] Executive Committee of the High Commissioner's Programme, Standing Committee, *Protracted Refugee Situations,* U.N. Doc. EC/54/SC/CRP.14 (June 10, 2004), p. 2, www .unhcr.org/40c982172.pdf; Parekh, *No Refuge,* p. 21.

near future. What could a right to economic belonging mean to non-citizens in a situation like this?

A right to have economic rights would parallel what Arendt says about human rights more broadly: It is a right to belong to some kind of meaningful economic community that can recognize you as a member. To be sure, it is not necessarily a community founded on speech and action, but one which includes individuals as equals. Recall what Arendt says about equality. Equality is not something guaranteed by God, founded on human nature, or something that we can rely on the state or laws to implement.[39] It can only be guaranteed through the commitment of individuals, through individual decision. While many will consider this insufficient, it is for her the only ground we can rely on in the realm of human affairs.

One way to think about a right to have economic rights is as economic integration for long-term non-citizen residents.[40] It is possible to envision economic integration of refugees taking many forms, if states were willing to include non-citizens in their economic communities. For example, most countries that host large numbers of refugees in the Global South do not permit refugees to work legally (Uganda, and more recently, Ethiopia, are notable exceptions). Most, of course, do work without authorization in order to meet their basic economic needs, but because they lack legal protections are exposed to various kinds of exploitation.[41] Western states could leverage their influence to encourage states to grant work permits. But there are even more concrete ways that Western states could aid economic integration.[42] While the focus on finding a durable solution for refugees, namely, a way that they can gain citizenship either through returning home or being resettled elsewhere, is admirable, it is important to support economic integration in the interim. Doing so would allow refugees a right to have economic rights.

Betts and Collier have argued that Western states should create "Special Economic Zones" in host countries that would provide tax incentives and allow lucrative trade deals with companies that hire refugees. For example, Germany might allow a company in Jordan favorable trading conditions if they hire a certain percentage of refugees. The host states would then gain the tax revenue from these enterprises.[43] The Jordan Compact of 2016 is an example of such an approach. It allowed Syrian refugees to work and in return Jordan was given grants, loans, and preferential trading status with the European Union.[44] Although it had problems in its implementation, it remains an example of a way to encourage economic

---

[39] Arendt, *Origins of Totalitarianism*, p. 297.

[40] S. Parekh, *Refugees and the Ethics of Forced Displacement* (New York: Routledge, 2017).

[41] Parekh, *No Refuge*; B. Rawlence, *City of Thorns: Nine Lives in the World's Largest Refugee Camp* (New York: Picador, 2016).

[42] Betts and Collier, *Refuge*.

[43] Ibid.

[44] V. Barbelet, J. Hagen-Zanker, and D. Mansour-Ille, *The Jordan Compact: Lessons Learnt and Implications for Future Refugee Compacts* (London: Overseas Development Institute, 2018).

integration of refugees and provides a model for how the international community can support a right to have economic rights or a right to economic belonging.

In closing, while both citizens and non-citizens need well-regulated markets in order to access their economic rights, they also need a more fundamental *right* to access such forms of economic inclusion. I have argued that theoretical accounts of what is needed for economic rights must be supplemented with a right to have economic rights, a right that translates in practice to a right to economic inclusion.

10

Human Rights Are Not Enough

Understanding Noncitizenship and Noncitizens in Their Own Right

Tendayi Bloom

INTRODUCTION

Within liberal theory, human rights are often seen as pre-institutional, and so are not tied, by definition, to any particular state. This differs from citizen rights, which derive from the individual–state relationship. Yet, in practice it is common for individuals to have to prove some citizen or quasi-citizen relationship with a particular state in order to claim their human rights. Expanding citizenship to include more individuals may provide a useful interim measure for some, but it leaves others behind and does not challenge the idea and practice of making access to human rights contingent on citizenship or quasi-citizenship.[1] In this chapter, I suggest that while human rights are important, they are theoretically and practically insufficient to ensure everyone's basic needs are met.[2] I argue that to address this, it is crucial to acknowledge that citizenship is not the only form of relationship that can exist between an individual and a state. It is also necessary in both theory and practice to recognize substantive relationships of "noncitizenship" as well as the rights claims that noncitizenship creates.

In this chapter, I offer noncitizen rights not as an alternative but as complementary to both human rights and citizen rights. I argue that noncitizenship is not a negation of citizenship, but another form of individual–state relationship produced

I acknowledge my thanks to participants on the panel "Malleable Nature and Challenges of Citizenship" at the International Political Studies Association World Congress 2018 in Brisbane for their feedback on an early version of this chapter, and to colleagues at the University of Connecticut for encouraging me to develop it. I am particularly grateful to Catherine Buerger, Jillian Chambers, Molly Land, Kathryn Libal, Jess Melvin, Narissa Ramsundar, Jo Shaw, Katherine Tonkiss, and Susan Williams for their critical reading of earlier drafts. Remaining errors are mine.

[1] *See also* L. Kingston, *Fully Human* (Oxford: Oxford University Press, 2019).

[2] Chapters 9 and 12 by Serena Parekh and Jaya Ramji-Nogales in this volume share similar concerns and frame their proposed solutions differently.

by the construction and reconstruction of states. The noncitizen relationship thereby generates obligations that are tied, by definition, to specific states.[3] Although human rights are conceptually important and have been useful in asserting rights for people who have struggled to access even the most basic rights in any other way, I argue that it is essential also to acknowledge the institutional, necessarily noncontractual, relationship of noncitizenship and the rights associated with it.

Noncitizenship rights arise from diverse existing philosophical theories for how a state is imbued with legitimacy. For example, state legitimacy may be thought to be founded on its ability to provide security and stability, protect human dignity, promote agency, and ensure coherent and self-governing national communities. States may appear to be justified insofar as they ensure these goods for citizens. However, in fulfilling these goals (to some extent) for some, states and the state system may also *actively impair* access to these goods for others. The way in which the provision of goods for some people harms those thereby excluded from those goods has implications for state legitimacy. It is, then, not enough to justify the state and the multistate system with respect to those who benefit from them. It is also necessary either to provide a justification for the state with respect to those who must bear the burden of its actions and find ways to live despite it or, at the very least, to explain why this justification is unnecessary.

Thus, I argue that relationships of both citizenship and noncitizenship are fundamental to most conceptions of state construction (whether acknowledged or not). Constructing and maintaining a modern state creates both types of relationship. They are not binary or opposites. Neither is derivative from the other. They represent different modes of relating to the state. This means that it is not possible to understand the state fully without understanding both noncitizenship and citizenship. As such, both must be part of the legitimation story of the state. On this basis, in this chapter I offer an alternative way of thinking about the relationship between rights and the institutions of states and of the multistate system. This framework could in turn drive a rethinking of institutional arrangements in ways that better recognize the rights claims of those who bear the heaviest burden of that system. Noncitizen rights are institutional and particular. They do not challenge, but complement (nonparticular) claims a person has to human rights by virtue of their humanity.

WHY NONCITIZEN RIGHTS

As Jaya Ramji-Nogales observes in Chapter 12, the lists of human rights as presented in existing international treaties represent the outcome of political negotiations

---

[3] The notion of "noncitizenship" is developed in detail in T. Bloom, *Noncitizenism: Recognising Noncitizen Capabilities in a World of Citizens* (Abingdon: Routledge, 2018).

among parties with different normative frameworks and interests within particular political contexts.[4] As she shows, despite the messiness with which they came into being, these treaties have been vital to establishing basic norms and are crucial in understanding how the claiming of human rights functions today. However, they are based on an understanding of human rights that is fundamentally state based.[5]

This is seen in the preamble to the Universal Declaration of Human Rights, where the Declaration is presented as a "common standard of achievement for all peoples and all nations."[6] That is, it is not directed toward individuals *per se* but rather as they are grouped into "peoples" and "nations," governed by states with the power to protect, grant, or withhold rights. The underlying assumption that human rights are dependent upon formal membership in a particular state ("citizenship") is pervasive in human rights literature. Most of the classic writers on the universality of human rights sometimes, if not as a matter of course, slip into the language of citizenship when they really mean personhood.

Thus, while human rights are theoretically pre-institutional, they are in practice institutionally derived and usually delivered through citizenship.[7] Human rights are harder to enforce in the absence of a legally recognized relationship with a state because it is difficult to establish a duty-holder. On the face of it, while negative rights (like the right not to be tortured or arbitrarily killed) most obviously give rise to perfect obligations against everyone (everyone, including every state official, has an obligation not to torture or arbitrarily kill), it is harder to establish this in the case of positive rights (like the right to subsistence or shelter).[8] However, even negative rights become more difficult to assign if they are associated with an underlying right to *be somewhere* un-tortured and thus become part of a community.[9] This means that while human rights might be universal in principle, in practice many people do not have a route to claiming even the most basic rights.

---

[4] Chapter 12.

[5] Dominant debates regarding the underlying politics of international human rights, and their implications, often do not engage with this state focus. Two key ways in which these debates are framed are found, e.g., in D. Thomas, *The Helsinki Effect* (Princeton, NJ: Princeton University Press, 2001) and S. Tharoor, "Are Human Rights Universal?" (2002) 16(4) *World Policy Journal* 1–6, respectively.

[6] Universal Declaration of Human Rights, December 10, 1948, United Nations General Assembly Res. 217A(III).

[7] H. Arendt, *The Origins of Totalitarianism* (San Diego, CA: Harcourt Books, 1994); *see also* J. Ramji-Nogales, "'The Right to Have Rights': Undocumented Migrants and State Protection" (2015) 63 *Kansas Law Review* 1045–1065; B. Blitz, "The State and the Stateless," in T. Bloom, K. Tonkiss, and P. Cole (eds.), *Understanding Statelessness* (Abingdon: Routledge, 2017).

[8] O. O'Neill, "Rights, Obligations and World Hunger," in F. Jiménez (ed.), *Poverty and Social Justice: Critical Perspectives: A Pilgrimage Toward Our Own Humanity* (Tempe: Bilingual Press, 1987), pp. 86–100.

[9] This is presented in different ways by J. X. Fan, "On the Two Sides of Human Rights" (2003) 9 *International Legal Theory* 79–86, and C. Fabre, "Constitutionalising Social Rights" (1998) 6 (3) *The Journal of Political Philosophy* 263–284.

My primary intention here is not to critique human rights, but to put forward a case for the recognition of an *additional* type of rights. This is needed for two main reasons. First, assumptions about human rights often slip into assumptions about citizen rights. Second, states rely on relationships of noncitizenship for their exist-ence and these relationships, I would argue, affect the state's legitimacy. In the construction and maintenance of states, relationships of both citizenship and non-citizenship are also constructed. That is, noncitizenship (not to be confused with the hyphenated "non-citizenship," as the negation of citizenship) is a real and founda-tional aspect of the modern state, and one which has thus far gone largely unacknowledged.

Some special statuses like refugee status, work visas, or residency have the same form as, but are not quite equivalent to, citizenship. I call these "quasi-citizen" statuses.[10] Although these statuses represent relationships between individuals and a state of which they are not citizens, what is *relevant* about these relationships is that they demonstrate an individual's almost-but-not-quite citizenship claim against a particular state. Quasi-citizenship is also related to notions of "denizenship." Sometimes this term refers to people with quasi-citizen statuses. Sometimes it is used more broadly to include all those who have a strong relationship with a state or with a community in a state, but are unable to access citizenship.[11] Like quasi-citizenship, denizenship is also defined in deference to citizenship. This is not the case for noncitizenship.

People with quasi-citizen statuses and those understood as denizens may in practice *also* experience strong noncitizen relationships with the states in question. This is because their relationships with those states cannot only be understood through citizenship and associated terminology. Citizenship is theorized in a number of ways, for example, as political status or recognition,[12] as bound up in rights and duties,[13] as membership connected with identity (variously

---

[10] The language of "quasi-citizenship" is developed in more detail throughout Bloom, *Noncitizenism*.

[11] For analysis of different uses of the language of "denizenship," see T. Golash-Bosa, "Feeling Like a Citizen, Living As a Denizen: Deportees' Sense of Belonging" (2016) 60(13) *American Behavioral Scientist* 1575–1589; T. Hammar, *Democracy and the Nation State: Aliens, Denizens, and Citizens in a World of International Migration* (Beatty, NV: Avebury, 1990); R. Bauböck, "Migration and Citizenship" (1991) 18(1) *New Community* 27–48.

[12] E. E., "United Stateless in the United States: Reflections from an Activist," in T. Bloom and L. Kingston (eds.), *Statelessness, Governance, and the Problem of Citizenship* (Manchester: Manchester University Press, 2021); R. Lister, "Dialectics of Citizenship," (1997) 12(4) *Hypatia* 6–26.

[13] T. H. Marshall, *Citizenship and Social Class* (1950), reprinted in J. Manza and M. Saunder (eds.), *Inequality and Society* (New York: Norton, 2009); interrogated in Y. Soysal, *Limits of Citizenship: Migrants and Postnational Membership in Europe* (Chicago: University of Chicago Press, 1994); J. Dunn, "Political Obligation," in D. Held (ed.), *Political Theory Today* (Stanford, CA: Stanford University Press, 1991); J. Rawls, *A Theory of Justice* (Cambridge, MA: Harvard University Press, 1999).

defined)[14] or shared values,[15] as a practice,[16] or, indeed, as some mix of these and other approaches.[17] Overall, theorizations of citizenship assume that somehow the interests of the citizen (or, in this case, the quasi-citizen) and those of the state are affected by each other. There is the idea that the citizen/quasi-citizen gives up power or resources or labor to the state and gets some form of altered power or protection back, or a share in communal goods. Underlying these ideas is the notion that citizens/quasi-citizens live well, or live, in one way or another *thanks* to the state.

Like citizenship, noncitizenship has no meaning outside the institutional arrangement of states. And like citizenship, noncitizenship is a relationship that gives rise to vulnerabilities and rights claims. Yet, unlike citizenship, which includes by definition some form of mitigation of the vulnerability and power disparity that it creates, noncitizenship does not include this mitigation.

Noncitizenship and citizenship are not mutually dependent or mutually exclusive, but equally fundamental. This means that a person could be in a citizen relationship (including a quasi-citizen relationship) with a particular state and at the same time be in a noncitizen relationship with that same state. For example, people may be recognized as citizens but, because of poverty or discrimination, be unable to make full use of their citizenship in some dimension or dimensions.[18] Such individuals struggle under the power of the state without citizen-mitigation of that power in key dimensions. They are, then, in both a citizen and a noncitizen relationship with that state. Others may be citizens of a state that they do not believe to be legitimate. They, too, can be described as being in both citizen and noncitizen relationships with the same state. This is clearest in the case of colonial states like the modern United States, in which there are populations for whom US citizenship is

---

[14] The notion of membership and identity is explored from different angles. M. Mamdani, "Beyond Settler and Native as Political Identities: Overcoming the Political Legacies of Colonialism" (2001) 43(4) *Comparative Studies in Society and History* 651–664; K. Tonkiss, *Migration and Identity in a Post-National World* (London: Palgrave, 2013); Y. Tamir, "United We Stand? The Educational Implications of the Politics of Difference" (1993) 12 *Studies in Philosophy and Education* 57–70; K. Belton, *Statelessness in the Caribbean: The Paradox of Belonging in a Postnational World* (Philadelphia: University of Pennsylvania Press, 2017).

[15] E.g., Tonkiss, *Migration and Identity in a Post-National World*; S. Sassen, "Towards Post-National and Denationalized Citizenship," in E. F. Isin and B. S. Turner (eds.), *Handbook of Citizenship Studies* (London: Sage, 2002), pp. 277–292; T. Miller, "Cultural Citizenship," in Isin and Turner (eds.), *Handbook of Citizenship Studies*; *see also* A. Shachar, *The Birthright Lottery* (Cambridge, MA: Harvard University Press, 2009).

[16] Essays in E. F. Isin and G. M. Nielsen, *Acts of Citizenship* (London: Zed, 2008).

[17] Joppke provides a way to frame this in C. Joppke, "Transformation of Citizenship: Status, Rights, Identity" (2007) 11(1) *Citizenship Studies* 37–48.

[18] Consider, for example: C. R. Epp, S. Maynard-Moody, and D. Haider-Markel, *Pulled Over: How Policy Stops Define Race and Citizenship* (Chicago: University of Chicago Press, 2014); S. T. Russell, "Queer in America: Citizenship for Sexual Minority Youth" (2002) 6(4) *Applied Developmental Science* 258–263; T. Bloom, "Endometriosis and Noncitizenship: What Makes Suffering Relevant?" (2020) 81 *Discover Society*, https://archive.discoversociety.org/2020/06/03/endometriosis-and-noncitizenship-what-makes-suffering-relevant/.

the only internationally recognized rights-generating status available, who at the same time reject the United States as a colonial power.[19]

Noncitizenship is a mode of relationship between an individual and a state in which the individual must live and pursue their ends to some extent *despite* that state. Though this is understood in a variety of ways, theoretically states aim to promote the wellbeing of citizens. The idea is that insofar as a person relates to a state as a citizen, that person is better off than if there had been no state. I suggest that noncitizenship functions differently. Insofar as a person functions as a non-citizen in relation to a state, the wellbeing of that person is not designed into the construction of that state. Often the implications of this for the person's life may be minimal, particularly where the person in question also has strong citizen relationships. However, where the noncitizen relationship is the overriding relationship that person has with the state with most power over them, it may present a significant impediment to that person's life.[20] Although some people in a noncitizen relationship may find ways to flourish, they do so *despite* a state that has significant power over their lives. Indeed, thanks to their noncitizen relationship, some people may be prevented from enjoying even basic goods. This is problematic for any liberal theory of the state that relies for its justification on the idea that the state makes the lives of those affected better.

Noncitizenship is not contingent on citizenship, but looking at citizenship can be helpful in developing a picture of how noncitizenship functions. An individual may be in a citizen relationship with many states at once. They may live in the state of which they are a citizen, or live far away from it. Their citizenship might be all-important or it might not be particularly important to them or to their life. Similarly, individuals can be simultaneously in *noncitizen* relationships with more than one state, though these relationships may have more or less relevance to their lives. A person can be in a strongly felt noncitizen relationship even with a state that is far away, but they may also be in a noncitizen relationship that is barely felt, even with the state on whose territory they are standing. For example, person G, an employee of an international firm living happily within a closed compound of compatriots in country X may not feel their noncitizen relationship with X very much at all. On the other hand, consider person H, who lives in state Y, downstream from powerful state

---

[19] See, e.g., K. Bruyneel, "Challenging American Boundaries: Indigenous People and the 'Gift' of US Citizenship" (2004) 18(1) *Studies in American Political Development* 30–43; N. T. C. Marques, "Divided We Stand: The Haudenosaunee, Their Passport and Legal Implications of Their Recognition in Canada and the United States" (2011) 13 *San Diego International Law Journal* 383–426; A. Witkin, "To Silence a Drum: The Imposition of United States Citizenship on Native Peoples" (1995) 21(2) *Historical Reflections/Réflexions Historiques* 353–383; T. Bloom, "Members of Colonised Groups, Statelessness and the Right to Have Rights," in Bloom, Tonkiss, and Cole (eds.), *Understanding Statelessness*.

[20] A person could potentially be in a noncitizen relationship with any state, but we are only interested here in the cases where that relationship has an impact on the way in which a person is able to live out their life.

Z that is syphoning or polluting their primary water source. H may feel their noncitizen relationship with Z strongly despite not being on its territory. In addition, although they are not *theoretically dependent* on each other, the noncitizen and citizen relationships that an individual has may *interact with and affect* each other. For example, perhaps G is also a citizen or quasi-citizen of a powerful country that can mitigate G's relationship with X, while Y is unable to do this for H.

A stronger noncitizen relationship gives rise to stronger claims. Consider the impact of CO_2 emissions and the global warming that results. Some countries produce significant levels of CO_2 emissions.[21] Everyone who must live well, or even just live, *despite* this is in a noncitizen relationship with the states concerned. However, some people are not affected as strongly as others. They may experience slightly different weather, but barely notice the effects. They are in a weak noncitizen relationship and this does not, then, give rise to strong claims. However, some people are affected much more strongly. This includes those whose traditional way of life has been made impossible (e.g., because crops no longer grow in the same way or animals can no longer survive).[22] It also includes those currently living in Kiribati, which is predicted to be the first state to be entirely submerged by rising sea levels.[23] In these cases, I suggest that affected individuals may have stronger noncitizen claims against polluting states. Even if it is true that the ability to select its citizenry is core to a state's sovereignty (which I'm not sure it is), recognizing noncitizenship means acknowledging that states have relationships with more individuals than those that they have selected as citizens.

Although there are similarities, noncitizenship functions differently to citizenship. Whereas notions of consent or reciprocity are built into various framings of citizenship, by definition noncitizenship functions differently. No matter your theory of citizenship or of the state, *noncitizenship* includes an element of the involuntary. This affects the rights that arise as a result. This involuntariness in the noncitizen relationship also applies to the state. In the world of modern states, I argue that even in *denying* an individual any formal relationship, a state is thereby creating a relationship with that individual, albeit one it would rather not have. And that this relationship gives rise to rights claims.

---

[21] International Energy Agency, "Global CO_2 emissions in 2019," February 11, 2020, www.iea.org/articles/global-co2-emissions-in-2019. *See also* discussion in S. Caney, "Just Emissions" (2012) 40 (1) *Philosophy and Public Affairs* 255–301.

[22] Presented already in the 1990s, e.g., in H. Le Houérou, "Climate Change, Drought, and Desertification" (1996) 34(2) *Journal of Arid Environments* 133–185; J. Snorek, "Contested Views of the Causes of Rural to Urban Migration amongst Patoralists in Niger," in B. Gebrewold and T. Bloom (eds.), *Understanding Migrant Decisions* (Abingdon: Routledge, 2016), pp. 59–79.

[23] M. Loughry and J. McAdam, "Kiribati – Relocation and Adaptation" (2008) 31 *Forced Migration Review* 51–52; M. Risse, "The Right to Relocation: Disappearing Island Nations and Common Ownership of the Earth" (2009) 23(3) *Ethics and International Affairs* 281–300; K. Wilkinson Cross and P. Kingi, "*Fonua* Cultural Statelessness in the Pacific and the Effects of Climate Change," in Bloom and Kingston (eds.), *Statelessness, Governance, and the Problem of Citizenship*.

NONCITIZEN RIGHTS AND GLOBAL JUSTICE

Noncitizen rights provide a way to understand how particular rights claims may be allocated to individuals within the multistate system, contributing to the global justice tradition. Global justice thinking challenges state-focused justice thinking as parochial, but it rarely engages with the problem of citizenship directly.[24] A dominant branch of global justice theory emphasizes the implications of global interconnectivity, focusing on the material injustices arising from existing arrangements[25] or the shaky legitimacy stories of underlying structures.[26] I suggest that one way to understand the concerns of global justice is by challenging the presumption that citizenship is the only way of relating to a state or to the system of states.[27] Recognizing noncitizen relationships as substantive and rights-generating can help to show that global justice claims are specific and attributable.

I argue that the construction of noncitizenship is inherent in the construction of the state and can be generated by its activities. This means that implications for noncitizens must be part of the state's legitimacy story, whatever form that legitimacy story takes. Moreover, it is necessary to present that justification *within* the real and limited global state structure. For example, there is not an infinite array of alternative and welcoming states and citizenries. To be justified, then, the theory of noncitizenism requires that a nationalist acknowledges and addresses how nationalist statehood both constructs noncitizenship and undermines coherent national group politics. A liberal may need to engage with the noncitizen relationship of both those excluded from a particular polity and those rejecting liberalism itself. And so on. The world is messy and each state's self-justification must take place within this messy system of unfair power structures and contemporary realities affected by painful histories. Noncitizen rights provide a tool to ensure that those who bear the heaviest burdens of existing structures are taken into account in their own right.

---

[24] Early proponents include a variety of approaches, such as H. O. Oruka, "The Philosophy of Foreign Aid: A Question of the Right to a Human Minimum" (1989) 8 *PRAXIS* 465–475; H. Shue, *Basic Rights* (Princeton, NJ: Princeton University Press, 1980); C. Beitz, *Political Theory and International Relations* (Cambridge, MA: Harvard University Press, 1979). For a presentation of the global problem of citizenship, see T. Bloom, "The Problem of Citizenship in Global Governance," in Bloom and Kingston (eds.), *Statelessness, Governance, and the Problem of Citizenship.*

[25] Beitz, *Political Theory and International Relations*; C. Beitz, *The Idea of Human Rights* (Oxford: Oxford University Press, 2009); T. Pogge, *World Poverty and Human Rights* (Cambridge: Polity Press, 2002).

[26] E.g., K. Nkrumah, *Neocolonialism: The Last Stage of Imperialism* (New York: International Publishers, 1966). Note that this was first published in 1965, while Nkrumah was president of Ghana.

[27] In fact, I suggest that painting over noncitizenship may have been an intentional strategy in the political philosophy that justified colonial expansion and grounds contemporary liberalism, e.g., Bloom, *Noncitizenism*, p. 31.

My conception of *noncitizen* rights shares characteristics with some "political" approaches to *human* rights. That is, according to a political approach to human rights, such rights "confront the ideology of arbitrary power and inherited or exclusive privilege."[28] My suggestion is that human rights as currently construed are also necessarily *tied up* with the arbitrary power and inherited or exclusive privilege that is the state and indeed the "nation state." The notion of noncitizen rights explicitly challenges this in a way that human rights cannot. In acknowledging noncitizen rights, one acknowledges that the mechanisms that institute and protect citizen and state power and privilege give rise to obligations toward those who are thereby deprived of their own power and freedom. That is, those who must live *despite* states and the state system that affect them have claims on those states and on that system. The approach of noncitizen rights differs from political approaches to human rights, then, in deriving from foundational questions about the legitimacy of the state. It argues that noncitizenship is not other or abstract from the state but instead part of what constitutes the state. This underlying difference in rationale also gives rise to a practical difference: noncitizen rights identify particular obligation-holders.

Considering the realities of "statelessness" in this context can illustrate both how noncitizen rights work and how this approach could be used to ground new directions for the protection of rights.[29] A person is considered "stateless" according to international law if they are not recognized as a citizen of any country under the operation of its law.[30] People excluded from formal citizenship in this way are often unable to assert their claim to even basic human rights. Such individuals can be left without any citizenship because of problems of administration or conflicts between citizenship regimes; it can also be intentionally produced through discriminatory practices.[31] However it arises, lacking citizenship can make it difficult for those affected to access their human rights either within the state in which they live or within the international community.

---

[28] M. Goodhart, "Human Rights and the Politics of Contestation," in M. Goodale (ed.), *Human Rights at the Crossroads* (Oxford: Oxford University Press, 2013), p. 33.

[29] E.g., W. Conklin, *Statelessness: The Enigma of the International Community* (Oxford: Hart, 2014); K. Staples, *Retheorising Statelessness: A Background Theory of Membership in World Politics* (Edinburgh: Edinburgh University Press, 2012).

[30] This definition comes from the Convention Relating to the Status of Stateless Persons, September 28, 1954, 360 U.N.T.S. 117, art. 1(1), except that the Convention refers instead to "national." As I do not have space here to enter into a discussion of the relationship between "national" and "citizen," I will stick to the word "citizen" that I have used throughout this piece. For more on this terminological distinction in this sort of context, see K. Tonkiss, "Statelessness and the Performance of Citizenship-As-Nationality," in Bloom, Tonkiss, and Cole (eds.), *Understanding Statelessness*.

[31] Expanded, e.g., in L. van Waas, *Nationality Matters* (Antwerp: Intersentia, 2008); and in different ways in the essays in Bloom, Tonkiss, and Cole (eds.), *Understanding Statelessness* and Bloom and Kingston (eds.), *Statelessness, Governance, and the Problem of Citizenship*.

Although the noncitizen relationship I defend can pertain between a formal citizen and their state of citizenship, statelessness represents the apotheosis of noncitizenship. The deprivations currently associated with lacking any citizenship provide a limit case for what can happen when, on the one hand, citizenship is both assumed necessary for rights and left up to states to bestow and, on the other hand, no other form of individual–state relationship is recognized as rights generating. When individual states can effectively decide who they want to protect, people can theoretically be – and in reality are – stranded in the world of states without being able to claim any recognized rights-generating relationship anywhere within it, and thus struggling to assert their status as humans.[32]

Recognition of noncitizen rights provides a way out of this, which is based, both theoretically and practically, upon how things are today. Among those working to end the rightslessness associated with statelessness, there is a strong tradition of promoting the expansion of access to citizenship or other statuses that would give individuals demonstrable claims against particular states. This is vital and urgent as part of a larger project. It can be seen, for example, in the academic literature[33] and in the United Nations High Commissioner for Refugees campaign to end stateless-ness by 2024.[34] There are many individuals whose lives could be made significantly better if they could just prove some sort of recognized rights-generating connection to the state with the most power over their lives. For these reasons, it is crucial that citizenships are made more accessible and protections against the revocation of citizenship made more secure.

But taken alone, the expansion of citizenship is inadequate for ensuring rights for everyone. It carries three major risks. First, focusing only on expanding citizenship and quasi-citizenship does not provide a solution for those who have no such relationship and have no clear route to obtaining it. That is, it is not enough to say "well, they *ought* to be citizens" if they are not. Second, it ignores cases where individuals are overwhelmingly affected by a state to which they have no obvious citizen claim. That is, it does not respond to the cases mentioned earlier of foreign occupation or of those affected by a polluting upriver state. Third, this approach does not allow for the political reality of individuals who want to *reject* the citizen-ship of the state(s) with overwhelming control over their lives without giving up their basic rights. Those who contest the existing constellation of states must currently do so while those states in fact mediate access to vital goods and even recognition.

---

[32] This is expressed by various writers with direct experience of statelessness. See, e.g., S. Zweig, *The World of Yesterday* (Lincoln: University of Nebraska Press, 1964), and E., "United Stateless in the United States: Reflections from an Activist."

[33] *See, e.g.,* Shachar, *The Birthright Lottery*; T. Kostakopoulou, *The Future Governance of Citizenship* (Cambridge: Cambridge University Press, 2007); *see also* M. Walzer, *Spheres of Justice: A Defense of Plurality and Equality* (New York: Basic Books, 1984).

[34] United Nations High Commissioner for Refugees, *Global Plan to End Statelessness 2014–2024* (Geneva: UNHCR, 2013).

Instead, there needs to be recognition of noncitizenship and the rights it generates, and eventually a means to access to those rights without the need to demonstrate any citizen or quasi-citizen status.

The terminology and framing of noncitizen rights provide vital tools for thinking about global justice. They force a recognition that global justice considerations are not abstract and the obligations that arise are not general. Instead, a state has specific and institutional obligations toward those people who bear the burden of its existence and of its actions. Acknowledging noncitizens in their own right means acknowledging that a state cannot unilaterally absolve itself of considering a person's interests and wellbeing. Whereas human rights are general and arise from a person's humanity, noncitizen rights are particular and arise from a person's relationship with a particular state or states.

CONTEMPORARY CITIZENSHIPS AND FUZZY CITIZEN RIGHTS

Citizenship, whether formally recognized or not, comes with certain rights and duties, the content of which is generally based on the legitimacy story of a particular state and the real-world construction of its citizenship. In the past decade or so, some scholars have suggested that there has been a detachment of citizenship from territory, so that citizens are increasingly able to function as citizens from afar.[35] This has been discussed mostly with regard to voting, a particularly symbolic citizen right for democratic states, with the creation of emigrant constituencies in national parliaments, for example.[36] Other scholars over the same period have suggested that some countries have been gradually detaching territorially based rights from citizenship so that even voting and the right to abode have become tied not to citizenship but instead to sustained regular residence. These two sets of observations could seem at first glance to be in conflict. That is, the traditional rights of citizenship are both decreasingly and increasingly associated with living on the territory of a state, and increasingly and decreasingly associated with formal citizenship. However, understanding how these two observations interrelate (and indeed some theorists make both observations) will be helpful in the discussion of noncitizenship and noncitizen rights.

First, citizenship has never had meaning only within the state to which that citizenship is attached. A particularly iconic symbol of citizenship, the passport, is intrinsically linked to movement across international borders, and so to the space outside the territory of the state of citizenship.[37] Meanwhile, states have long offered

---

[35] E.g., G. Davies, "'Any Place I Hang My Hat?' or: Residence is the New Nationality" (2005) 11(1) *European Law Journal* 43–56.

[36] M. Collyer, "A Geography of Extra-Territorial Citizenship: Explanations of External Voting" (2014) 2(1) *Migration Studies* 55–72; R. Bauböck, "Expansive Citizenship – Voting beyond Territory and Membership" (2005) 38(4) *Political Science and Politics* 683–687.

[37] Consider, e.g., J. Torpey, *The Invention of the Passport: Surveillance, Citizenship and the State* (Cambridge: Cambridge University Press, 2000, 2018) and M. Salter, *Rights of Passage: The Passport in International Relations* (London: Lynne Rienner, 2003).

a range of diplomatic and consular services to citizens outside their territories and are now increasingly extending voting rights to citizens living far away. As of July 2020, 75 percent of countries had had some form of overseas voting in their most recent elections.[38] States also offer a range of other social services and forms of assistance through their consulates.

In select cases, citizens of powerful states have even been excused from complying with local justice systems, thanks to consular intercession. Consider, for example, the case of Gillian Gibbons, a British teacher who was facing punishment for blasphemy in Sudan, having named a class teddy bear "Mohamed."[39] Thanks to support from the government of the United Kingdom and intercession from the President of Sudan, Gibbons was eventually released and returned to the United Kingdom.[40] This suggests that in some cases citizens are able to access the rights of citizenship from afar and even be protected by the laws of their country of citizenship outside its territory, affecting the nature of their relationship with the countries on whose territories they stand. For the most part, the recognized rights of citizens *qua* citizens outside their states of citizenship are discretionary and dependent upon the interests and relative power of the states involved. In this case, Gibbons' citizenship of the United Kingdom helped to neutralize her noncitizenship in relation to Sudan.

Meanwhile, some countries have specific forms of overseas citizenship that do not carry these benefits. Consider the United Kingdom, which intervened on behalf of Gillian Gibbons. During the process of disentangling itself from an empire (and so from a contiguous political space) that spanned a large part of the globe, the United Kingdom has constructed a variety of citizenships. This includes citizenships that do not provide the right to live in the country of citizenship, or which include specific constraints on children inheriting citizenship from their parents. These two elements came to a head in the case of the grandchildren of people displaced from the Chagos Islands. In 1965, the United States expressed a desire to build a military base on Diego Garcia, the main island of the Chagos Islands. At the time, the Chagos Islands was part of Mauritius, which was under UK control. The United Kingdom separated Chagos from Mauritius to create the British Indian Ocean Territory (BIOT), which was then lent to the United States for its military base. The people living in Diego Garcia were forcibly relocated, mostly to other parts of Mauritius. They had citizenship of the British Indian Ocean Territory but were not allowed to live in it. In 1968, Mauritius declared Independence from Britain.[41] In 2002, an Act

---

[38] "Voting From Abroad Database – World," *International Institute for Democracy and Electoral Assistance*, www.idea.int/data-tools/world-view/52 (last visited July 30, 2020).

[39] *See, e.g.*, R. Crilly, "The Blasphemous Teddy Bear," *Time*, November 26, 2007.

[40] J. Gettleman, "Calls in Sudan for Execution of British Teacher," *The New York Times*, December 1, 2007; M. Weaver, "'Muhammad' Teddy Teacher to Be Freed," *The Guardian*, December 3, 2007.

[41] *See Legal Consequences of the Separation of the Chagos Archipelago from Mauritius in 1965*, International Court of Justice, February 25, 2019.

of the UK Parliament (along with some specific amendments) meant that those who had been displaced from the Chagos Islands were eligible for UK citizenship. Their children were also eligible for UK citizenship. Their grandchildren were not.[42] As a result, Chagossians in exile potentially had citizenship of a country that they could not visit and citizenship of another that they could not pass on. Not only did these citizenships not neutralize noncitizenships in relation to other countries, they also did not neutralize noncitizenships in relation to the United Kingdom.

Alongside the literature on extraterritorial citizenship is a discourse relating to an increasing importance of residency over citizenship within a state. For example, scholars presenting what they refer to as "post-national" citizenship emphasize that an individual has rights and duties in relation to the state where they live because they are a resident, they engage in its daily life, and they are affected by its political structures.[43] Although some of these texts offer empirical claims, for the most part their claims are normative. The argument is that individuals *should* be able to relate to a state in this way, even if currently they cannot. Where rights *are* accessible in this way, they are mostly social or civil (access to health care, for example). Insofar as there are political rights associated with regular residence, they are mostly only on the local level (i.e., voting in local elections but not general elections or referenda). In addition, these rights of residents sit against a backdrop of liminality, since continued "regular" residence itself is not a given. They are citizen-like or quasi-citizen claims in a context where that relationship is contested or vulnerable.

Most residents in most states are citizens.[44] For those that are not, in order to be a "regular" resident a person must have some sort of special status that might derive from a work visa, refugee status, student visa, multilateral or bilateral agreement, or some other arrangement approved by the rights-granting state. That is, a quasi-citizen status. What is key is that these statuses approximate citizenship. This means that, while regular residence is important to rights and is often a precursor to citizenship,[45] for our purposes, it should not really be seen as *replacing* citizenship as the primary locus for rights claiming. These alternative routes to rights claims have gained more relevance, but only insofar as they represent some form of quasi-citizenship.

---

[42] E.g., L. Jeffery, "'Unusual Immigrants,' or, Chagos Islanders and Their Confrontations with British Citizenship" (2011) 18(2) *Anthropology in Action* 33–44.

[43] Soysal, *Limits of Citizenship*; J. Bhabha, "Belonging in Europe: Citizenship and Post-national Rights" (1999) 51 *International Social Science Journal* 11–23; Tonkiss, *Migration and Identity*.

[44] There are exceptions to this. For example, according to data from the Government of Kuwait, in 2019 so-called non-Kuwaitis made up 70 percent of the Kuwaiti resident population. "Population Estimates," *Central Statistics Bureau, Government of Kuwait*, www.csb.gov.kw/Pages/Statistics_en?ID=67&ParentCatID=%201 (last visited July 30, 2020).

[45] E.g., S. Robertson, "Contractualization, Depoliticisation and the Limits of Solidarity: Noncitizens in Contemporary Australia" (2015) 19(8) *Citizenship Studies* 936–950.

The changing relationship between residence and citizenship is tied also to a global shift in approaches to dual and plural formal citizenship. Arguably, this also represents a formalization of some aspects of the transnationalism identified in the 1990s,[46] as well as an attempt to control the messy and mixed feelings that many individuals, in fact, have of citizenship.[47] Dual and plural formal citizenship have long been seen as deviant and anomalous.[48] It was assumed that a person could not simultaneously have full allegiance to more than one country. The reality of international migration, the need for gender equality in nationality law, and the desire of states to engage with their diasporas have all contributed to a context in which dual and plural citizenships are now accepted by many states and are normalized on the international level, though this comes alongside localized concerns regarding the loyalty that can be expected from dual or plural citizens.

As shown, relevant also is the global context in which the relationships between states affect the nature of their citizenships and noncitizenships and the rights associated with them. This means that even if everyone in the international community were a formal citizen of a recognized state, this would still not be enough to ensure human rights for all. There are three main reasons.

First, in most states many formal citizens experience noncitizen relationships, in some dimensions at least, with respect to their states of citizenship. This may result from overt discrimination or from material poverty and other inequalities that make it difficult for individuals to assert their citizenship.

The particularity of these individual–state relationships can be seen through the illustrative case of Zambians in relation to other countries in the context of extracting Zambian copper. Since 2008, the government of Zambia has led a series of tax reforms to try to enforce higher tax burdens on copper mining companies operating in the country. While tax money received as a result of these reforms is higher than it had previously been, significant profits from copper extraction in Zambia are made and remain outside the country.[49] During the 1990s and early 2000s, and on the basis of recommendations from German and UK companies,

---

[46] R. Rouse, "Mexican Migration and the Social Space of Postmodernism" (1991) 1(1) *Diaspora: A Journal of Transnational Studies* 8–23; R. Bauböck, *Transnational Citizenship: Membership and Rights in International Migration* (Cheltenham: Edward Elgar, 1994).

[47] A. Ong, *Flexible Citizenship: The Cultural Logics of Transnationality* (Durham, NC: Duke University Press, 1999).

[48] E.g., C. Joppke, "Citizenship between De- and Re-Ethnicization" (2003) 44 *European Journal of Sociology* 429–458; T. Brondsted Sejersen, "'I Vow to Thee My Countries' – The Expansion of Dual Citizenship in the 21st Century" (2008) 42(3) *International Migration Review* 523–549.

[49] O. Lundstøl and J. Isaksen, "Zambia's Mining Windfall Tax," WIDER Working Paper 2018/51; G. Zucman, *The Hidden Wealth of Nations* (Chicago: University of Chicago Press, 2016). It is also interesting to consider this in the context of discourse relating to Chinese involvement in Zambian copper mining. See, e.g., H. Yan and B. Sautman, "'The Beginning of a World Empire'? Contesting the Discourse of Chinese Copper Mining in Zambia" (2013) 39(2) *Modern China* 131–164.

Zambia's extraction industry was privatized and its taxation rates reduced.[50] This period also saw a 24 percent rise in unemployment and a decrease in Zambia's position in the Human Development Index from 110th in 1990 to 166th in 2005. This led to a period of rethinking, including the Zambian civil society report "For whom the windfalls."[51] The report expressed concern that Zambia's resources, and so also its ability to meet the needs of its citizens, were being lost to foreign companies. I propose that this put each Zambian citizen also into a relationship with the countries from which those companies operate and into which the wealth was being funneled. This relationship was one of noncitizenship. It is particular and it is rights generating.

Third, the language of noncitizenship helps to illustrate how citizenship itself can constrain rights. This is seen particularly clearly in colonial and post-colonial contexts. For example, while there are those in post-Soviet space who struggle for citizenship, others struggle against particular citizenships or cannot explain their relationships with existing states through citizenship alone.[52] Consider, for example, citizenship dynamics in the Crimea. Most recently, the Crimea was an autonomous region of Ukraine until annexation by the Russian Federation in Spring 2014. Although Crimeans were forcibly made Russian citizens, some retained their Ukrainian citizenship. Officially, Ukraine does not allow dual citizenship (though its Citizenship Law includes a provision for those who have not taken foreign citizenship voluntarily). This has put individuals living in the Crimea at risk of losing their Ukrainian citizenship, even if against their wishes. Some in the region reject both Ukrainian and Russian citizenships in favor of citizenship of unilaterally declared republics such as Donbass and Donetsk, which are not internationally recognized, while others make strategic use of different citizenships in different contexts.[53] The terminology of noncitizenship alongside that of citizenship provides a more nuanced way to explain these complex relationships.

Noncitizenship can help us to understand aspects of the international system that cannot be easily described using the language of citizenship and of human rights alone. However, while noncitizen rights are a distinct institutional category of rights, in the world as it is, noncitizen relationships and citizen relationships interact and affect each other. It is the existing states that are able to grant or withhold citizenship from individuals. And it is the existing states that are able to recognize or not recognize the citizenship-granting statehood of other political entities. This means

---

[50] Lundstol and Isaksen, "Zambia's Mining Windfall Tax," pp. 5–8.

[51] A. Fraser and J. Lungu, *For Whom the Windfalls? Winners and Losers in the Privatisation of Zambia's Copper Mines* (Lusaka, Zambia: CSNTZ/CCJDP, 2007).

[52] K. Swider, "Why End Statelessness?," in Bloom, Tonkiss, and Cole (eds.), *Understanding Statelessness*.

[53] N. Kasianenko, "Internal Legitimacy and Governance in the Absence of Recognition: The Donetsk People's Republic," in Bloom and Kingston (eds.), *Statelessness, Governance, and the Problem of Citizenship*.

that a system of rights that is purely citizen based reinforces existing structures of international power and control and stifles dissent. Noncitizenship, then, and noncitizen rights are also needed in order to liberate human rights and citizenship from the risk of being coercive.

CONCLUSION: UNDERSTANDING NONCITIZENSHIP AND NONCITIZENS IN THEIR OWN RIGHT

Human rights and citizen rights play important theoretical and practical roles in ensuring basic needs are met and protected in the world as it is. But they are not enough. This is because they fail to represent an important type of individual–state relationship that has largely been left unacknowledged. Noncitizenship is a relationship between an individual and a state that arises necessarily in the construction of the modern state in a world of states. It arises when people find themselves living – and flourishing – *despite* the state. This is theoretically important. It makes it possible to recognize a crucial dimension of how people relate to states, and to acknowledge the burden that this places upon them. It is also practically essential. It provides the terminology necessary for challenging the dominance of citizenship in framing basic rights and explaining that a relationship of contest between an individual and a state is still a relationship in its own right

Recognizing this relationship and its role in the construction of the state challenges state legitimation stories. It problematizes the idea of a multistate system constructed for those people who states wish to include in it, on terms set by states. It is necessary either to justify the state to people in noncitizen relationships with it or to defend why this justification is not needed. I suggest that this legitimacy challenge generates particular rights claims against states and can help to drive a framing of global justice that is based in relationships that are often obscured. The language of noncitizenship and noncitizen rights helps to show how an individual could have particular claims against a state even when either that state or the individual rejects any relationship. It also makes it possible to examine how citizenships and noncitizenships interact and the implications of this for rights. Finally, it provides a vehicle for considering the implications for rights when citizenship itself is seen not as emancipatory but as a constraint. A theory of noncitizen rights advocates holding states accountable to those who bear the greatest burden for their existence, without requiring those affected to contort themselves into citizen or quasi-citizen relationships. It provides a way to understand noncitizens in their own right.

11

Uncertainty and Educational Mismatch

Schooling and Life Pursuits in Contexts of Illegalization

Susan Bibler Coutin

This chapter draws on the literature on liminality, uncertainty, and precarity to analyze the complicated mismatches between the lives of immigrants and the forms of deservingness produced through US immigration enforcement initiatives. Since passage of the Illegal Immigration Reform and Immigrant Responsibility Act (IIRIRA) in 1996, the mechanisms through which undocumented noncitizens could regularize their status in the United States have been highly restricted.[1] Access to asylum has been increasingly curtailed, presence bars have made it hard for noncitizens to qualify for family visa petitions, and hyper-criminalization, over-policing, and stiffened border enforcement have created records that disqualify many from consideration.[2] Avenues for relief have increasingly taken highly liminal forms, such as Temporary Protected Status (TPS) or Deferred Action for Childhood Arrivals (DACA), which have to be renewed at regular intervals, confer only limited rights (such as work authorization and relief from deportation), and are vulnerable to being overturned, as the Trump administration attempted to do.[3] In such an atmosphere of heightened enforcement and limited opportunity, "deservingness" has been defined in a constrained fashion that privileges sacrifice, achievement, personal responsibility, and law abidingness. This limited definition defines "deservingness" as an individual character trait, ignoring the structural conditions that shape whether or not individuals are able to do things like excel in school, graduate, work, advance in careers, and avoid behaviors that could lead to accusations of

---

[1] N. Morawetz, "Understanding the Impact of the 1996 Deportation Laws and the Limited Scope of Proposed Reforms" (2000) 113(8) *Harvard Law Review* 1936–1962.

[2] J. M. Chacón, "Overcriminalizing Immigration" (2012) 102(3) *Journal of Criminal Law and Criminology* 613–652; R. Gomberg-Muñoz, "The Juárez Wives Club: Gendered Citizenship and US Immigration Law" (2016) 43(2) *American Ethnologist* 339–352.

[3] C. Menjívar, "Liminal Legality: Salvadoran and Guatemalan Immigrants' Lives in the United States" (2006) 111(4) *American Journal of Sociology* 999–1037; S. B. Coutin et al., "Deferred Action and the Discretionary State: Migration, Precarity and Resistance" (2017) 21(8) *Citizenship Studies* 951–968.

criminality. The very circumstance of being undocumented may compel individuals to use false Social Security numbers, work without authorization, drive without licenses, and reenter the country to join family members.[4] Immigration law thus makes otherwise legitimate activities – working, studying, traveling, being with family – appear as markers of undeservingness. Legal definitions of "deservingness" are therefore misaligned with the realities of living in the United States without authorization.

Aligning definitions of deservingness with the realities of immigrants' lives is key to ensuring respect for human rights. The most inclusive basis for granting people rights in international law is humanity.[5] Basic human rights, such as the right to life, liberty, equality, and freedom from persecution are to be enjoyed by "all members of the human family."[6] Such ideals inspired the immigrant rights' slogan "no human being is illegal."[7] In contrast to such notions of universality, political membership has been seen as a basis for limiting rights. Drawing on the theory that there is a social contract between citizens and state,[8] notions of political membership limit specified political and civil rights to those who are party to this contract. Grounding rights in notions of political membership, rather than humanity, draws distinctions between those who are and are not members of a given society. Alongside theories of membership, however, are understandings of disadvantage, according to which certain vulnerable groups are considered deserving of rights regardless of their formal citizenship status. Such groups include women, children, refugees, workers, the indigenous, and racial and ethnic minorities.[9] These groups are thought to have unique needs that cannot be adequately captured in universal declarations.

The gaps between universal human rights, bounded political membership, and particular disadvantage make educational pursuits particularly fraught for undocumented students, as individualized notions of deservingness collide with the forms of exclusion to which they and their families are subjected. In the United States, the Supreme Court decision in *Plyler* v. *Doe* established that public education cannot be denied to K-12 students on the basis of immigration status.[10] As a result, schooling

---

4 H. Lewis and L. Waite, "Asylum, Immigration Restrictions and Exploitation: Hyper-precarity as a Lens for Understanding and Tackling Forced Labour" (2015) 5 *Anti-Trafficking Review* 49–67.

5 Y. N. Soysal, *Limits of Citizenship: Migrants and Postnational Membership in Europe* (Chicago: University of Chicago Press, 1994).

6 Universal Declaration of Human Rights, December 10, 1948, United Nations General Assembly Res. 217A(III), pmbl.

7 M. M. Ngai, "No Human Being Is Illegal" (2006) 34(3/4) *Women's Studies Quarterly* 291–295.

8 J. F. Collier, B. Maurer, and L. Suarez-Navaz, "Sanctioned Identities: Legal Constructions of Modern Personhood" (1995) 2(1–2) *Identities* 1–27.

9 D. Reynaert, M. Bouverne-de-Bie, and S. Vandevelde "A Review of Children's Rights Literature since the Adoption of the United Nations Convention on the Rights of the Child" (2009) 16(4) *Childhood* 518–534; P. Thornberry, "Confronting Racial Discrimination: A CERD Perspective" (2005) 5(2) *Human Rights Law Review* 239–269.

10 *Plyler* v. *Doe*, 457 U.S. 202 (1982); L. J. Abrego and R.G. Gonzales, (2010) "Blocked Paths, Uncertain Futures: The Postsecondary Education and Labor Market Prospects of

is something of a protected space and life stage in which the impacts of being undocumented, or of having undocumented relatives, are muted.[11] Yet in other ways, schooling is one of the arenas where the contradiction between legal measures of deservingness and the structural conditions that limit opportunity play out. Children who are undocumented or who have relatives who are at risk of deportation experience anxiety,[12] material deprivation, and restrictions on travel, all of which can influence their school experiences.[13] Furthermore, as undocumented children reach adolescence, they "awaken to a nightmare"[14] in which driver's licenses, identity documents, work authorization, and the financial resources needed to attend college are often beyond their reach. Some states, such as California, have attempted to ease these burdens, and DACA has helped, but DACA's future is highly uncertain, and state and local measures do not go far enough. Navigating schooling in a context of illegalization can therefore be like walking through a minefield.

To explore how this highly punitive environment shapes educational pursuits, this chapter draws on two sets of data: (1) interviews that the author conducted between 2006 and 2010 with 50 1.5 generation young adults, that is, immigrants who were born in El Salvador, immigrated to the United States as children, and were raised in Southern California, thus falling between the first generation (born outside of the country) and the second generation (born in the United States), and (2) interviews that the author and colleagues carried out between 2014 and 2017 with Latinx and Asian and Pacific Islander individuals who either had DACA or who had hoped to apply for deferred action under the Deferred Action for Parents of Americans program that the Obama administration announced in 2014 but that never went into effect. The 2006–2010 interviews with Salvadoran 1.5 generation youth in Southern California focused on interviewees' experiences of the Salvadoran civil war, journeys to the United States, childhoods in Southern California, family circumstances, identities, return trips to El Salvador if any, transitions to adulthood, legal histories, and future aspirations. Educational experiences were a key focus in these interviewees' discussions of their childhoods, current circumstances, and goals. Interview results therefore indicate how immigration law

---

Undocumented Latino Youth" (2010) 15(1–2) *Journal of Education for Students Placed at Risk* 144–157.

[11] R. G. Gonzales and L. R. Chavez "'Awakening to a Nightmare': 'Abjectivity and Illegality in the Lives of Undocumented 1.5-Generation Latino Immigrants in the United States" (2012) 3 *Current Anthropology: A World Journal of the Sciences of Man* 255–281.

[12] J. Dreby, "The Burden of Deportation on Children in Mexican Immigrant Families" (2012) 74 (4) *Journal of Marriage and Family* 829–845.

[13] H. Castañeda, *Borders of Belonging: Struggle and Solidarity in Mixed-Status Immigrant Families* (Stanford, CA: Stanford University Press, 2019); C. Getrich, *Border Brokers: Children of Mexican Immigrants Navigating US Society, Laws, and Politics* (Tucson: University of Arizona Press, 2019).

[14] Gonzales and Chavez, "Awakening to a Nightmare."

shaped schooling in the period before DACA. The interviews that were carried out in 2014–2017 in the post-DACA era also included accounts of schooling and of educational goals, particularly in the case of interviewees who had or hoped to qualify for DACA. Pseudonyms have been used for all interviewees. Together, this interview material reveals the ways that racialization, illegalization, and precarization shape educational opportunities, even in a state that welcomes immigrants, such that the educational achievements that might be considered hallmarks of deservingness are placed beyond the reach of many, regardless of their individual talents or abilities. This material also reveals the resourceful strategies through which interviewees, their families, and some educators pushed back against these forces to attain educational goals.

Theory regarding illegalization, precarity, and uncertainty suggests that defining deservingness as an aspect of individual identity ignores the structural forces that shape individuals' lives. Scholars have examined illegalization in order to emphasize that individuals, families, and communities are not intrinsically "illegal" and therefore "undeserving"; rather, they are constituted as such by state and other actors as an ongoing part of daily life.[15] Furthermore, the illegalization literature suggests there is not a dichotomy between being undocumented and having status, as there are gradations of partial and temporary statuses.[16] This sort of differentiation in status has implications for educational opportunities, as it influences travel, financial resources, mental health, material conditions, and ability to plan. Likewise, educational institutions can play a role in furthering or mitigating this process. Illegalization is closely connected to precarity, which has been defined as "that politically induced condition in which certain populations suffer from failing social and economic networks of support and become differentially exposed to injury, violence, and death."[17] Immigration status contributes to precarity by limiting access to employment, healthcare, family, safety, and more. The condition of precarity extends across multiple contexts, thus creating commonalities between noncitizens

---

[15] C. Dauvergne, "Making People Illegal," in M. Crock (ed.), *Migrants and Rights* (New York: Routledge, 2017), pp. 74–94; L. F. Plascencia, "The 'Undocumented' Mexican Migrant Question: Re-Examining the Framing of Law and Illegalization in the United States," 38(2) *Urban Anthropology and Studies of Cultural Systems and World Economic Development* 375–434; L. Schuster, "Turning Refugees into 'Illegal Migrants': Afghan Asylum Seekers in Europe" (2011) 34(8) *Ethnic and Racial Studies* 1392–1407; P. E. Villegas, "Assembling a Visa Requirement against the Mexican 'Wave': Migrant Illegalization, Policy and Affective 'Crises' in Canada" (2013) 36(12) *Ethnic and Racial Studies* 2200–2219; P. E. Villegas "Fishing for Precarious Status Migrants: Surveillant Assemblages of Migrant Illegalization in Toronto Canada" (2015) 42(2) *Journal of Law and Society* 230–252.

[16] S. Chauvin and B. Garcés-Mascareñas, "Becoming Less Illegal: Deservingness Frames and Undocumented Migrant Incorporation (2014) 8(4) *Sociology Compass* 422–432; M. Reeves, "Clean Fake: Authenticating Documents and Persons in Migrant Moscow" (2013) 40(3) *American Ethnologist* 508–524.

[17] J. Butler, "Performativity, Precarity and Sexual Politics" (2009) 4(3) *AIBR. Revista de Antropología Iberoamericana* at ii.

and other marginalized and racialized groups.[18] Precarity impacts access to education, as well as the material conditions within which schooling occurs, making it difficult for youth to be the "high achievers" that are lauded in narratives about "DREAMers" who are cheerleaders or high school valedictorians but are also undocumented. Lastly, uncertainty is a key facet of both illegalization and precarity, given that immigration law and policy change over time, temporary statuses are vulnerable to political exigencies, and pathways to regularization may be blocked or shrouded.[19] Uncertainty makes it hard for noncitizens to plan for the future, understand the rules to which they are subject, and know whether adverse records about them have been created. Planning and record-keeping are key to educational pursuits, so again, schooling can be impacted by and in turn shape individuals' experiences of uncertainty in ways that make educational achievement difficult to demonstrate.

EDUCATION AND ILLEGALIZATION PRE-DACA

Interviews conducted between 2006 and 2010 with 1.5 generation Salvadoran immigrants in Southern California shed light on the relationships between illegalization, precarity, uncertainty, and education during the period before the DACA program recognized graduation from US high schools as a marker of deservingness. While a few of these interviewees reported being impacted due to immigration status, for the most part it was illegalization and precarization more generally that affected their school experiences, rather than legal status in particular. Illegalization impacted their parents' employment opportunities, which in turn led their families to live in neighborhoods characterized by poverty, racial tensions, crime, and pressures to join gangs. In this context, instead of being places of safety, schools became one place where children experienced violence and discrimination. Moreover, all too often, interviewees reported school officials and policies that exacerbated educational disadvantage by, for example, treating language skills as a measure of academic ability or requiring students to complete grade levels that they had already completed in their country of origin. Sometimes, however, school programs, counselors, or teachers intervened to mitigate illegalization, precarization, and educational disadvantage, such as by enrolling children in gifted classes, helping them graduate, or steering them toward college. Children and their families also resisted disadvantage through self-advocacy and developing support networks. The transition to college or the workplace was nonetheless challenging to these young people. In

---

[18] L. Goldring and M.-P. Joly, "Immigration, Citizenship and Racialization at Work: Unpacking Employment Precarity in Southwestern Ontario (2014) 22 *Just Labour* 94–121.

[19] M. B. E. Griffiths, "Out of Time: The Temporal Uncertainties of Refused Asylum Seekers and Immigration Detainees" (2014) 40(12) *Journal of Ethnic and Migration Studies* 1991–2009; I. Hasselberg, *Enduring Uncertainty: Deportation, Punishment and Everyday Life* (New York: Berghahn Books, 2016).

California, Assembly Bill 540 gave undocumented high school graduates the right to pay in-state tuition,[20] but the inability to qualify for federal financial aid or work legally placed college and therefore educational achievements out of reach for many. For those who managed to attend college anyway, universities provided the opportunity to organize new programs to overcome educational disadvantage.

Interview material suggested that, even though undocumented and immigrant children had the legal right to attend public schools, these institutions were not isolated from the broader social pressures that impacted children's families and neighborhoods. Interviews were replete with references to poverty, gangs, and violence. Adelmo Ariel Umanzor, whose family fled El Salvador during the civil war, observed, "If you were Salvadorian you were [presumed to be] like straight-MS. You know and nobody liked MS or – That kind of created a lot of like conflict … between students you know. Because that's why I didn't go to Belmont High School. I went to Pacific Palisades. Because in Belmont High School, gee, they were like all kinds of gangs in there." Jessica Morales explained how attending a middle school in a low-income neighborhood impacted her:

> That [going to Virgil Middle School] was probably the worst experience I've had in any of my schooling …. For some time I felt like somewhat ashamed of being Latino. I really did, because the kids were just trouble-makers. They were tagging. They were, you know, in gangs. And here I am as goody-two-shoes and I have to adapt to that very quickly. So, in 6th grade I didn't really have too many friends. I really didn't. There was a lot of girls that didn't like me and loved to pick on me because I was … an easy target. By 7th grade, similar to my brother, I got tired of being a target, so then I started getting into trouble. I started dressing more like them.

Note the way that Jessica equated "trouble-making" with race and ethnicity, while Adelmo commented that merely being Salvadoran gave him a presumed gang affiliation. In fact, racial and ethnic tensions were pervasive in the public schools attended by interviewees. Marta Dominguez reported that her school actually experienced riots: "I was teased a lot by Mexicans …. Within Latinos we are so diverse that Mexicans kids were always being like 'Oh you Salvi' and you know, this and that. So there was a lot, like, so much more riots at school because of that." Thus racialization impacted students' school experiences in ways that made it difficult for them to excel.

Instead of being neutral institutions, school policies and personnel in some ways contributed to these tensions and forms of marginalization. Salvadoran children who were viewed as troublemakers, for example, were suspended or otherwise disciplined, thus making them appear undeserving, often for reasons beyond their

---

[20] L. Abrego, "Legitimacy, Social Identity, and the Mobilization of Law: The Effects of Assembly Bill 540 on Undocumented Students in California" (2008) 33(3) *Law & Social Inquiry* 709–734.

control. Cesar Quintanilla, the United States-born son of Salvadoran parents, reported that he was deeply distrusted by his English teacher:

I was bleeding, because I used to get bloody noses all the time. And I used to be bleeding. And then like, I'm already there holding my nose, and I was like, "Mr. [name deleted], I'm bleeding. I need to go to the bathroom." And he's like, "Cesar, stop it." And I'm here bleeding, and holding my nose, and I'm like, "Mr. [name deleted], I'm bleeding, look, there's blood." And he's like, "Cesar, stop it!" And I just couldn't take it. I just left! I just went to the bathroom. I think I got in trouble for that. And it was just funny how he thought I was lying, with blood on my hands, you know?

Another common practice, according to interviewees, was placing children in grades that they had already completed, thus making them stay in school more years than necessary. Marta Dominguez, who eventually became a staff person at a four-year college, recalled:

Math, that's all they gave me. No other thing because, I guess, because I couldn't speak the language. And, then they would, I thought it was kind of weird because I wasn't, they put me back in third grade when I came. So it was kind of upsetting because I wanted to go to fourth grade. And, uhm, they gave me a lot of like easy stuff. Like, uhm, multiplication and divisions with just one digit. And, I was already doing fractions in El Salvador.

Numerous interviewees felt that they were evaluated on the basis of their language skills or immigrant status instead of their academic qualifications. Ernesto Duran complained that he was inexplicably held back for a year in elementary school, Bayardo Morazan stated that a high school counselor wanted to put him in remedial classes rather than honors due to his accent, and Sandra Mejillas went from testing into a gifted program at one school to being placed in English-as-a-second language (ESL) classes in another. Several interviewees reported that even though they eventually performed well at four-year institutions, their high school counselors had steered them toward community college or military enlistment. They saw such "guidance" as racially biased.

In the worst-case scenario, illegalization, precarization, and school policies that disadvantaged Salvadoran children resulted in dropping out of school, an outcome that contrasted with the DREAMer narrative of high-achieving immigrant youth. Manuel Cañas had this experience. During the second semester of 9th grade, Manuel's mother was working the night shift and needed Manuel to watch his siblings during the day so that she could sleep. He tried to go to night school to complete his high school degree, but felt the pressure to earn money. So, he accepted a 9th grade diploma and in addition to caring for his siblings and cousins, he did piece work at a factory, worked in a restaurant, and, at the time of our interview, had become a baggage handler at the airport, a job he was able to get due to having work authorization as a TPS recipient. Definitions of deservingness that emphasized educational achievement were misaligned with the pressures of Manuel's life.

While schools frequently contributed to or failed to protect Salvadoran children from marginalization, there were instances when schools, programs, teachers, or counselors supported interviewees in ways that mitigated the impacts of precarization and illegalization. Some students attended schools that had more resources. Juana Rocio related, "I think it was an advantage coming at such an early age, 3 years old … I was like Sponge Bobs, sponging everything that I learned," while Verónica Reina recalled happily that her parents gave her "the perfect childhood experience." As a recent arrival, Marta Dominguez perceived her school as a place of abundance: "I loved the school because it had like, all these wonderful things. And, toys, and letters like, really cute decorated. I was, like, I was amazed with the school. And, then the fact that they fed us [laughs]. That was just like, new to me." Some interviewees singled out a teacher who had made a difference in their lives. Mónica Ramirez spoke of a teacher who "saw me like a daughter and I still remember her," while Adelmo Ariel Umanzor appreciated teachers who noticed that he was from El Salvador and gave him books about the Salvadoran Civil War. Saul Henriquez recognized a counselor who believed in him. She told him, "you're doing B- work. This is not you. You can do this [other] type of work." Interviewees also described teachers who fought for them, getting them transferred into honors classes or college-bound programs. Cesar, who had been mistrusted by his English teacher, attributed his success in college at least partially to a mentorship program. As a fourteen- or fifteen-year-old, Cesar's mentor would "take me to places, to events, to college trips. He would just take me anywhere, anywhere he would take me, I used to love it, because it was a place that I wouldn't go if I would not have met him. So to the museum, to the opera, to the orchestra." Such individuals and programs helped to counter educational disadvantage wrought by poverty. But interviewees seemed to see them as exceptions, "rare to find a teacher like that," as Mónica Ramirez put it.

Interviewees also resisted educational marginalization, primarily through work-arounds, self-advocacy, family and peer support networks, and "passing." Jessica Morales was slated to attend an inner-city high school where her older brother had gotten into trouble. Jessica persuaded her parents to use someone else's address so that she could enroll in a middle-class high school in the San Fernando Valley. Graciela Nuñez successfully fought to be transferred to honors classes. She related:

And then I got to high school … . I remember I had integrated science and I was really mad because I really wanted Biology and then Chemistry, and Physics – the sciences separate. And I told the counselor and then the counselor was like, "No we can't do that." And then I talked to like the head counselor and then she said, "No, we can't pull you out for some reason." And then she said, "If you do really well, we could put you in Physics next year." So then I did really well that year and that's how I got to go into the Honors Program at the school.

Peers and family were also sources of support. Araceli Muñoz's grandmother sent a grammar book from El Salvador so that Araceli would not forget Spanish, Manuel Cañas made friends who helped him acclimate to elementary school, and Walter Olivar's friends encouraged him to make his first public speech in English, despite having an accent: "Come on you can do it. Walter, you can do it. Come on go, you can do it." Lastly, some interviewees reported that they "passed" as Mexicans, to avoid being stigmatized as Salvadorans, and as citizens, to avoid being accused of illegality. Marta Dominguez said, "There was a lot of, like, Salvadorans, when I was growing up, because of that tension that there was in school, the majority were Mexican, they would deny who they were so they wouldn't get, like, beat up. Or picked on. Yeah, it was sad because we had to, like, pretend to be Mexican." Likewise, Jessica Morales recalled being ashamed to be a permanent resident rather than a citizen. She stated, "I remember when I was in junior high I think somebody was talking about being a citizen and they said, 'Oh, but you were born here right? You're a citizen?' And I lied and I said, 'Yes.'" These forms of resistance – work-arounds, self-advocacy, social support networks, and passing – helped individuals navigate public schools in ways that made them appear deserving, but did not actually change oppressive structures that produced education disadvantage.

Unlike K-12 education, where legal status did not pose a barrier to enrollment, transitioning to college was significantly impacted by legal status, as has been well documented.[21] In 2001, California approved Assembly Bill 540 (AB-540), which allowed undocumented high school graduates to pay in-state tuition at public colleges and universities,[22] so during the 2006–2010 period in which these interviews were conducted, interviewees were eligible for this more affordable tuition rate. Nonetheless, lack of work authorization, the inability to drive legally, and ineligibility for financial aid placed college beyond the reach of many. Beatriz Gonzalez, an activist in the California Dream Network, described her own experience:

> And so, end of junior year, I wanted to go to college, I got to visit [UC] Davis. So I remember feeling, "No! I can't just not go to college. That's not an option. And I don't want to go to a community college" because I had like a 4.1 GPA, and was like, "No, I want to go to UC."
> So AB-540 became law, and I applied for every possible scholarship that I could get ahold of. At the end of my senior year, I had fundraised $500. And so, during that time, UC Davis, the quarter system, so it's three quarters and it was $1450 per quarter. So it was like, I did the math and "well, I have enough money for my tuition." And so I talked to my parents, and I said, "You know, can you guys help me pay for my rent?" And they said, "if it's something around $250. No more than $300 a month, then we can help you. If not, then you should really consider staying here." And I said, "No, no. I'll find out."

[21] Gonzalez and Chavez, "Awakening to a Nightmare."
[22] Abrego and Gonzales, "Blocked Paths, Uncertain Futures."

And so it worked. I went up there and did some homework and found a place to share for that amount. Got in the newspaper and found a job as a caregiver for a quadriplegic woman. And so that's how I was able to start in Davis. Because I knew I had enough money for my tuition.

And so I went there all my four years, and I, every year, was that same pressure. So again, it's like, I guess too the common thread or theme is that to be undocumented means to have to walk the unconventional path. And so, so you know, while I remember everybody feeling like, "Yes! Finals are over!" And like, "let's relax!" I remember thinking, "Yes! Finals are over! Oh, gosh" you know, "I gotta keep on searching, I gotta keep on asking, "where can I get money?"

While Beatriz succeeded in graduating from UC Davis, her college experience was shaped by continual worry about financial resources. Deservingness, in her case, was not an individual attribute but a product of circumstances. Such worries were shared by other interviewees who were frustrated by lack of immigration reform. As a TPS holder who had employment authorization, Tomás Marino-Vargas was working his way through college. But delays in government renewals of TPS put his job at risk. Although he was able to get a sticker showing that the US government had extended his expired Employment Authorization Document (EAD), Tomás' employer doubted the validity of this document. Only when the new EAD, valid for eighteen months, arrived, was his employer satisfied. Meanwhile, these difficulties had caused Tomás to withdraw from school. Consumed by uncertainty, Tomás related:

I've put my life, like, on hold, you know, to getting married and all that because I don't want to have that whole double issue of dealing with that until I get at least myself – my affairs straightened out . . . . School, um – I kinda felt – I felt cheated by the system because so many people get money, you know, to go to school and – and um, for their expenses, that when it came to me, it's like, hey, you know, I'm trying to do the same, but because I'm not here legally, I guess you could say, um, I have no rights to that.

One way that students fought against uncertainty was by organizing for policy change so that definitions of deservingness would better align with their lives. Schools were a place that afforded students the opportunity to form clubs and organizations, launch campaigns to pass the federal Dream Act, which would have created a pathway to legal status and eventually citizenship for undocumented students. As well, at the state level, students successfully fought for passage of the California Dream Act, which gave them access to state financial aid. In high schools, students formed AB-540 clubs, where they came together with other students who were also undocumented. Marisol Sanabria explained how she organized one such club at her high school, and then continued her activism in college. After revealing her undocumented status to a teacher to explain why she could not participate in a field trip to Washington, DC, he told her:

"Tomorrow we're going to have meeting and you're going to start a club, you know. Not only for immigrants, but for everybody. And you're going to fundraise to have scholarship for you – for you guys, you know." And that's how I became open. And I started going to places, talking to people. And ... now in college we have come to my high school from Cal Poly Pomona trying to make people apply to our school. And then I'm there just talking to people like – and we have a section for AB-540, and we tell them, "You know what, you're not alone .... The government can't help you financially, but there are people like out there [who can], you know."

Students also used college campuses as a platform for organizing. At California State University, Los Angeles, several Salvadoran students formed a student club known as USEU, the Unión Salvadoreña de Estudiantes Universitarios, or the Salvadoran University Student Union. USEU members sought to counter popular images of Salvadorans as gang members by highlighting their own status as university students. In addition, they worked with local high schools to educate undocumented and other students about opportunities to attend college. Cesar Quintanilla, who helped found this group, explained, "What we're trying to do with this organization, we're trying to show, like, we're trying to go out to the community and go out to the high schools, and not just our Salvadoran youth, we're going to focus on them, but not just them, just show our history, why we're here. Nobody tells us that." Salvadoran youth also promoted social change through their own research, scholarship, and creative work. Through organizing, activism, and becoming scholars in their own right, students helped to lay the groundwork for DACA.

ILLEGALIZATION, PRECARIZATION, AND UNCERTAINTY POST-DACA

Interviews conducted between 2014 and 2017 with individuals who had or hoped to apply for deferred action suggest that the combination of DACA and state and local integrative policies helped to mitigate but did not entirely overcome the impacts of illegalization and precarity. Students had more opportunities for academic success in the post-DACA era, but again, structural conditions shaped their lives in ways that deviated from narratives that treated educational achievement as an individual attribute. Unlike the 2006–2010 interviews with 1.5 and second-generation Salvadoran youth whose families immigrated to the United States during the Salvadoran Civil War, the 2014–2017 interviews were conducted with members of two generations: those who potentially could have applied for deferred action through DAPA, had it gone into effect, and college-age students who had DACA or potentially could have applied. The former group tended to be over thirty-five (many were parents), and the latter group tended to be in their twenties. Moreover, the 2014–2017 interview participants were from a range of countries, most commonly Mexico, but also Peru, Central America, Korea, Ethiopia, and China. Although the younger generation of 2014–2017 interviewees had entered the US educational system later than the 2006–2010 interviewees, there were striking similarities in their experiences. Many faced challenges acclimating to US schools when they were young and many also went through the traumatic adolescent experience of discovering that they were undocumented and therefore faced curtailed educational opportunities. For some, DACA and California state policies provided the means of pursuing college, often at high personal sacrifice, but the illegalization and precarization to which their families were subjected still created financial challenges. Educational institutions therefore helped to mitigate but could not overcome the impacts of illegalization. In the best-case scenario, schools, colleges, and universities were places of advocacy and empowerment, but in the worst-case scenario, educational institutions denied opportunities, thus exacerbating illegalization and precarization. Moreover, continued uncertainty over DACA, the intensification of enforcement, and an increase in overt xenophobia and racism made many interviewees anxious about their future prospects.

The early school experiences of the post-DACA interview group were not unlike those of pre-DACA interviewees. Mireya, a college student in her twenties at the time of our interview, was one of the few who described being directly impacted by immigration law as young children. Mireya had wanted to learn the violin, but her mother, who was undocumented, was unwilling to sign the form for her to check out an instrument. Mireya lamented, "I've always thought that, had I been given the opportunity to do that [learn violin], I would have been a composer .... So that educational goal went flying away." Many interviewees reported that their initial school experiences were traumatic, not because of legal status specifically, but rather due to language and cultural differences. Imelda described school as "a struggle," recalling, "I was very shy because I didn't know anybody or anyone and ... I started off in kindergarten so most of the kids already knew the language." Marisol, a housecleaner who was in her forties, recounted that when her four-year-old son entered the US school system, he was so traumatized that he began vomiting and she had to pick him up from school: "He says, 'Mommy, they don't talk like me in the bus and the teacher kept asking me questions and I didn't know what she was saying,' so I started crying with him and I just said what did I do but I told him you can do it, you are going to learn English and you will be able to speak it. He then sat down and okay mommy." Despite such early challenges, interviewees expressed pride in their educational achievements. Joaquin had been frightened during kindergarten, but, he said, "after kindergarten, I went to bilingual classes, by 2nd grade, I had entered into honors already. I made great progress." Some post-DACA interviewees also reported that the intervention of supportive teachers or counselors made a difference in their educational trajectories. Stephanie, whose family immigrated to the United States from South Korea, commented, "my fourth grade teacher was very patient with me. She sat one on one with me, she helped me learn how to write, and then pronounce. Like I think one of the reason I got better was because of her. She was remarkable."

College-age post-DACA interviewees reported that it was during their teenage years that the reality of being undocumented hit them in ways that impacted them academically. Some, such as Mireya, were already aware of their immigration status. Others only learned that they were undocumented when they tried to apply for college, obtain financial aid, or qualify for driver's licenses. These interviewees found that any protections that they had experienced during K-12 schooling evaporated. Catalina, for example, told us "I didn't really know I was undocumented until I was like 14 or 15, and then I – my junior year, no my whole entire high school career, I was like how am I going to pay for college? Like that's not even possible." Bryce, who had immigrated to the United States from Thailand, discovered his undocumented status when he applied for his first job: "I tried to get a part-time [job] being a lifeguard. I got my certification and went out to apply and I eventually got turned down and they told me I couldn't work because my paperwork was kind of messed-up. I didn't have a social, like that worked properly and after that I kind of like, 'What?'" Bryce described the moment when his parents explained his status as "surreal." Teenage years were a life stage when some were under pressure to join gangs, drop out of school in order to work, or assume family responsibilities. Imelda, quoted earlier, recalled of her own high school, "not a lot of kids would graduate." Added concerns about immigration status made such pressures more acute. Their teenage years were also a time when the impact of legal differences between themselves and their siblings became apparent. Older siblings, who had reached college age before DACA, had experienced greater educational disadvantage, whereas younger siblings who may have been United States citizens, were able to pay instate tuition and qualify for financial aid. Some interviewees felt guilty about their own opportunities, but also resentful about the disadvantages they faced.

Interviewees who qualified for DACA by attending or completing high school experienced some relief from educational disadvantages associated with immigration status. Bryce, who had feared that it would be impossible to complete college and attend medical school, stated, "with the [deferred] action itself like all of a sudden I have these rights that I never had before. I felt a lot more accepted and the community I was felt like my home. Yeah, when it came out I was just very thrilled about it . . . . When DACA came out that's when I really realized like hey, the future might not be as dark as I really anticipated . . . . All the hopes and goals I had suddenly became more plausible." California law also made a difference in expanding their educational opportunities. For example, Imelda, who had imagined that she would be restricted to community college and would have to take out many loans, related, "I always knew it would be tough for me to go to college . . . . I'm so thankful for the California Dream Act because that will help me so much . . . . Now I could go to UC." Similarly, Lupita, who was majoring in Public Health Policy with a minor in Civic and Community Engagement, said, "When I found out I could apply to AB 540 and the Dream Act and all that, I was like, 'Oh, cool.'" With in-state tuition and financial aid, for Lupita, education became affordable.

Yet, despite DACA and California state policies, some interviewees still faced reduced opportunities. Not everyone qualified for DACA. Sonya, who was undocumented, completed a medical assistant degree but was turned away from an internship because she did not have a Social Security number. This experience was emotionally devastating. Choking up as she told the story, Sonya related, "I remember that I cried and cried. I walked for blocks and blocks without making my way towards home. I just wanted to clear my mind (*desahogarme*)." Even with financial assistance, college was still expensive. Nidia, for example, had to take a couple of semesters off to work so that she could help her family financially, while Alessandra, who had DACA, had to repeatedly take time off to work in order to pay for her education. She had been in college for eight years at the time of our interview. Some interviewees passed over opportunities to attend more prestigious universities for financial reasons. Joaquin, who was undocumented, recalled the educational challenges that he had faced:

> It was hard to accept, year after year, not being able to transfer. You know, I was stuck at community college for seven years. And I didn't know if I was going to finish or make it. But I was starting to lose hope. And then along the way, I also had to sacrifice a lot of things .... I had actually dreamed with going to Berkeley. I got admitted every year that I applied .... In 2010 I tried to commit suicide, and I, I regret it, but I think it was a waking moment.

Finally, uncertainty about DACA's future coupled with the impacts of immigration enforcement created additional hardship for college students and their families. Catalina, who had DACA and was attending college at the time of our interview, worried,

> I've always had a plan, right? I think that's something that I've always tried to do. But it's also been like this like kind of struggle with myself is that accepting that that probably won't be the case .... If I could have any kind of security in the future which is I think that something that I yearn for just because it's so much of my life has been unstable and going around it, trying to like going day by day, you know.

In the post-DACA era, educational institutions played complex roles in the lives of noncitizens who, in contrast to the notion of individual achievement celebrated in the DREAMer narrative, were subject to educational marginalization through illegalization, precarization, and legal uncertainty. On the one hand, institutions sometimes countered these processes, creating opportunities for inclusion, empowerment, and activism. Some high schools had special programs, such as Early Academic Outreach Program (EAOP) that enabled interviewees to prepare for college. Imelda, who went to high school in Compton, recalled that EAOP "helped me out with the college process and teaching me about the Dreamer [California Dream Act] and how to fill it out." Nidia's public school in Santa Ana provided educational materials in Spanish, which allowed her parents to participate in school activities. Catalina, who had never had health insurance, accessed health care through a student insurance program. Joaquin, who had taken ten years to complete his undergraduate degree, was able to envision pursuing a doctorate. Bryce learned how to apply for DACA through an educational organization, E4FC (Educators for Fair Consideration). Bryce then became active with an E4FC off-shoot, Pre-Health Dreamers, which intervened with medical schools nationally to encourage them to admit undocumented students. Mireya obtained legal and financial assistance for the DACA process from her university, which also helped her siblings complete the DACA application. Dreamer Centers were particularly important sources of community for undocumented students. The parents we interviewed also stressed the ways that schools had enabled them to volunteer, attend workshops, and advocate for their children. Records of their volunteer activities also helped to document their time in the United States. Thus, the resources and programs that educational institutions provided allowed many interviewees not only to pursue their own educational goals, but also to become activists working for social, educational, and legal change.

On the other hand, though educational institutions were potentially empowering, schools, colleges, and universities also were in some ways that place where illegalization, precarization, and uncertainty occurred. Alessandra felt that she was discriminated against at school. She stated, "Because some of the schools, when it came to appointments, they ask you stuff like your social or you need to fill out an application and they ask you for a social and you have no social, like, they'll leave you just like that, you know, they won't even give you the appointment. I don't know, their tone of voice completely changes." Mauricio graduated from high school in Peru, and so did not qualify for AB-540. Because he had to pay nonresident tuition rates, he could not attend a university. Herminia did not qualify for DACA and had struggled to attend college, dropping out when she was only a few credits short of completing her degree. With exasperation, she commented, "I'm thirty-nine years old now, and I'm still trying to become, you know, legal. And yet I feel like my life has gone by and I haven't done much. And it's very frustrating because if I had had my residency when I was going to college, I would have finished and I would have a good job right now." Karina had DACA and was able to pursue her educational goals, but her father had been caught crossing the US–Mexico border and therefore would likely never be able to obtain legal status in the United States. Regardless of Karina's educational achievements, she was still potentially subject to being separated from her father through deportation. Some interviewees reported that their schools and universities were not well informed about DACA, AB-540, or the California Dream Act. They found themselves educating counselors, rather than vice versa. Some universities took insensitive actions, such as inviting the border patrol to campus to participate in a career fair or to speak in class. In that their admissions policies, record-keeping practices, advising procedures, and financial assistance was not always designed to accommodate the needs of undocumented students, educational institutions could be exclusionary, reproducing educational disadvantage, preventing social mobility, and exacerbating uncertainty.

DISCUSSION AND CONCLUSION: EDUCATIONAL MISMATCH

The pre- and post-DACA interview material analyzed in this chapter demonstrates that definitions of deservingness that treat educational achievement as a measure of individual merit are out of sync with the ways that educational institutions further illegalization, precarization, and racialization. When schools deny access based on immigration status, charge higher tuition to noncitizens, or administer programs that require documentation that immigrant students lack, then schools are themselves perpetuating illegalization in ways that can prevent educational success. The precarization to which noncitizens are subjected also shape educational experiences. Impoverished communities also have under-resourced schools; poverty requires parents to work long hours, thus impacting their abilities to be involved in their children's schooling; and financial pressures may lead students to enter the workforce at young ages, or to care for siblings so that parents can work. Racialization and criminalization exacerbate these disadvantages, as schools treat students as potential gang members, or use discipline policies that alienate students. At the same time, this interview material also reveals that students, families, and educators have proven resourceful in pushing back against illegalization, precarization, and racialization. Interviewees described teachers and counselors who intervened positively in their lives, recognizing students' abilities, conveying information about college, and advocating for students within educational institutions. Families sometimes resorted to workarounds, such as using different addresses, to gain access of educational opportunities, while students engaged in self-advocacy in order to enroll in accelerated programs. In some cases, schools served as a platform for organization and empowerment, providing students with resources to apply for DACA, develop clubs and advocacy groups, build community, and forge alliances.

The complex roles that educational institutions play in relation to illegalization, precarization, and racialization are evidence that living in the United States without authorization undermines noncitizens' ability to demonstrate the "deservingness" that immigration policies often require. In other words, the undocumented are held accountable for the conditions that produce illegality, even though US policies create these conditions. For example, educational achievements are one way to show "deservingness," and in recent years, the DREAMer narrative has been celebrated, generating public sympathy for undocumented students.[23] Yet, school systems are not always designed to support these students. Discipline practices may treat students of color as suspect, as described by Cesar, whose teacher did not allow him to go to the restroom even when he was bleeding. Schools sometimes treat language skills as a measure of academic achievement, placing non- or limited-English speakers in remedial classes or lower-grade levels. College opportunities

---

[23] W. J. Nicholls, *The DREAMers: How the Undocumented Youth Movement Transformed the Immigrant Rights Debate* (Palo Alto, CA: Stanford University Press, 2013).

may be beyond the reach of some high school graduates, due to their immigration status or to the expense of college. A lack of educational achievement can be a product of the immigration system rather than a measure of noncitizens' own abilities. For these and related reasons, the DREAMer narrative has undergone considerable critique in recent years.

The similarities in interviewees' experiences pre- and post-DACA suggest that temporary measures, such as DACA, though valuable, are insufficient to counter both the intensity of illegalization, and the financial pressures of paying for college. The uncertain nature of DACA, which could potentially be dismantled through legal action or presidential policy, makes it difficult for students to plan. In fact, on June 18, 2020, in *Department of Homeland Security* v. *Regents of the University of California,* the US Supreme Court ruled that the Trump administration's rescission of the DACA program violated the Administrative Procedures Act (APA), due to being arbitrary and capricious.[24] The DACA program has been allowed to remain in place, for the time being. Yet, a new rescission order that complies with the APA could be issued in the future, making the circumstances of DACA recipients precarious. Furthermore, even if DACA is allowed to remain in place, a new generation of undocumented students who did not immigrate to the U.S. before 2007 will be ineligible for DACA benefits. These students will face increased educational and other challenges. Even if state policies enable undocumented students to attend college, lack of work authorization could make it impossible for them to work professionally. Moreover, the high cost of college affects undocumented students, students with DACA, and low-income students. Creating campuses that are truly sanctuaries requires making college accessible to all who qualify, regardless of their immigration status or income. Continued advocacy for affordable education, the rights of undocumented students, and programs that more effectively integrate English language learners in the public schools is needed. Transformative advocacy could establish transnational educational partnerships, bridging boundaries within and beyond national borders, and placing students rather than politics and economics at the center of educational programming. In such a future, illegalization itself would be dismantled, not through legalization but rather by limiting the divisiveness of borders themselves in ways that allow all to enjoy the right to have rights.

---

[24] *Department of Homeland Security v. Regents of Univ. of Cal.*, 140 S. Ct. 1891 (2020).

12

Constructing Human Rights

State Power and Migrant Silence

Jaya Ramji-Nogales

This chapter analyzes the role of states in framing the scope and applicability of human rights protections. The limited perspective of the sovereign has constructed a system that, while ostensibly universal, prioritizes the power of the state while erasing the interests of migrants. The chapter argues that this flaw at the conceptual core of human rights contributes to contemporary migration-related challenges and demands radical rethinking.

Responding to the horrors of the Second World War, the project of human rights law described itself as a movement that would extend rights to all people by simple virtue of their humanity. This was a noble cause, but its ambition was hampered by the process and structure of international human rights treaties. Drafted by representatives of states, who were also the central subject and primary enforcer of these laws, multilateral human rights treaties perhaps unsurprisingly maintained the sovereign interest in border control. This profound state prerogative also manifested itself in the content of international human rights law itself – or perhaps more accurately, in human rights law's silences.

Migrants are of course protected by numerous basic international human rights that attach to all people regardless of migration status. Human rights law constrains state behavior with respect to these rights, including the right to life, the right to be free from torture, and the right to freedom of thought and religion. Yet, when it comes to rights that would impinge on the sovereign's ability to control its borders, such as the right to enter into, the right to safe transit to, and even the right to remain in a destination state, international law falls silent.

Destination states in the Global North have expanded their power into that gap, building a variety of mechanisms to keep migrants away from their borders. From the "Pacific Solution" to "Operation Sovereign Borders," Australia has kept its sea borders clear of migrants (see Chapter 4 in this volume). Through agreements with North African and Middle Eastern states such as Libya and Turkey as well as the

Dublin Regulation,[1] Europe has attempted to minimize the number of migrants reaching its shores. The United States has used a variety of harsh border control methods in an effort to deter migrants from approaching its southern land border (see Chapter 3 in this volume). Migrants pay the cost of these deterrence and border control programs financially, physically, and emotionally, as they are subject to extortion, exploitation, and abuse during their journeys. Yet these humans are not and will not be deterred from moving, as they seek freedom from harsh conditions in their countries of origin, pursuing the exercise of their human autonomy (see Chapter 6 in this volume). These deterrence policies increasingly encompass measures designed to strip migrants of their human dignity, and come at the cost of degrading the humanity of destination states.[2]

In the contemporary era of widespread anti-immigrant sentiment, it is hard to imagine states ceding power to protect migrants. Nevertheless, a critical analysis of the current structure of human rights law and its consequences points to the possibilities of an approach that takes the voices of migrants into account: a new human rights treaty focused on migrants rather than states.[3] A human rights instrument that fully represents migrant interests is not likely to be signed by any destination states any time soon, but could still be a worthwhile drafting exercise in terms of its expressive function. This instrument might not be law in the traditional sense, but the process would bring together a variety of groups from civil society to corporations to diaspora to transnational families. A representative catalogue of migrants' rights could help to frame the debate, persuade the public, and focus activist energies in lobbying states for change.

THE PROJECT OF HUMAN RIGHTS LAW

From its inception, international human rights law has represented itself as a project that extends rights to all people by simple virtue of their humanity. Although human

---

[1] Adopted in 2003, the Dublin Regulation determines which member state of the European Union is responsible for adjudicating an asylum seeker's protection claim. The responsibility normally lies with the country where the asylum seeker first entered the EU. European Parliament and Council Regulation (EU) No 604/2013, *Establishing the Criteria and Mechanisms for Determining the Member State Responsible for Examining an Application for International Protection Lodged in One of the Member States by a Third-Country National or a Stateless Person* (June 26, 2013).

[2] Bhabha, "Zero Humanity."

[3] This treaty would differ from the International Convention on the Protection of the Rights of All Migrant Workers and Members of Their Families in that it would provide rights that are fundamental to protecting undocumented migrants, such as the right to territorial security. International Convention on the Protection of the Rights of All Migrant Workers and Members of Their Families, July 1, 2003, 2220 U.N.T.S. 3; J. Ramji-Nogales, "Undocumented Migrants and the Failures of Universal Individualism" (2014) 47 *Vanderbilt Journal of Transnational Law* 699–763 at 722–739. The treaty would contain much stronger protections for the rights of undocumented migrants than the UN Global Compact for Safe, Orderly, and Regular Migration, which has been widely criticized for failing to make any meaningful changes to existing international law, particularly with respect to protection for undocumented migrants.

rights law has undoubtedly contributed to a variety of expanded protections for many individuals, it has not fulfilled this original promise. There are of course many reasons for this shortcoming; this chapter focuses on one key factor: the role of sovereigns of the Global North in drafting and enforcing human rights law, and the resultant gaps in its protections.

Contemporary international human rights law, including in its canon treaties such as the Covenant on Civil and Political Rights, the Convention on the Elimination of All Forms of Racial Discrimination, and the Covenant on Economic, Social and Cultural Rights, was drafted in the wake of the Second World War.[4] The United Nations describes the creation of international human rights law as an effort by the international community to ensure that the human rights abuses perpetrated during the war never occurred again.[5] However, critical scholarship has described human rights law, which was created contemporaneously with independence movements in the Global South, as a continuation of "colonial ideology and practices"[6] that "represent[ed] Western ideas of the individual, state, and society."[7] In other words, from the start, the project of human rights law portrayed itself as universal while privileging a particular worldview.

The United Nations website describes the Universal Declaration of Human Rights as "a roadmap to guarantee the rights of every individual everywhere."[8] This proclamation leaves open at least one core question about the scope of international human rights: exactly which rights are being guaranteed? The description appears to rely on an unsurfaced assumption that the content of these rights is universally agreed upon, or "[reflecting] a common sense of justice, fairness, and decency."[9] Even if international human rights law was somehow able to locate a set of rights that reflected the moral tenets of the vast and diverse membership of

---

4   *See* P. Alston, "Does the Past Matter? On the Origins of Human Rights" (2013) 126 *Harvard Law Review* 2043–2081 at 2065 (reviewing J. S. Martinez, *The Slave Trade and the Origins of International Human Rights Law* (New York: Oxford University Press, 2012)) (explaining that "the most common starting point for modern histories of human rights is the United Nations Charter of 1945 and the Universal Declaration of Human Rights of 1948" but suggesting that projects to pinpoint precisely a single origin are flawed).

5   United Nations, "Universal Declaration of Human Rights: History of the Document," www.un.org/en/sections/universal-declaration/history-document/index.html; *cf.* S. Moyn, *The Last Utopia* (Cambridge, MA: Harvard University Press, 2010), p. 7.

6   B. Rajagopal, *International Law from Below: Development, Social Movements and Third World Resistance* (Cambridge: Cambridge University Press, 2003), p. 176; *see also* J. Reynolds, *Empire, Emergency and International Law* (Cambridge: Cambridge University Press, 2017), pp. 115–116. *But see* M. Mazower, *No Enchanted Palace: The End of Empire and the Ideological Origins of the United Nations* (Princeton, NJ: Princeton University Press, 2009), pp. 94–96.

7   A. Anghie, *Imperialism, Sovereignty, and the Making of International Law* (Cambridge: Cambridge University Press 2005), p. 254.

8   United Nations, "Universal Declaration of Human Rights."

9   L. Henkin, *The Age of Rights* (New York: Columbia University Press, 1990), p. 2; *see also* Universal Declaration of Human Rights, December 10, 1948, United Nations General Assembly Res. 217A(III), pmbl.

humanity, the guarantee also of course relies on states to guarantee these rights to "all members of the human family."[10] It is quickly apparent where this plan might fall short: states are not likely protectors of the humans at the margins of their societies, particularly those who might in the state's view be undesirable.[11] Undocumented migrants present both of these challenges to the human rights canon: they demand rights that may not be universally accepted and they are generally disfavored by states, who prize the ability to exclude as a manifestation of their sovereign ability to control their territorial borders.

Though the idea of human rights arose much earlier, the evolution of rights in international law has a particular and contingent history that contributed to this gap between the story that human rights law tells about itself and its application on the ground. Anthony Anghie locates the foundations of modern international law in the colonial encounter between the Spanish and Indigenous people in the Americas.[12] He explains that the doctrine of sovereignty arose from Francisco di Vitoria's struggle to create a legal system that managed relations between these two societies and their disparate cultural orders.[13] Vitoria created the idea of natural law, which enabled the Spanish to insist that their cultural practices were a universally valid baseline that could and should be enforced both externally and by ensuring that their colonial subjects and others internalized these claims to universality.[14] In addition, Martti Koskenniemi explains that the Spanish theologians' theoretical approach to universal and individualized rights focused on ensuring horizontal justice between individuals rather than vertical justice between the individual and their community.[15] Their theories supported territorial notions of sovereignty as well as ownership rights over private property. Koskenniemi describes this pre-Westphalian international legal regime in terms that are equally apt today, as a "powerful and long-standing type of informal imperial domination that is achieved through a worldwide pattern of acquisition and exchange of private property by which ... formal state policies are also controlled, enabled, or undermined, as befits the global market."[16]

In the same way, the fundamental rights conceptualized in the French and American Revolutions promised more than they delivered. The radical move to identifying the people (rather than the crown) as the source of political authority required a natural rights justification that could exist independent of the state. Unfortunately, social and historical realities simply did not match up with the idea

---

[10] Universal Declaration of Human Rights, pmbl.
[11] E. Goffman, *Stigma: Notes on the Management of Spoiled Identity* (New York: Simon & Schuster, 1986).
[12] Anghie, *Imperialism*, p. 15.
[13] Ibid., p. 16.
[14] Ibid., pp. 21–23.
[15] *See* M. Koskenniemi, "Empire and International Law: The Real Spanish Contribution" (2011) 61 *University of Toronto Law Journal* 1.
[16] Ibid., at 32.

that power came from the people, who as a result held inalienable and universal rights.[17] Statehood was born of armed conflict, not from the inherent authority of the people. These allegedly fundamental rights were narrow in scope and applied only to a select few individuals; they were hardly universal in practice.[18] And similar to the Spanish theologians, this new approach to rights created a division between the private or economic sphere and the public or political sphere.[19] Though this change was justified as furthering the interests of all people, on the ground, it established new power relationships that furthered some interests more than others.[20]

It was against this rather flawed backdrop that international human rights law was created. The new treaties drafted in response to the Second World War claimed universality yet extended a politically determined set of rights selectively. For example, the International Covenant on Civil and Political Rights (ICCPR) failed to extend certain key rights to groups such as undocumented migrants.[21] In particular, human rights law reinforced the Western liberal democratic order by prioritizing individual and political rights over distributive and economic justice. While the ICCPR established binding obligations on its member states and required compliance in the short term, the International Covenant on Economic, Social, and Cultural Rights was characterized as an aspirational document that encouraged member states to make every effort to comply in the long term.[22] This hierarchy that elevated civil and political rights above economic and social rights offered many eloquent provisions discussing the individual right to equality yet no opportunity to challenge the deep inequalities of global economic order.[23]

International human rights law can be understood as part of a longer historical phenomenon that fundamentally altered the basis for governance, yet entrenched a particular framework for social change that is amenable to economic interests that

---

[17] N. Stammers, "Human Rights and Power" (1993) 41 *Political Studies* 70–82 at 72–73.

[18] Ibid., at 75.

[19] T. Evans, *The Politics of Human Rights* (London: Pluto Press, 2005), pp. 15–16.

[20] Ibid., p. 16.

[21] *See* L. Bosniak, "Human Rights, State Sovereignty and the Protection of Undocumented Migrants under the International Migrant Workers Convention" (1991) 25 *International Migration Review* 737 at 737 (concluding that "the [ICCPR]'s ability to substantially ameliorate the human rights situation of irregular migrants is significantly constrained by its over-riding commitment to the norms and structures of sovereign statehood").

[22] International Covenant on Civil and Political Rights, December 10, 1984, 999 U.N.T.S. 171, art. 13; International Covenant on Economic, Social and Cultural Rights, December 16, 1966, G.A. Res. 2200 (XXI), U.N. Doc. A/6316.

[23] Evans, *The Politics of Human Rights*, pp. 43–44; *see* A. Kirkup and T. Evans, "The Myth of Western Opposition to Economic, Social, and Cultural Rights?: A Reply to Whelan and Donnelly" (2009) 31 *Human Rights Quarterly* 221–238 at 226–232 (discussing the private-sector-fueled backlash to the idea of including social and economic rights in any list of universal rights).

seek to subjugate rather than emancipate.[24] Human rights law's claims to universality mask political choices that prioritize certain interests over others. The coverage of these rights is narrower than the label "universal" might suggest; different levels of protection are allocated to more and less powerful individuals. Individual and political rights are prized while structural and economic harms are obscured. All the while, the language of universal individualism can be used to camouflage the perpetuation of extant power structures.

THE HUMAN RIGHTS OF MIGRANTS

Undocumented migrants present a particularly illuminating case study through which to examine the limitations of international human rights law. Though they are on paper accorded the same fundamental rights provided to all human beings, undocumented migrants are much less likely to be able to access these protections on the ground due to their precarious status. Moreover, the rights that are most important to the undocumented – safe transit, entry, and to remain – are found nowhere in the canon of human rights law.[25]

Though human rights law appears to provide universal protections, the obstacles to enforcing those rights means that vulnerable populations face limited access to those rights in practice. Migrants are particularly vulnerable in transit, suffering harms ranging from murder to brutal sexual assault to extreme financial extortion.[26] Even after undocumented migrants are able to enter the territory of their destination, they are targets for violence and exploitation at the hands of a variety of actors. The undocumented are rendered vulnerable through their immigration status; even if they know that there is a legal remedy for the harms they suffer, they may be unable to report these abuses to and seek protection from local authorities because they fear deportation.[27] Many of the undocumented migrate to seek employment,

---

[24] *See, e.g.,* U. Baxi, "Voices of Suffering and the Future of Human Rights" (1998) 8 *Transnational Law and Contemporary Problems* 125–70 at 163–64 ("This new [trade-related, market friendly, human rights] paradigm reverses the notion that universal human rights are designed for the dignity and well being of human beings and insists, instead, upon the promotion and protection of the collective rights of global capital in ways that 'justify' corporate well-being and dignity over that of human persons."); Rajagopal, *International Law from Below,* p. 246 (describing the "uncritical acceptance of the counter-sovereignty liberal rights rhetoric, without examining the socioeconomic and cultural foundations of rights and sovereignty" as one of two weaknesses that "have greatly reduced the transformatory potential of international human-rights discourse, and instead made it into a handmaiden of particular constellations and exercises of power").

[25] I should note here that by "international human rights law" I mean to discuss only multilateral human rights treaties. Regional human rights law such as the American Convention on Human Rights and the European Convention on Human Rights offer some contestation around a few of these rights.

[26] invisiblesfilms, www.youtube.com/user/invisiblesfilms.

[27] *See, e.g.,* P. Bouckaert, *Prohibited Persons: Abuse of Undocumented Migrants, Asylum-Seekers, and Refugees in South Africa* (New York: Human Rights Watch, 1998); J. J. Lee, "Redefining

often finding jobs available to them only in dirty, degrading, and dangerous sectors. When their employers refuse to pay them, these migrants may fear that identifying themselves to law enforcement will result in their deportation; indeed, employers can prey on these fears and threaten to call migration control if migrants attempt to assert their rights. Some migrants brave enough to report these and other violations to law enforcement are then exploited and abused by government actors. Undocumented migrants belonging to relatively isolated linguistic groups face even greater obstacles to understanding and accessing their rights, and can be preyed upon by members of their community, who may demand usurious fees to provide them with faulty or obvious information.

Human rights law is not responsive to the needs of these migrants. Though empirical studies of population preferences are hard to come by, it seems fairly safe to assume that undocumented migrants would prize the right to enter their destination state lawfully, the right to travel safely to that state, and the right to remain safely once on the territory of that state. The first right, to entry at will, is not accorded to any set of migrants, even refugees, who otherwise benefit from preferential treatment. Though the Universal Declaration of Human Rights envisioned a right to asylum that would have enabled refugees to enter any country to seek protection, that aspirational provision failed to find its way into any multilateral human rights treaty.[28] The right to travel safely is similarly absent from human rights law. Though migrants in transit are in theory protected by international human rights treaties signed by transit countries, they face perhaps even greater challenges in enforcing those rights than undocumented migrants in the host state because of the increased level of vulnerability implicated in travel. More importantly, human rights law does not authorize migrants to access safe carriers, relegating them to dangerous journeys by foot, in cramped and often airless trunks and shipping crates, and on top of trains. Finally, the plain text of human rights treaties does not offer undocumented migrants the right to remain in their host state. Treaty interpretive bodies have refused to read that right into any of the multilateral human rights treaties.[29]

---

the Legality of Undocumented Work" (2018) 106 *California Law Review* 1617–1656, at 1624–1626; M. J. Gibney, "Outside the Protection of the Law: The Situation of Irregular Migrants in Europe" (2000) Refugee Studies Center, Working Paper No. 6, p. 21; "The Law Was Against Me": Migrant Women's Access to Protection for Family Violence in Belgium (New York: Human Rights Watch, 2012), www.hrw.org/report/2012/11/08/law-was-against-me/migrant-womens-access-protection-family-violence-belgium.

[28] UDHR, art. 14(1) ("Everyone has the right to seek and to enjoy in other countries asylum from persecution."). *Cf.* Organization of American States, *Montevideo Convention on Political Asylum* (December 26, 1933), www.refworld.org/docid/4f3d18oa2.html (providing a regional right to asylum); D. Acosta, "Free Movement in South America: The Emergence of an Alternative Model?" *Migration Information Source* (August 23, 2016), www.migrationpolicy.org/article/free-movement-south-america-emergence-alternative-model.

[29] Ramji-Nogales, "Undocumented Migrants" at 725–727.

While human rights law claims to be universal in its scope and applicability, it fails in some cases and refuses in others to speak to the rights that are crucial in protecting undocumented migrants. International human rights law has not strayed far from its roots; the continuities with colonial rule are unmistakable. The rights contained within the human rights canon obscure the underlying assumption that all humans have equal autonomy and access to justice. Those who have been rendered less than autonomous through global economic inequality and the legacies of colonialism – undocumented migrants being just one example – fall outside the scope of protection. Human rights law is unmistakably silent on the question of how to protect these populations.

HUMAN RIGHTS LAW'S SILENCES

The protection gap that human rights law constructs and obscures creates an opportunity for migrant destination states to flex their sovereign muscle through a variety of mechanisms to prevent the undocumented from reaching their borders.[30] These deterrence-based border control policies perhaps unsurprisingly do not prevent migrants from undertaking their journey, but instead amplify the dangers that migrants face in transit. Although human rights protections against mistreatment and abuse may apply in theory, migrants in transit are rarely able to enforce those rights. Without the right to enter, transit safely, or remain, the undocumented are subject to harsh treatment at the hands of states and private actors. Moreover, the images of hundreds of migrants approaching the borders of destination states in the Global North make ideal fodder for nationalist politicians seeking to expand their own power through xenophobic fearmongering.

For at least the past twenty years, migrant destination states have pushed their border enforcement well beyond their physical borders through programs such as the "Pacific Solution" in Australia and "Fortress Europe," as well as lesser-known programs such as Programa Frontera Sur in the United States and Mexico. Australia has been the most successful at preventing migrants from crossing its borders, effectively "stopping the boats" as its nativist politicians promised as part of their campaign platforms. This cruel policy began in 2001, when the Norwegian freighter, the MV *Tampa*, rescued more than four hundred Afghanis and Iraqis who had traveled by sea from Southeast Asia to seek asylum in Australia.[31] The Australian government refused to allow these asylum seekers to land on Australian territory, instead unloading them into a naval vessel that transported them to the remote

---

[30] For a comprehensive treatment of the topic, see D. FitzGerald, *Refuge beyond Reach: How Rich Democracies Repel Asylum Seekers* (Oxford: Oxford University Press, 2019).

[31] C. Inglis, "Australia: A Welcoming Destination for Some," *Migration Information Source* (February 15, 2018), www.migrationpolicy.org/article/australia-welcoming-destination-some.

island of Nauru. There, the Australian government was able to detain these migrants in an asylum processing center they had previously created.

These detention centers, as well as similar centers in Manus Island, have been the subject of criticism by human rights treaty actors and academics.[32] The analysis is telling: "offshore processing" is "neither explicitly prohibited nor authorized under the Refugee Convention and its Protocol and the relevant human rights treaties."[33] Although the treatment of migrants in detention centers violates human rights law, it has been difficult for migrants to enforce those rights given their distance from Australian territory and precarious status.[34] The detention centers were briefly closed down by the Labor Party when it took power in 2007, but then reinstated in 2012 after sea arrivals began to increase.[35] In the 2013 election, candidate Tony Abbott campaigned on a "stop the boats" slogan that ushered him into the prime ministerial suite.[36] Using methods that afforded no deference to human rights law, such as turnbacks and towbacks, migrants arriving by boat have been returned to their home countries.[37] As an island nation, Australia has ensured that undocumented migrants, including refugees, cannot enter their territory. Human rights law's gaps in protections, in this case the absence of a right to safe transit or entry, enable states to engage in extraterritorial processing. Moreover, though some existing human rights might offer some protections to undocumented migrants on paper, migrant vulnerability creates substantial obstacles to enforcing those rights.

Europe has also undertaken an array of programs to prevent migrants from reaching its borders. Regional human rights law has played an important role; though it has not established a right to entry, the European Court of Human Rights has held that member states exercising jurisdiction outside of national territory must process individual migrants' claims to protection before returning

---

[32] B. Doherty, "'Affront to Human Rights': Top UN Official Slams Australia's Offshore Detention," *The Guardian* (September 10, 2018), www.theguardian.com/law/2018/sep/11/affront-to-human-rights-top-un-official-slams-australias-offshore-detention.

[33] M. Gleeson, "Protection Deficit: The Failure of Australia's Offshore Processing Arrangements to Guarantee 'Protection Elsewhere' in the Pacific" (2019) XX *International Journal of Refugee Law* 1–49 at 4.

[34] Ibid., at 4, 10; United Nations High Commissioner for Refugees, *Submission by the Office of the United Nations High Commissioner for Refugees on the Inquiry into the Serious Allegations of Abuse, Self-Harm and Neglect of Asylum-Seekers in Relation to the Nauru Regional Processing Centre, and Any Like Allegations in Relation to the Manus Regional Processing Centre* (November 12, 2016).

[35] Inglis, "Australia"; Gleeson, "Protection Deficit" at 6; Andrew and Renata Kaldor Centre for International Refugee Law, University of New South Wales, "Offshore Processing: An Overview" (May 9, 2017), www.kaldorcentre.unsw.edu.au/publication/offshore-processing-overview.

[36] A. Rourke, "Tony Abbott, the Man Who Promised to 'Stop The Boats', Sails to Victory," *The Guardian* (September 7, 2013), www.theguardian.com/world/2013/sep/07/australia-election-tony-abbott-liberal-victory.

[37] Kaldor Centre, "Offshore Processing."

them.[38] Human rights law does not, however, prohibit member states from preventing migrants from reaching their jurisdictions. The European Union and its member states engage in capacity-building efforts with border guards in home and transit states, establish readmission agreements with countries of origin and transit, and create mobility partnerships that require states of origin and transit to sign onto border control reforms and readmission agreements in order to create temporary migration opportunities for a limited set of workers.[39] Though human rights actors have expressed concern with the manner in which these agreements are enforced and their potential for violating the rights of migrants, human rights law's silence around entry and safe transit creates the opening from which these policies can grow.

For at least forty years, the United States has prevented migrants from reaching its sea and land borders through a variety of externalization policies. In 1981, the Reagan administration signed an agreement with the Haitian government that enabled the US Coast Guard to interdict on the high seas boats carrying Haitians and push the passengers back to Haiti.[40] Nearly ten years later, the US Supreme Court held that the Refugee Convention's *nonrefoulement* protections did not apply on the high seas, allowing the George H. W. Bush administration to push back Haitians without screening their claims to refugee status.[41] Since 1994, interdicted migrants have been detained at the US naval base in Guantánamo, Cuba; at times they have been screened for refugee status and at times they have simply been held awaiting return to Cuba or Haiti.[42] On land, the US government has allocated substantial resources toward ensuring that Mexican authorities prevent Central American migrants from arriving at its southern land border.[43] Through the Mérida Initiative and Programa Frontera Sur, the Obama administration provided financial and logistical assistance to Mexican border enforcement.[44] Under the

---

[38] *Hirsi Jamaa and Others v. Italy*, Eur. Ct. H.R., App. No. 27765/09 (Grand Chamber, February 23, 2012).

[39] *Report of the Special Rapporteur on the Human Rights of Migrants, François Crépeau*, pp. 14–17, U.N. Doc. A/HRC/23/46 (April 24, 2013); *Communication from the Commission to the European Parliament, the European Council, the Council and the European Investment Bank on Establishing a New Partnership Framework with Third Countries under the European Agenda on Migration*, COM(2016) 385 (June 7, 2016).

[40] B. Frelick et al., "The Impact of Externalization of Migration Controls on the Rights of Asylum Seekers and Other Migrants" (2016) 4 *Journal of Migration and Human Security* 190–220 at 199; *Interdiction Agreement Between the United States of America and Haiti*, 33 U.S.T. 3559 (September 23, 1981).

[41] *Sale v. Haitian Centers Council*, 509 U.S. 155, 187 (1993).

[42] Frelick et al., "The Impact of Externalization" at 199–200.

[43] C. Ribando Seelke and K. Finklea, *U.S.–Mexican Security Cooperation: The Mérida Initiative and Beyond* (Washington, DC: Congressional Research Service, 2016), pp. 6–8.

[44] A. Castillo, *The Mexican Government's Frontera Sur Program: An Inconsistent Immigration Policy* (Council on Hemispheric Affairs, 2016), www.coha.org/wp-content/uploads/2016/10/The-Mexican-Government%E2%80%99s-Frontera-Sur-Program-An-Inconsistent-Immigration-Policy.pdf.

Remain in Mexico program and the Asylum Cooperative Agreement, the Trump
administration pushed some migrants back into Mexico to await their court hearings
and sent others to Guatemala to pursue their claims for protection.[45] Without a right
to safe transit or entry under international law, domestic governments can interpret
human rights law's silences to enable their externalization policies, with harsh
consequences for the migrants subject to those policies.[46]

FILLING THE SILENCES WITH MIGRANTS' VOICES

Despite its claims to universality, international human rights law does not adequately
reflect the interests and preferences of undocumented migrants. Without key rights
relating to movement, namely, the rights to safe transit, entry, and to remain,
migrants suffer substantial vulnerability and face serious obstacles to accessing the
human rights to which they are ostensibly entitled. Destination states are able to
leverage human rights law's silences to implement increasingly harsh measures to
prevent migrants from even reaching their borders. By inflicting inhumane harms on
humans on the move, these methods of border externalization also degrade the
humanity of the societies the migrants seek to enter. Human rights law's colonial
roots prevent it from fulfilling its potential as a project of emancipation.

An emancipatory approach to international human rights law might instead
take the human seriously, beginning from the perspective of the law's subject: the
migrant. A reimagined canon would identify and foreground the voices of those in
precarious situations, asking what protections are needed to minimize their vulnerability. Those inquiries might well lead to a right to safe transit, entry, and to
remain, but an emancipatory response must rest on empirical study to catalogue
and uplift the migrant's perspective. This challenging task has yet to be performed,
though several scholars are developing thoughtful and robust methods to collect
migrant voices.[47]

---

[45] K. M. Nielsen, *Policy Guidance for Implementation of the Migrant Protection Protocols*
(January 25, 2019), www.dhs.gov/sites/default/files/publications/19_0129_OPA_migrant-protec
tion-protocols-policy-guidance.pdf; *Agreement between the Government of the United States of
America and the Government of the Republic of Guatemala on Cooperation Regarding the
Examination of Protection Claims*, 84 Federal Register No. 224 at 64095–64099 (November
20, 2019).

[46] A. Isacson, "*I Can't Believe What's Happening – What We're Becoming": A Memo from El Paso
and Ciudad Juárez* (Washington, DC: The Washington Office on Latin America, 2019); *Fact
Sheet: Is Guatemala Safe for Refugees and Asylum Seekers?* (Washington, DC: Human Rights
First, 2019).

[47] H. Crawley et al., *Destination Europe? Understanding the Dynamics and Drivers of
Mediterranean Migration in 2015* (Coventry: MEDMIG, 2016), www.medmig.info/research-
brief-destination-europe.pdf; G. Sanchez, "Critical Perspectives on Clandestine Migration
Facilitation: An Overview of Migrant Smuggling Research" (2017) 5(1) *Journal on Migration
and Human Security* 9–27.

The year 2020 seems perhaps an unlikely juncture from which to demand radical reform in favor of the interests of undocumented migrants. As destination states sink to new depths of inhumanity toward humans on the move, one might reasonably argue that any changes to international law are more likely to diminish rather than expand the rights of migrants. Yet contemporary attitudes and policies toward migrants foreground the urgency of a response that underscores the humanity of the undocumented. Moreover, the unsettled political ground on which destination states currently stand can create unexpected openings, perhaps as citizens of these countries begin to realize the cost of inhumane border enforcement for migrants and for their own societies.

Although the governments of destination states may be unlikely in the current political climate to sign a multilateral human rights treaty that represents migrant interests, several other paths to generating a new set of migrant-centered human rights standards present themselves. Regional human rights bodies and other regional organizations might offer a location that is more amenable to migrant interests. In December 2019, the Inter-American Commission on Human Rights adopted the Inter-American Principles on the Rights of All Migrants, Refugees, Stateless Persons, and Victims of Trafficking, taking a first step in this direction.[48] Cities may also provide a space for generating human rights standards, whether binding or expressive, that represent the interests of migrants.[49] Other groups, from civil society to transnational social movements, might also seek to expand the source of human rights law beyond the state. Though a catalogue of rights generated by one of these groups will obviously not be binding law, it could offer a starting point for reframing perceptions of migrants and their rights through a process that rejects the state-centered focus of international law. Diaspora, transnational families, and others can similarly invoke conceptions of human rights that more clearly track the interests of migrants, either by adopting instruments and definitions created by other groups or by drafting their own language to represent the interests of their friends and loved ones. These groups and others, perhaps even including corporations and religious figures, could help to push forward a new framing of migrants' rights, which could be used to help persuade and remind citizens of destination states of the humanity of those on the move. It is a daunting road, but only by hearing and uplifting the voices of undocumented migrants can we push human rights law closer to its emancipatory potential, redeeming the humanity of migrants and citizens of destination states alike.

---

[48] Comisión Interamericana de Derechos Humanos, *Principios interamericanos sobre los derechos humanos de todas las personas migrantes, refugiadas, apátridas y las víctimas de la trata de personas*, December 7, 2019, Res. 04/19, www.oas.org/es/cidh/informes/pdfs/Principios DDHH migrantes - ES.pdf.

[49] C. Lasch et al., "Understanding 'Sanctuary Cities'" (2018) 59 *Boston College Law Review* 1703–1773.

Index

9 781108 823975